What ~~people are saying~~ about
The New Politics of Old Values

"During an era of media absorption in the trivia of political personality and political mechanisms, one welcomes this volume with its
emphasis on the crucial role of values and institutions and the link-
ages between them."
  —James MacGregor Burns, author of *Roosevelt: The Lion and
  the Fox*

"John White's description of the strategic imperatives that underpin
Ronald Reagan's 1980 presidential victory captures more faithfully
what *really* happened than anything else now in print."
  —Richard Wirthlin, Ronald Reagan's presidential pollster

"John White pulls together a wide range of materials—from ballots and ballads to surveys and speeches—weaving them into a nar-
rative description of the fabric of contemporary American elections.
Through it all, he demonstrates the central role of shared values as
the building blocks of leadership."
  —Peter D. Hart, Democratic pollster

"By helping us understand better one main source of Ronald
Reagan's remarkable appeal, John White also tells us much about
contemporary American politics."
  —Everett C. Ladd, Executive Director, Roper Center for Public
  Opinion Research

"John White documents the nature of Reagan's influence and uses
rigorous but imaginative critical methods to follow it where it leads
—into the deeper rhythms of American life and feeling."
  —Ralph Whitehead, Jr., University of Massachusetts, Amherst

"Absolutely fascinating. John White weaves a pattern of history into
a tabloid of culture to produce a remarkable explanation of our
nation's political process, and along the way truly defines the Ronald Reagan presidency."
  —Eddie Mahe, Jr., Republican campaig

D1607825

THE NEW
POLITICS
OF OLD
VALUES

THE NEW
POLITICS
OF OLD
VALUES

JOHN KENNETH WHITE

UNIVERSITY PRESS OF NEW ENGLAND

HANOVER AND LONDON

University Press of New England
Brandeis University
Brown University
Clark University
University of Connecticut
Dartmouth College
University of New Hampshire
University of Rhode Island
Tufts University
University of Vermont

© 1988 by University Press of New England

Printed in the United States of America

Library of Congress Cataloging-in-Publication Data
White, John Kenneth, 1952–
  The new politics of old values
  Bibliography: p.
  Includes index.
    1. Reagan, Ronald. 2. United States—Politics and government—1981–   . 3. Values—Political aspects—United States. 4. Presidents—United States. I. Title.
  E877.2.W48 1988   973.927′092′4   87–40513
  ISBN 0–87451–445–2 (cloth)
  ISBN 0–87451–438–X (paper)

5 4 3 2 1

Permission to reprint an excerpt from "The Hollow Men" in *Collected Poems 1909–1962* by T. S. Eliot, copyright 1936 by Harcourt Brace Jovanovich, Inc.; copyright © 1963, 1964 by T. S. Eliot. Reprinted by permission of the publisher. Also reprinted by permission of Faber and Faber Ltd. from *Collected Poems 1909–1962* by T. S. Eliot.

This book is dedicated to my parents,
Harold and Margaret White,
who instilled their values in me.

CONTENTS

Acknowledgments   ix

Introduction   1

1. The (un)Making of
   Ronald Reagan   7

2. Visions and Values   23

3. A Transforming Election   37

4. The Encore   56

5. The Parties: Us Against Them   74

6. Echoes in the Marketplace   103

7. A Sense of Return   122

Notes   145

Further Readings   173

Index   183

ACKNOWLEDGMENTS

While writing this book I incurred more than the usual obligations of most authors. At the State University College at Potsdam, I am indebted to the members of the Political Science Department—Richard DelGuidice, David Brown, Sanford Schram, and John Massaro—for their encouragement and insightful comments on the manuscript. Arthur Johnson of the History Department also read the manuscript and gave useful commentary . I am also grateful for the research assistance provided by Marie Keller and the staff of the Frederick Crumb Library at Potsdam College. Finally, I owe a special debt of gratitude to Anthony Catana, the director of the college's Star Lake Campus, and Anita Figueras, his administrative assistant, for providing me with wonderful facilities where I could write this book.

This book would not have been possible without the assistance provided by presidential poll taker Richard B. Wirthlin. Since our very first meeting in 1983, we have engaged in prolonged discussions about the nature of U.S. politics, the Reagan presidency, and the special role that values played in shaping the presidential campaigns of 1980 and 1984. These conversations have enriched my thinking about American politics, and have resulted in a deep and abiding friendship. Dr. Wirthlin made available much of his polling data and campaign memoranda, which added texture to this book. I also want to express my appreciation to Dr. Wirthlin's executive assistant, Bryce Bassett, who facilitated my travels and in other ways—both great and small—made the crooked roads straight.

I am also indebted to readers of successive drafts of the manuscript. Norman Zucker of the University of Rhode Island and Jerome Mileur of the University of Massachusetts saw this project through from start to finish, providing much-needed advice and encouragement. James MacGregor Burns of Williams College, Everett Ladd of the University of Connecticut, Peter Colby of the University of Central Florida, and Lawrence Radway of Dartmouth College also contributed mightily to the manuscript's development.

The editorial assistance Betty Seaver provided proved invaluable once again.

I also wish to thank Ludlow Music, Inc. and TRO Essex Music Limited for granting permission to use the lyrics to Woody Guthrie's "This Land Is Your Land" in the text. Also I wish to thank Harcourt Brace Jovanovich and Faber and Faber Limited for permission to reprint a portion of T. S. Eliot's poem "The Hollow Men."

Finally, I would not have been able to complete this book without the love of my mother, Margaret, and my sister, Janet, each of whom sustained me when the going got rough. This book is dedicated to my parents, my late father, Harold, and Margaret White, whose values they instilled in their son.

Potsdam, New York   J.K.W.
November 1987

THE NEW
POLITICS
OF OLD
VALUES

INTRODUCTION

Reagan certainly held us spellbound. I shall always wonder whether it just happened or if he calculated that it would happen.
—Peter Jennings, ABC News broadcast, 23 April 1987

The vice president of the United States had just completed a note to a supporter, thanking him for his words of encouragement. In it, he urged his loyalist to "continue your very effective speeches," adding: "You have the ability of putting complicated technical ideas into words everyone can understand. Those of us who have spent a number of years in Washington too often lack the ability to express ourselves in this way."[1]

Richard M. Nixon's 1959 letter to Ronald Reagan was prophetic. Ever since Reagan's successful run for governor of California in 1966, he has occupied center stage in the American political drama. Thirty years after that letter was written the fortieth president will be leaving the White House, forever to be remembered as the "Great Communicator."

That Reagan should have gained the title at all is something of a political miracle. During his first six years in the White House, he defied the odds. From John F. Kennedy's administration to Jimmy Carter's, the presidential record has been noticeably devoid of successes. Kennedy's assassination extinguished the promise; Johnson's Vietnam War eclipsed the Great Society; Nixon's Watergate brought him down; Ford's pardon of his predecessor destroyed his hope of being elected to the office; and Iran's hostages wrecked Carter's chance for a second term. This litany of failure lingered in the minds of Reagan and those who accompanied him to national power in 1981. Yet for longer than anyone ever expected, Reagan avoided the perception of defeat—until the Iran-Contra affair was exposed. Perhaps the scandal was inevitable, given the lackluster appointments Reagan made in his second term, his management style as described by the Tower Commission,[2] and his general inattention to the details of the office.

Still the question remains: How did Reagan maintain his standing for so long? And how has he always managed to recover so quickly even after serious setbacks? His enormous personal popularity certainly has been a major asset. In fact, popular approval is the fuel that drives the presidential engine. Lyndon B. Johnson, for one, understood that. After his landslide win in 1964, he told administration lobbyists that he wanted to accelerate the pace of congressional legislation before the gas tank read empty:

I was just elected by the biggest popular margin in the history of the country, fifteen million votes. Just by the natural way people think and because Barry Goldwater scared the hell out of them, I have already lost two of these fifteen and am probably getting down to thirteen. If I get into any fight with Congress, I have already lost another couple of million, and if I have to send any more boys into Vietnam, I may be down to eight million by the end of the summer.[3]

For six years, Reagan's popularity has been the driving force of the American political engine. More than three-fourths of all citizens said they liked him, even if they did not approve of his policies. Democrats charged that Reagan actually did little to enhance the folk values to which he so often paid homage: family, work, neighborhood, peace, and freedom. Yet they could not deny Reagan's ability to establish a connection between these values and himself.

Democrats repeatedly claimed that Reagan advanced the interests of the well-to-do at the expense of the poor and middle class. The declaration by the Secretary of Agriculture in 1981 that henceforth ketchup was to be considered a vegetable in school lunch programs became a standard line in the Democratic counterattack. Later, many of the loyal opposition took up the cause of the budget deficits. Reagan's trillion-dollar deficits, more debt than that accumulated during the presidencies of George Washington to Jimmy Carter combined, were threatening the economic security of the average American family. Former Speaker of the House Thomas P. "Tip" O'Neill called Reagan a "rich man's president," saying: "He has shown no care or compassion for the poor, or for the working person. But when it comes to giving money to the Pentagon or tax breaks to the wealthy, this guy has a heart of gold."[4]

O'Neill's attacks, and those of his party, fell mostly on deaf ears. Even after the revelation that the United States had been secretly selling arms to Iran's Ayatollah Khomeini, with the profits diverted to the Nicaraguan Contras, Reagan remained relatively popular. If it was merely Reagan's genial personality that was the secret to his success, then the so-called Reagan Revolution would have been quite an ephemeral one.

It was not, and a considerable body of evidence confirms it was more than just a matter of personal popularity. Polling done for the White House shows that at the height of Reagan's popularity in 1984, only eight percent said they supported the president because of his charming smile and winning ways. This equalled the number of those who backed Walter Mondale for the same reason—this despite Mondale's wooden image.[5]

Some observers argue that the politics of redistribution had much to do with Reagan's effectiveness. Many years ago the political scientist Harold Lasswell defined politics as "who gets what, when, and how."[6] Implicit here is the fact that an effective scattering of federal monies can make for a popular president. During the 1930s, Franklin D. Roosevelt molded a new Democratic party in part by making sure that his supporters "got theirs." Myriad federal agencies were established to accomplish the task, including the Civilian Conservation Corps, the National Youth Administration, the Works Progress Administration, and the Public Works Adminstration. These, with Social Security, constituted the New Deal. Roosevelt's successors sought to augment the New Deal by sharing the wealth with their supporters, thus enhancing their own political popularity. Harry S Truman's Fair Deal offered Medicare to the elderly and the GI Bill to former members of the armed services. John Kennedy's New Frontier extended the New Deal to black Americans through tough enforcement of civil rights laws. Lyndon B. Johnson's Great Society enlarged FDR's program to include those who had been previously excluded.

Ronald Reagan's vision, however, ran contrary to the national trend. Indeed, with regard to federal social expenditures, the hallmark of his administration was "making do with less." He proposed cuts in the most popular government programs: loans to college students, revenue sharing for the states, school lunch programs, and other middle-class entitlements. Time and again the Reagan budgets were pronounced "dead on arrival" at Capitol Hill. Yet he remained popular with the voters and, hence, a force to be reckoned with by the recalcitrant legislators.

Over the years I have become convinced that politics is more than "who gets what, when, and how." Instead, I believe that those who succeed politically—from the president to the county sheriff—somehow convince voters that they are "like us." On the eve of the 1980 election, Reagan was asked by a reporter what Americans saw in him. His response was revealing: "Would you laugh if I told you that I think, maybe, they see themselves and that I'm one of them? I've never been able to detach myself or think that I, somehow, am apart from them."[7]

Beginning with his first try for an elected office in 1966, Reagan has usually managed to present himself to voters as "one of us." Reagan's communicative skills were not diminished by the fact that his life before politics was steeped in the mythology of Hollywood—something few Americans have experienced. And his life style continued to remain aloof from that of ordinary voters long after his movie career was over. "Tip" O'Neill charges that "Reagan forgot where he came from and started picking up a different set of values." He added:

For years he's been surrounded by wealthy friends, to the point where he no longer knows any working people—not to mention anyone who's actually poor. He's been out of touch with how regular Americans live and the problems they face. His whole world is Hollywood.[8]

Yet Reagan's estrangement from the ordinary details of the workingman's life, as O'Neill points out, has not threatened his title as the Great Communicator. In fact, Reagan's success rests in his ability to convey a sense of *shared values*—not different ones—that transform him into "one of us." With his role as the Great Communicator firmly established, Reagan has been able to do what those presidents who make their mark on history must: become an agent of change. George Will writes, "Because politics is 95 percent talk, and the Presidency is 98 percent talk, there's nothing the President can do on his own except move the country, and by moving the country with his rhetoric move Congress, and once Congress is moved, then, but only then, can he govern."[9] In 1980 Reagan set about to move the country by focusing on the traditional values of family, work, neighborhood, peace, and freedom—themes that resonated with much of the electorate.

These are not simply nice-sounding platitudes, but romantic visions that voters seek to emulate in their own lives. Consequently, most want reassurances from their political leaders that such dreams can be made real. In early 1987 Governor of New York Mario Cuomo sought to give the schoolchildren of New York City such encouragement. Speaking to ninth and tenth graders about the dangers of drug usage, Cuomo described the beauty of life, its opportunities, and how drugs posed a threat to their future. After he finished, Cuomo asked if what he had said made sense. Most nodded. But one boy, no more than fifteen years old with a chipped front tooth, looked at the governor impassively, a mask of skepticism adorning his face. Sensing the lad's doubts Cuomo asked, "Didn't you agree with me? That your life is too precious to give away to drugs?" The youngster responded: "I'm not sure. The stuff you said sounded good, but I don't really know. I'm not sure what my life is for, why we're here. I really don't understand it." Cuomo said later that he was "stunned by his answer. By its simplicity. By its staggering profundity. I was at a loss."[10]

Reagan, like Cuomo, probably would have been at a loss, too. But politicians neither look for nor often get such thoughtful responses. Instead, they spend most of their time painting themselves as "one of us" and their opponents as "one of them." Few citizens would identify with the fifteen-year-old Cuomo described. Most of us recall our childhoods as more idyllic. A typical remembrance might be the one given voice by the Great Communicator himself: "There were woods and mysteries, life and death among the small creatures, hunting and fishing . . . Waiting and hoping for the winter freeze without snow so that we could go skating on the Rock River . . . swimming and picnics in the summer, the long thoughts of spring, the pain with the coloring of the falling leaves of autumn. It was a good life."[11]

Ronald Reagan's tender depiction of his upbringing is one many Americans can identify with. After painting such a Norman Rockwell-like image of the past, Reagan added: "I have never asked for anything more, then or now."[12] Most Americans would nod in agreement. It is with such rose-tinted protraits that Reagan, in the apt description of ABC News anchor Peter Jennings, "held us spellbound."[13] After a decade that included such debacles as the Vietnam War, Watergate, political assassinations, and hostage taking, voters wanted traditional values reaffirmed in 1980. Reagan provided the anitdote, shrewdly understanding the needs of his audience. Reagan's value-laden rhetoric fueled his popularity, prompting Jennings to speculate, "I shall always wonder whether it just happened or if he calculated that it would happen."[14] Whatever his intentions were, political party strategists, both Democratic and Republican, are now beginning to focus on Reagan's attention to values and are attempting to emulate him with mixed success.

During the heat of the 1984 presidential campaign, Walter Mondale declared: "When the true story of this election is written I suspect it will not be about me, or Mr. Reagan—but about you." Mondale believed the contest was over our values and perceptions, "the kind of people we are."[15]

This book is not so much about Ronald Reagan's presidency as it is about how we want to see ourselves—about who we Americans are. In this vein, Reagan provides the quintessential case study of how widely shared values can be utilized to garner public support and move a nation. Chapter 1 describes the world Ronald Reagan inhabits—an environment the voters created for him. Chapter 2 focuses on the importance of values in the American polity, and the historical disagreements over how the instruments of government should be used to achieve them. Chapter 3 describes the 1980 Reagan-Carter contest, explaining how the Reagan campaign devised a "strategy of values" to oust an incumbent president. Chapter 4 describes how President Reagan persisted with his values strategy—not only as an instrument with which to govern the nation, but as a campaign device to win reelection. Chapter 5 relates how values act as bonding agents to form party coalitions. Chapter 6 then examines the American culture, showing how the values Reagan espoused and the chords he struck with the citizenry are reflected in television, movies, and print. Finally, Chapter 7 studies the impact of Reagan's attention to values on the nation's governing agenda, the future of the Democratic and Republican parties, and lessons his immediate successors can derive from the Great Communicator.

1

THE (UN)MAKING OF RONALD REAGAN

We live in a world of perceptions, not realities.
—Lieutenant Colonel Oliver L. North in a message to National
Security Adviser John Poindexter, 15 July 1986

In politics, the persona—the role that a politician assumes to communicate his conscious intentions to himself and to others—is the starting point for success or failure. Any consideration of Ronald Reagan's public persona must begin with the tale of the man Reagan portrayed on the movie screen—Notre Dame's most famous football player, George Gipp.

The George Gipp story was one his coach, Knute Rockne, liked to tell. In a 1930 issue of *Colliers* magazine, Rockne recounted how his star football player had absented himself from several classes at Notre Dame during the 1919 spring term, saying he was ill. His professors, no doubt less charitable, found the excuse wanting, and he was expelled. To gain readmittance he submitted himself to an oral examination conducted by a board of examiners. Rockne's account of that day is gripping:

Gipp went into that examination-room with the whole school and the whole city awaiting the outcome. Some of his inquisitors were not football fans. They were prepared to stop his scholastic run with tough tackling questions and blocking from the books. His professors knew that Gipp was no diligent student. He made no notes. But he astonished everybody by what he knew when it came to cross-examination. He passed back into school, and there was general rejoicing. Not, however, by Gipp. Calmly, as usual, he accepted victory; but it was observed that he was more regular in attending class.[1]

One small flaw mars Rockne's account: *it never happened*. Sure enough, George Gipp was expelled from Notre Dame on March 8,

7

1919, for missing too many classes. The reason was not illness but laziness. During the ensuing six weeks after his dismissal, Gipp could be found in a pool hall hustling customers. The local papers reported his success playing pool, as well as the offers he received from other colleges to play on their football teams. Considerable pressure was exerted on Notre Dame's president by local citizens and college alumni who saw Gipp's presence on the team as essential and the whiling away of his time in pool halls as unbecoming. Finally, the college readmitted him on April 29, 1919—*without* Gipp's having taken that infamous oral examination.[2]

Gipp, according to Rockne, had "fewer than the usual faults of star athletes"[3]; but a more truthful rendering of Gipp's life is filled with those "usual faults"—and then some. He was lazy, undependable, and not particularly well liked by his teammates. One can understand why. Gipp's deportment was deplorable. In 1917 he was three weeks late arriving on campus and four weeks tardy for the start of football practice. A year later, Gipp skipped his final examinations altogether. Still, there were no recriminations. During his last two years at Notre Dame, Gipp lived alone at the Hotel Oliver in South Bend. There, free from the discipline imposed by the Roman Catholic priests, he could play pool and cards without fear of punishment. In 1919, after being readmitted following that "astonishing" oral exam performance, Gipp vanished for a week between the Army game and the Michigan A & M contest. To this day, no one knows where he went. He also secretly played professional football. He bet large sums—on occasion as much as four hundred dollars, real money in 1919—on his teammates. At one point Gipp wrote a friend that he felt "all wrong. I'd like to give up . . . chuck everything and go anywhere." He morosely concluded, "Now I know that I'm unlucky."[4] As if to fulfill his fateful prophesy, Gipp died on December 14, 1920, at the age of twenty-five. The death certificate listed the cause as viral pneumonia.

Even in death—especially in death—the myth of Gipp the paragon grew stronger. In that same *Colliers* article, inappropriately titled "Gipp the Great," Rockne related a final meeting with his star player. Gipp's eyes "brightened in a frame of pallor" as he said these last words: "'Some time, Rock, when the team's up against it, when things are wrong and the breaks are beating the boys—tell them to go in there with all they've got and win just one more for the Gipper. I don't know where I'll be then, Rock. But I'll know about it and I'll be happy.'"[5]

That tear-jerking scene, like the oral examination described earlier, was a product of Rockne's hyperactive imagination. Two of Gipp's classmates later said that the story did not ring true—in part because his teammates never referred to him as "the Gipper," nor did he himself do so.[6] Another writer states flatly that the tale is patently false, since Rockne was not at Gipp's bedside when he died.[7]

No matter. Eight years went by after Gipp's death without a word from Rockne about Gipp's "parting words." Then came 1928, a year when Rockne was coaching a demoralized, losing squad. The team lost four games—one-third of all the losses Rockne was to suffer during his entire coaching career.[8] The night before a pivotal game against Army, Rockne told sportswriter Grantland Rice: "You know, I'm worried about this game and might have to use George Gipp to win it."[9] Sure enough, at halftime, with the score tied 0–0, Rockne related the dying Gipp's "last words." Suddenly, in Rockne's account, the team came out of the locker room "exalted, inspired, overpowering."[10] The 1940 movie *Knute Rockne-All American* shows one inspired player scoring the winning touchdown on the strength of Gipp's "last words." Injured on the play, the actor is carried off the field saying: "That's the last one I can get for you, Gipper."[11] Clearly the team was motivated, for Notre Dame defeated Army, 7–6.

That was not the first time Rockne resorted to fiction to inspire greater effort. One recalled another game in which Rockne came into the locker room at halftime with several telegrams urging the team to victory. Only one of the messages mattered to him, he said. It was from "my poor sick little boy, Billy, who is critically ill in the hospital." Rockne, with a lump in his throat, read the wire: "I want Daddy's team to win." The team did win, and when the players returned to South Bend, there waiting to greet them at the railroad station was "sick" Billy Rockne.[12]

Near the century's close little has changed from its beginning. There are many individuals like Gipp who bear scant resemblance to reality. Most use the medium of television to transmit their public personas. Among the most notable are Frank Bartles and Ed Jaymes. The cleverly done wine cooler commercial depicts, in the words of its creator, "two old fogies on a porch" who run a small business, pay mortgages, and live in a small town.[13] They are characteristically courteous: Bartles always signs off saying, "Thank you for your support"; Jaymes never speaks.

But the Bartles and Jaymes story is not true: *there are no Bartles and Jaymes*. The television characters are actually two nonprofessional actors. And the company they represent is not little old, down-home "Bartles and Jaymes," but the largest wine-maker in the United States, Ernest and Julio Gallo. Nearly every news organization has revealed the identity of these characters and their company. No matter. The public persona given Bartles and Jaymes resulted in an enormous increase in sales—from number forty to number one within several months after they were introduced to the public in 1985. Those who watch the commercials strongly identify with Frank Bartles and Ed Jaymes, believing them to be somehow "like us." Some viewers have actually sent money to Ed Jaymes to help on the mortgage. To Hal Riney, the man behind the advertising campaign, the success of the commercial lies in the emotions it evokes: "I don't like to think about where my emotions come from. I hate that kind of analysis. But I'd be a liar if I didn't say there's a bit of a game to it all."[14] Clearly, the line between storytelling and reality—between myth and manipulation—is thin.

The essence of the accounts about Gipp's career, Rockne's prowess as a coach, and the fictional Bartles and Jaymes lies not in the facts—or lack thereof—but in the *values* espoused by those doing the telling. Concluding his tribute to Gipp, Rockne said, "A boy does well indeed who, so young, leaves the clean glory of a name behind."[15] Fifty-one years later, the man who portrayed Gipp in movie houses recalled his on-screen character while addressing the 1981 graduates of Notre Dame University. Ronald Reagan began by telling the audience, "Now, today I hear very often, 'Win one for the Gipper,' spoken in a humorous vein." Then, more seriously, he asked his listeners to "look at the significance of that story":

Rockne could have used Gipp's dying words to win a game at any time. But eight years went by following the death of George Gipp before Rock revealed those dying words, his deathbed wish.

And then he told the story at halftime to a team that was losing, and one of the only teams he had ever coached that was torn by dissension and jealousy and factionalism. The seniors on that team were about to close out their football careers without learning or experiencing any of the real values that a game has to impart. None of them had known George Gipp. They were children when he played for Notre Dame. It was to this team that Rockne told the story and so inspired them that they rose above their personal animosities. For someone they had never known, they joined together in a common cause and attained the unattainable.[16]

Reagan never cited Gipp's actual longing to "give up" and "chuck everything." Instead, he asked, "Is there anything wrong with young people having an experience, feeling something so deeply, thinking of someone else to the point they can give so completely of themselves?" Reagan answered his own question: "There will come times in the lives of all of us when we'll be faced with causes bigger than ourselves, and they won't be on a playing field."[17]

"The Gipper"

After *Knute Rockne—All American* was released in 1940, Warner Brothers sponsored a promotional visit by the cast to Notre Dame. There Reagan described the film's recounting of Gipp's career and concluded, "I hope my performance will win another for the Gipper. I sure wouldn't want to disappoint all those scores of Notre Dame fans."[18] The next day Reagan received a tremendous ovation in a local movie theater after the film had been shown. His response: "I guess we really won one for the Gipper."[19]

The public associated Reagan the man with his public persona as "the Gipper." So identified was he with Gipp, that during the 1980 presidential campaign many voters believed Reagan actually had attended Notre Dame. (Reagan, of course, was a graduate of tiny Eureka College.) Reagan was cognizant of the public's perception and he soon began to link himself with the mythical Gipp.[20] In a pep talk to the United States Olympic team on the opening day of the 1984 games, he told the athletes: "Set your sights high, and then go for it. For yourselves, for your family, for your country—and will you forgive me if I just be a little presumptuous—do it for the Gipper."[21] During the 1984 campaign Reagan sought refuge in the role once more. He urged crowds to "help spread the word, get out the vote, and win 'em for the Gipper."[22] In his public persona as the Gipper, Reagan compared the choosing of a president with the selection of a football coach: "Well, making our economy bear the burden of [Mondale's promised] tax hike would be like having a coach tell an Olympic swimmer to do the laps with a ball and chain. Come November, the American people are going to get to vote on their coaches. And come November the American people are going to tell Coach Tax Hike to go find another team someplace else."[23]

Nancy Reagan has understood and embellished Reagan in this role. At the 1984 Republican National Convention, the former movie actress addressed the delegates. Her speech consisted of just one line: "Make it one more for the Gipper."[24] As if by magic, a smiling apparition appeared behind her—there on a gigantic television screen was "the Gipper" waving to the First Lady, the delegates who were about to renominate him, and the voters who were about to give him a second term in office.

Reagan well understood the power he held over audiences as the Gipper. Even when not invoking George Gipp by name, Reagan continued to employ themes like family, hard work, and self-sacrifice that had come to be associated with Gipp. In a 1983 Saturday radio speech commemorating Mother's Day, Reagan extolled the nation's mothers as "quiet, everyday heroes," noting that from them "we first learn about values and caring and the difference between right and wrong." He added, "They're raising children in a fast-paced world where basic values are constantly questioned. Their monumental challenge is to bring their children into adulthood, healthy and whole, nurturing their physical and emotional growth while avoiding the pitfalls of drug abuse and crime." The president then asked those who were not mothers to "always remember, reward, and recognize them and use their examples of love and courage as inspiration to be better than we are." He signed off, saying, "Till next week, thanks for listening and God bless you."[25] The Democrats have had a hard act to follow.

Reagan has often resorted to apocryphal tales about Americans who embody the values he so deeply cherishes. Campaigning for the presidency in 1980, he told of a B-17 pilot whose plane was badly shot up in a World War II bombing mission. A crew member was badly wounded and could not be extricated from the damaged bull-turret. As the craft began to lose altitude, the commander ordered the crew to bail out and then lay down beside the injured man. According to Reagan, the officer took the young man's hand and said, "Never mind son, we'll ride it down together." Reagan ended his tale: "Congressional Medal of Honor posthumously awarded."[26]

There is no record of the B-17 incident. No evidence of a Congressional Medal of Honor so awarded. And because both men in the tale died, reporters wondered who had survived to spread the word. *Chicago Sun Times* columnist Mike Royko wrote a scathing column satirizing Reagan about the story.[27] It was later discovered that Reagan's account bore a striking resemblance to the plot of the 1944 movie *A Wing and a Prayer*, whose star, Dana Andrews, says, "We'll take this ride together."[28] Despite the story's having been proved a fabrication, Reagan did not drop it. On a visit to West Germany in 1982, he retold it to U.S. soldiers stationed there—this time contrasting the airman's heroism with the dastardly deeds of the Soviets.

The story of the bomber pilot is one of many in Reagan's repertoire. Another was used while campaigning in Cedar Rapids, Iowa, near the close of the 1984 presidential campaign. Reagan related how in 1948 Warner Brothers sent him to England to film *The Hasty Heart*. One evening at a four-hundred-year-old pub he was served by a "nice, matronly woman." While sipping his beer, Reagan spoke with an elderly gentleman. After a time the woman approached Reagan and asked, "You're an American, aren't you?" When Reagan said yes, she related an incident that he repeated to the Iowans some forty years later. "'During the war there were a bunch of your lads, a great bunch of them, stationed just down the road. They would come here in the evenin' and we'd have a song fest. They began calling me Mom and called the old man Pop. And then, one Christmas Eve, we were in here all alone, and the door burst open and there they was. They came in and they had presents for us.'"[29] At this point, she looked past Reagan, a "tear on her cheek." Then she said, "Big strapping lads they was from a place called Iowa." As the Iowa crowd began to laugh, sensing that the events were unreal, "the Gipper" astutely added: "When she said this, I could just picture those big strapping lads. And then I had a tear on my cheek."[30]

Reagan is a storyteller, a craft he learned well in his former profession. Shortly after being inaugurated president in 1981, he invited members of the Baseball Hall of Fame to a White House luncheon.[31] After the meal Reagan swapped stories with his guests about his days as a baseball broadcaster for Iowa radio station WHO. He recalled that in 1933 as he was announcing a Cubs game, the wire went dead. In those days radio announcers did not attend baseball games but relied on coded messages relayed from the field. Reagan realized he had two choices: he could tell his audience what had happened and then play transcribed music, thereby causing many to turn their dials to another station broadcasting the game, or he could hold their attention by making something up. He chose the latter. Reagan had Billy Jurges, the batter, foul a ball from pitcher Dizzy Dean. A foul ball is the only play not recorded in the record books; thus, Reagan would not be caught in a lie. After one foul ball Reagan eagerly looked to the control booth, but the technician shook his head, indicating that the wire was still dead. Reagan had Jurges put another of Dean's pitches out of play. Then he described a fight between two children trying to retrieve the ball. Next Reagan had the batter foul another pitch—this one just missed being a home run. As the wire continued dead, Reagan began to wonder if he was setting a record for the most fouled pitches by a batter but reassured himself that no one keeps accounts of that kind. Finally, the wire resumed its hum and its first message caused Reagan to burst out laughing: Jurges had popped out on the first ball pitched.

This oft-told story about Reagan's early days is instructive because prior to 1933, Reagan had never attended a major league baseball game. Football had always been his preferred sport, for unlike the baseball game he reported, "I knew . . . how it felt to be on the field, and the smell of sweat and the taste of mud and blood."[32] Still, Reagan projected an air of authenticity about baseball, conjuring the mythical Dean-Jurges tale in such a way as to convince his listeners that what was happening was real. Later as host of television's "G. E. Theatre" and "Death Valley Days," Reagan continued to tell parables that were entertaining—they had to be to win an audience—but were also strongly infused with moral virtues. William A. Henry III writes that Reagan understands the "purpose of a storyteller is not to gain new information, but to recapture experiences that the listener already had, to reaffirm views of the world they already had."[33]

The accuracy of Reagan's stories is often in doubt, but those like Royko who poke fun at Reagan for his memory lapses or ridicule his mistakes miss the point. It is the moral of the stories, the values reaffirmed, that count with his listeners. In a bicentennial address on July 4, 1976, Reagan declared that the American people had "never fallen for the line of a few fashionable intellectuals and academics who in recent years would have us believe ours is a sick society—a bad country."[34] Later, as president, he told the American Bar Association, "One of my dreams is to help Americans rise above pessimism by renewing their belief in themselves."[35] In large measure Reagan accomplished this. A Des Moines businessman told an interviewer in 1987, "The reason this country is getting better is because we've been led to believe it's getting better. I believe we can be led into doing that. I believe Reagan projects that."[36]

Reagan has never deviated from his optimistic view that the nation can be made better if we are true to ourselves. Another tale illustrates the point. Trying to escape the fury of the Iran-Contra affair in April 1987, he left the capital for Indiana, and at the West Lafayette airport Reagan told of a letter he had received about a boy named Billy. Billy's father was an avid reader of the Sunday newspapers, but Billy himself preferred to play baseball. To stall his son for a while, Billy's father gave him the formidable task of reassembling a newspaper map of the world that had been cut into little pieces. Reagan recounted that, after just seven minutes, Billy put the map together again. Asked by his father how he did it so quickly, Billy responded, "On the other side of the map there was a picture of a family, and I found that if you put the family together the world took care of itself." Reagan then reported that Billy and his father went outside to play ball. When the president finished the crowd applauded.[37] Few took the parable at face value, but everyone understood its point: the importance of the family. Nancy Reagan, who knows her husband better than anyone, maintains, "There's a certain cynicism in politics. You look back of a statement for what a man really means. But it takes people a while to realize that with Ronnie you don't have to look in back of anything."[38]

"The Link Is Broken"

In his tribute Rockne wrote that George Gipp "was really a master showman . . . The lad had brilliance and a sense of dramatic opportuneness of doing the right, unpreconceived thing at exactly the right, unpreconceived moment."[39] In a way every president is a showman, with the more successful ones having Gipp's sense of timing. As John Adams once said of George Washington, "If he was not the greatest President he was the best Actor of the Presidency we ever had. His Address to the States when he left the Army: his solemn Leave taken of Congress . . . his Farewell Address to the people when he resigned his Presidency. These were all in a strain of Shakespearean and Garrickal excellence in Dramatic Exhibitions."[40]

Washington established the role that his successors must play. Although each president confronts different crises, the electorate, remembering Washington, expects each to exhibit the characteristics of the role. Foremost among the presidential persona is honesty, far outranking intelligence.[41]

In 1966, when Reagan was brought forth as a candidate for governor of California, one movie mogul said it was miscasting: "No, Jimmy Stewart for Governor. Reagan for best friend."[42] Reagan, however, played the gubernatorial role, if not the office, well and was awarded two terms. When he captured the presidency in 1980, Reagan, more than his immediate predecessors, understood the role he was expected to play. He gave a bravura performance. Cuomo, for one, gives Reagan a rave review: "By his personal conduct when he's shot, when he's told he has cancer, when he goes to Normandy—the way he's deported himself has been a moral instruction to my children."[43]

Reagan's attention to role playing was not lost on his subordinates. In a July 1986 memorandum to National Security Adviser John Poindexter, Lieutenant Colonel Oliver North alluded to the public stage upon which he was operating: "We live in a world of perceptions, not realities."[44] Subsequently, when North testified before Congress on his role in the Iran-Contra affair, Lance Morrow wrote in *Time* magazine, "He played brilliantly upon the collective values of America, upon its nostalgias, its memories of a thousand movies (James Stewart in *Mr. Smith Goes to Washington*, John Wayne in *They Were Expendible*) and Norman Rockwell Boy Scout icons . . . In the fading seasons of Reagan's presidency, young Ollie North was splendid at the Old Man's game."[45]

The president-as-actor is an important function vested in the office. When presidents, or would-be presidents, fail to live up to the role, they are disposed of summarily. Richard Nixon had no choice in 1974 but to leave the presidency in disgrace after tape-recordings showed he had lied about his participation in the Watergate affair. In 1987, Gary Hart removed himself from the race for the Democratic presidential nomination after the press reported his dalliance with Donna Rice. Hart's account of the time he spent with the twenty-nine-year-old model and aspiring actress raised questions about his character and credibility. In exiting from the contest, Hart complained that media attention to his personal life had driven the issues he wanted to raise off the front pages: "That link with the voters that lets you listen to their concerns and often your ideas and proposals" had been broken.[46]

In much the same fashion the link between Reagan and the public was frayed, but not broken, as a consequence of the Iran-Contra affair. News of his sale of arms to Iran, with the proceeds going to the Nicaraguan Contras, came upon the heels of the swap of a Soviet espionage agent for U.S. reporter Nicholas Daniloff—a swap that Reagan said was not a swap—and a summit with Mikhail Gorbachev in Reykjavik, Iceland—a summit that Reagan said was not a summit. These were just the surface.

The underbelly of the Reagan administration was corroded by what many referred to as the "sleaze factor." More than a hundred appointees were accused of malfeasance, a record. These included former Reagan aide Michael Deaver, who was indicted for perjury; Rita Lavelle, assistant administrator of the Environmental Protection Agency, who was convicted of the same charge; her superior, Anne Burford, who resigned after disclosures that she bent regulations for certain industrial polluters; Attorney General Edwin Meese, who twice underwent investigation by independent counsel about his activities as a member of the first-term Reagan White House staff; Lyn Nofziger, another former Reagan aide, who was indicted for influence peddling; James Beggs, the chief administrator of the National Aeronautics and Space Administration, who was indicted for defrauding the government while an executive of General Dynamics.[47]

The allegations of wrongdoing, many of which were known before the Iran-Contra affair became public, undermined Reagan's ability to project a Gipper-like image. Garry Wills writes that when Rockne was caught telling lies, he "just admitted them, certain that they were justified if they worked for the team."[48] Most of the time, however, Rockne did not have to admit to them, for as Wills points out, he was "so good at convincing others, with his heartfelt pleas, that he convinced himself."[49]

"Coach" Reagan could not sell the proposition that the arms sales to Iran "worked for the team." Although he may have convinced himself of the wisdom and sincerity of his actions, most of the public remained unconvinced. In December 1986, 37 percent believed Reagan was telling the truth when he asserted he did not know that profits from the arms transactions with the Ayatollah Khomeini were diverted to the Contras in Nicaragua; 47 percent thought Reagan was lying. By May 1987, those believing Reagan misrepresented his involvement rose to nearly three of five Americans; those who still believed Reagan's account amounted to fewer than one in four.[50] Ronald Reagan, in the starring role as the Gipper, was a less believable character.

It is surprising that Reagan abandoned his longtime public persona. Only once before had he done so. That was when he was divorced from actress Jane Wyman in 1940—a time when divorce was still frowned upon. Wyman's career was on the rise, while Reagan's was at a nadir.[51] That undoubtedly would be a source of friction in any marriage—especially in 1940 when most women listed their occupation as "housewife." Wyman told reporters that she was tired of hearing Reagan constantly talking politics, and that she could not bear to watch *King's Row*, Reagan's favorite movie and one in which he played the lead, one more time. After learning of the impending divorce, Hollywood columnist Louella Parsons wrote: "No marital separation since I broke the story that Mary Pickford, America's sweetheart, was leaving Douglas Fairbanks has had the effect of the parting of the Reagans . . . Jane and Ronnie have stood for so much that is right in Hollywood . . . That's why this hurts so much. That's why we are fighting so hard to make them realize that what seems to have come between them is not important enough to make their break final."[52]

Reagan and Wyman divorced nonetheless. Several years later he resumed his Gipper image by marrying Nancy Davis, a union that has been likened by one author to a world of "make-believe."[53] But it was not so much a world of their own making as one we made for them. Reagan's famous 1984 "It's Morning in America" advertisement—created by the same Hal Riney who makes the Bartles and Jaymes commercials—depicted a community of friends and neighbors who espoused homespun values. A new bride hugs her mother. An old man and a police officer hoist the flag while schoolchildren pledge allegiance to it. The announcer proclaims that "America today is prouder, stronger, better. Why would we want to return to where we were less than four short years ago?" There was no mention of Reagan's name, but it showed a world Americans wanted to see, even if they could no longer live there.

When Reagan destroyed that world with the Iran-Contra affair, he was punished in much the same way that other actors are when they want to depart from their established roles. Even at the age of twenty-six, Mickey Rooney played Andy Hardy, a lovesick high school senior. Audiences loved him as the perpetual adolescent, and in 1939, 1940, and 1941 he was the nation's number-one box-office draw. Similarly, other actors have had their public personas shaped by their movie roles. Lana Turner was typecast as the sophisticated girl, and June Allyson was the girl next door. Ava Gardner, Rita Hayworth, and Marilyn Monroe were accepted by moviegoers as love goddesses. John Travolta won acclaim in *Saturday Night Fever* and *Grease* in which he played a high school student. Yet later he fared poorly because, according to one movie executive, "The public wasn't interested in seeing him grow up. They liked him as king of the disco and as king of the prom."[54] When actor Kirk Douglas played Vincent van Gogh in the film *Lust for Life*, his friend John Wayne took him aside and said: "How dare you play a weakling, an artist who commits suicide?" Douglas laughed, saying: "Come on, it's all make-believe." Wayne, serious, responded: "No. Tough guys like us have an obligation to keep that image for the audience."[55]

Before the Iran-Contra affair, Reagan could have continued to refurbish his image by playing the Gipper. But Reagan chose to act contrary to his public persona by selling arms to the Ayatollah Khomeini. Until that act, voters believed Reagan was the embodiment of the mythical Gipp and, therefore, the embodiment of all that is right with America. Like Rooney and Travolta, Reagan's image was bruised when he acted out of character.

Until late 1986, Reagan occupied an exalted place in American politics—especially when compared to his immediate predecessors. Somewhat typical of the way we have viewed recent presidents is the case of Richard Nixon. Few were ambivalent about him, for Nixon had more than his share of ardent admirers and detractors, though often it seemed that his enemies outnumbered his supporters. Nixon biographer Stephen Ambrose details their passions:

To millions of Americans, including at that time this author, the man seemed utterly insincere. We believed that everything he did was coldly calculated, the opposite of spontaneous, unrelated to any interest other than Richard Nixon's own. His motives were always the lowest. Everything he did was a put on. We could see nothing good in him whatsoever. His face on the television screen filled us with fear and loathing.[56]

Widespread detestation of Nixon gave rise to the sobriquet "Tricky Dick" and the line, "Would you buy a used car from this man?" Thus, when Watergate happened, the public was not surprised—it had always assumed, even as it hoped against hope, that certain unpleasant aspects of the Nixon character were still there.

Reagan was an altogether different story. Patrick Buchanan, who worked in both the Nixon and Reagan White Houses, observed that Nixon liked to skewer his enemies, whereas Reagan was a genuinely genial man. Presidential pollster Richard B. Wirthlin reports that more than three-fourths of all Americans say they like Reagan personally. Hence, it is all the more surprising that Reagan, having worked so long to establish himself as the Gipper, momentarily shed the role. He is likely to spend the rest of the presidency trying to resurrect it. His success in doing so does not depend on the scripts handed to him—like the late 1987 summit with Mikhail Gorbachev concluding an arms control agreement—but whether the Gipper can restore his credibility as the all-American hero.

Life in the Shadows

Between the idea
And the reality
Between the motion
And the act
Falls the Shadow.[57]

These lines, penned some years ago by the poet T. S. Eliot, say much about the Reagan years. The essence of the Reagan presidency lies not in its promulgated policies—though they have changed America—but in its shadows. In his first term Reagan was attacked for not living up to the values he espoused. Veteran ABC News White House correspondent Sam Donaldson maintained:

I think if you somehow got into the Oval Office, past the Secret Service, and told [Reagan] you were down on your luck and needed some help, he would literally give you the shirt off his back. But there is another side to the man that is cold and calculating. While you are gratefully putting on his shirt, he will sit down at his desk in his undershirt and happily sign legislation that would take your worthless relatives off welfare, and remove your children from the school lunch program—all in the name of his political ideology.[58]

Reagan's critics became frustrated as he sought refuge in his public persona as the Gipper. During the 1984 campaign, Democratic vice-presidential candidate Geraldine Ferraro charged that Reagan was un-Christian because his policies were so unfair.[59] Exiting from politics, Mondale blamed himself for the overwhelming defeat he suffered at the Gipper's hands, saying he had "fundamentally mishandled" the case against Reagan.[60] Surely, the movie persona of Gipp could not be as mean-spirited, unfair, and un-Christian as Mondale and Ferraro charged. This was vividly demonstrated in an encounter House Speaker Tip O'Neill had with an ex-construction worker. The man, having suffered a spinal cord injury after falling off a roof, was angry because the Reagan administration wanted to tax workmen's compensation benefits. After getting a sympathetic ear from the Speaker, the disabled hardhat ventured yet another complaint. "Tip," he said, "I've voted for you all my life, but I think you're too tough on the president." O'Neill, stunned, responded, "Who do you think is cutting your benefits?" The injured man answered, "Not the president. He's got nothing to do with it. It's the people around him."[61] Indeed, the public persona of the Gipper was such that the president and the presidency became separate entities. The Democrats became so irritated with their failure to make their accusations against Reagan stick that one of them, Congresswoman Pat Schroeder of Colorado, coined the phrase "the Teflon president."

The critics failed to make their case because, instead of vaunting themselves as representives of cherished American values, they allowed Reagan to dominate the field. Garry Wills wrote that Reagan became a "symbol of America," an "angel of our better natures," a "reconciler of our meaner aspects into a smiling strength," a "folksy commander of a worldwide empire." He added, "[A]ll these were images too high or too deep for ordinary political criticism. How he came to that eminence was a matter of shared history between him and the American electorate—shared innocence about the responsibilities of great power, about what he deplores as 'govment' in keeping the accounts of a great nation and a world power."[62]

Reagan's magic remains unparalleled, even in the wake of the Iran-Contra affair. In retrospect the scandal, although important, came to be seen as a relatively small stain on Reagan's Norman Rockwell-like portrait of America—a masterpiece whose broad brush strokes of family, work, neighborhood, peace, and freedom evoked admiration and contentment. The painting ignored the blotches of racism and poverty that exist in any true-to-life depiction of American life. In that respect, it was not all that different from other portraits drawn by Reagan's predecessors. Some years ago when John F. Kennedy was accused by his critics of "managing the news," Daniel Boorstin wrote:

Nowadays everybody tells us that what we need is more belief, a stronger and deeper and more encompassing faith. A faith in America and in what we are doing. That may be true in the long run. What we need first and now is to disillusion ourselves. What ails us most is not what we have done with America, but what we have substituted for America. We suffer primarily not from our vices or weaknesses, but from our illusions. We are haunted, not by reality, but by those images we have put in place of reality.[63]

The America that Daniel Boorstin described and that Reagan inhabits is not so much a product of Reagan's imagination as it is of our own. With the Iran-Contra affair, Reagan destroyed what Coleridge referred to as his audience's "willing suspension of disbelief," an open conspiracy between actor and audience—each knows that what is happening is not real, yet each plays along.

At the height of the Iran-Contra affair in July 1987, presidential pollster Wirthlin told a national television audience, "I think Ronald Reagan could likely win another landslide in 1988."[64] The Constitution prevents Wirthlin's hypothesis from being put to the test. Nevertheless, the Reagan presidency raises the question: How did he accumulate such an astonishing degree of popularity? The answer lies in his ability to conjure for a willing, and eager, audience visions of values that have roots in our collective subconscious: family, work, neighborhood, peace, and freedom. This public persona, with its emphasis on traditional values, constitutes the motif of the Reagan presidency. How these values became part of American folklore, and the different ways politicians have used them to win a following are the subject of the next chapter.

2

VISIONS AND VALUES

"*I want a house!*" Those were the last words Andre Sakharov's wife, Yelena Bonner, spoke upon leaving the United States in 1986 to return to the Soviet Union. Her dream was the quintessential American dream: to be oneself in one's private dwelling place. "A house," said Bonner, "is a symbol of independence, spiritual and physical." At age sixty-three the Soviet dissident mourned, "I've never had a house . . . [not even] a corner I could call my own." She sadly concluded, "My dream, my own house, is unattainable for my husband and myself, as unattainable as heaven on earth."[1]

Yelena Bonner's "dream" is not so much about home ownership per se as it is a longing for freedom. Observers of that peculiar species called Americans have often described their values by employing metaphorical devices. "The Star Spangled Banner" proclaims the United States to be the "*land* of the free" and the "*home* of the brave." Most countries, including ours, pour considerable quantities of mortar and brick into mausoleums that immortalize national heroes. But the United States has devoted a nearly equal amount of building materials to erect monuments to and representations of an idea: on Ellis Island, the Statue of Liberty; in Philadelphia, the Liberty Bell and Independence Hall; in Boston, the Freedom Trail.[2] These symbols are not mere icons passed from generation to generation but meaningful symbols of our values. A second-generation citizen told of his immigrant forebears' reverence for the Statue of Liberty: "She was America to my parents. They talked about her like she was alive. To them, I guess, she was."[3]

As these symbols demonstrate, the American polity is not a structure of government, but a contract between the government and its people whose clauses contain shared values. Among the most cherished is freedom. A blue-collar worker in the early 1960s said:

My God, I work where I want to work. I spend my money where I want to spend it. I buy what I want to buy. I go where I want to go. I read what I want to read. My kids go to the school that they want to go tō, or where I want to send them. We bring them up in the religion we want to bring them up in. What else—what else could you have?[4]

A 1986 poll found little change in the sentiments expressed by that worker: 88 percent believed that "freedom and liberty were two ideas that make America great."[5]

The value of freedom arrived with the first settlers. From afar William Pitt captured this aspect of the colonists when he told the British House of Lords in 1770: "I love Americans because they love liberty."[6] Six years later Thomas Jefferson elaborated on this theme in the Declaration of Independence: "We hold these truths to be self-evident, that all men are created equal, that they are endowed by their Creator with certain unalienable rights, that among these are Life, Liberty and the pursuit of Happiness."

As the years passed, an ideology that was uniquely American took hold. Gilbert K. Chesterton, after visiting the United States in the 1920s, concluded, "America is the only nation in the world that is founded on a creed."[7] In fact, Chesterton discovered the "Rosetta stone" of our society: the core of the American creed is a belief in the malleability of the future by the individual. At the conclusion of their daily "PTL" television show Jim and Tammy Bakker would remind their viewers: "You *can* make it!" The sentence became the couple's signature. Most often, however, the phrase "American dream" is the expression commonly used.[8]

The American dream is as old, and as young, as the United States itself. Regarding the presidency of John Quincy Adams, historian James Truslow Adams wrote that Adams believed his country stood for opportunity, "the chance to grow into something bigger and finer, as bigger and finer appealed to him."[9] More than 150 years later, little has changed. Like the sixth president, people everywhere continue to hope that their lives and their children's lives will be better. But, unlike the United States, few countries express themselves in terms of a national dream. Indeed, the parlance among Western nations is devoid of references to a French, German, or

British dream. The term "American dream" has come to stand for the ability of the individual to get ahead. At a 1983 news conference, Ronald Reagan put it this way: "What I want to see above all is that this country remains a country where someone can always get rich. That's the thing that we have and that must be preserved."[10]

Today, Americans of every political stripe extol the American dream. Accepting the Republican presidential nomination in 1960, Richard Nixon told the delegates: "I believe in the American dream because I have seen it come true in my own life."[11] Mario Cuomo echoed Nixon when he chronicled the struggles of his immigrant parents:

Poppa came in 1926 without a penny. Half a century later the family he and Momma started here are enjoying the milk and honey of the greatest and most abundantly blessed nation in the world. Just the idea that I am considered a possible choice for governor is a dramatic illustration of what this country means. It is the definition of the word "opportunity."[12]

A steelworker interviewed by Studs Terkel captured the sentiments expressed by Nixon and Cuomo more forcefully: "If my kid wants to work in a factory, I'm gonna kick the hell out of him. I want my kid to be an effete snot. I want him to be able to quote Walt Whitman, to be proud of it. If you can't improve yourself, you improve your posterity. Otherwise life isn't worth nothing."[13]

When asked by the Roper Organization in 1986 what the American dream meant to them, most spoke in terms of education and property. Eighty-four percent said the American dream symbolized a high school education; 80 percent said freedom of choice was part of the dream; 70 percent said it was owning a home; 77 percent thought it was their children's receiving a college diploma and 68 percent said it was getting a college education for themselves; 64 percent said financial security was part of the dream; 61 percent said it was realized in "doing better than my parents"; 58 percent said it was owning a business; 52 percent said it meant progressing "from worker to company president."[14]

The freedom to excel is an important component of the American dream. But another value is also inherent in the concept: equality of opportunity. Americans have been nearly fanatical in their devotion to this particular value. Max Berger wrote that the most indelible impression nineteenth-century British travelers had of their former colonies was "the aggressive equalitarianism of the people."[15] In the film *Knute Rockne—All American* Rockne's father claimed that only in America could his Norwegian son start on an "equal basis with all other children." This is followed by an on-screen commentary: "Among millions like themselves, simple hard-working people from the old countries following the new road of equality and opportunity which led to America, the Rockne family settled in Chicago."[16] As background, the orchestra plays "God Bless America."

Faith in aggressive equalitarianism has made the American dream especially appealing to the ordinary citizen. Indeed, it is the common man and woman who figure most prominently in the dream's persistence. They gave birth to it; they sustain it. Nixon realized this. Accepting the Republican presidential nomination for a second time in 1968, he told the delegates that it was the "great majority of Americans, the forgotten Americans" who "give lift to the American dream."[17]

"Forgotten Americans" still believe that with enough diligence and energy they can, like Nixon, see the American dream come true—if not in their lives, then in the lives of their children. This conviction has a long history. In his 1782 essay "What Is an American?" Jean de Crevecoeur found the answer in the American penchant for hard work:

Here the rewards of his industry follow with equal steps the progress of his labour; his labour is founded on the basis of *self-interest*; can it want a stronger allurement? Wives and children, who before in vain demanded of him a morsel of bread, now, fat and frolicsome, gladly help their father to clear those fields whence exuberant crops are to arise to feed and to clothe them all; without any part being claimed, either by a despotic prince, a rich abbot, or a mighty lord.[18]

Glorification of the work ethic has endured. In the 1940 film about his life, the pre-Notre Dame Knute Rockne is described this way: "In the great melting-pot of Chicago the Viking boy added a rich sense of humor to his lust for life, and a sturdy body to a level head. But ten years of hard work and sacrifice only strengthened the one dream in his heart."[19] As this narration appeared on theater screens, the orchestra played "America the Beautiful."

More than forty years later most Americans still believe the dream rests on their individual efforts. A 1984 National Opinion Research Center poll found 84 percent agreeing with the following statement: "America has an open society. Whatever one achieves in life no longer depends on one's family background, but on the abilities one has and the education one requires."[20] A 1987 study conducted by the same firm shows 66 percent saying that "hard work" is the most important factor in getting ahead; just 15 percent think "luck" is crucial.[21]

No wonder that Martin Luther King, like so many before him, seized on the American commitment to equalitarianism to woo supporters to the civil rights cause. Addressing thousands gathered at the Lincoln Memorial in 1963, King said in his speech, "I have a dream that my four little children will one day live in a nation where they will not be judged by the color of their skin but by the content of their character."[22]

Americans are also aggressively equalitarian when it comes to making individual choices. A 1981 Decision/Making/Information study asked respondents to choose between a "Mr. Smith" and a "Mr. Jones." "Mr. Smith believes that consenting adults ought to be able to do whatever they want in private." Mr. Jones, on the other hand, says, "There ought to be laws against certain kinds of behavior since many private actions have social consequences." Despite concerns about pornography and lack of moral standards, 66 percent said they agreed "strongly" or "somewhat" with Smith; just 32 percent agreed with Jones.[23] Pollster Daniel Yankelovich says Americans want to act as they choose, and people should be able to conduct themselves according to their own lights.[24]

This predilection for pluralism extends to highly unpopular views and unconventional lifestyles. National Opinion Research Center studies show considerable public tolerance of persons who are against churches and religion, admitted communists, racists, homosexuals, or who are antidemocratic. In each case, solid majorities believe they should be allowed to speak freely and have books that advocate such beliefs on the shelves of the community library.[25]

The American Consensus

The values of freedom, liberty, and equality of opportunity are dominant themes in U.S. history. They explain, for example, why so many Americans admire successful entrepreneurs. In the nineteenth century, Horatio Alger created a role model for many. By the late twentieth century, Chrysler Board Chairman Lee Iacocca had become a folk hero.

Business people are celebrated principally because they embody the American dream. Not surprisingly, then, Americans are obsessed with property (and property rights), largely because they are the tangible products of a triumphant political creed. James Q. Wilson described the tendency of Southern Californians to display the fruits of their labors: "Each family had a house; there it was for all to see and inspect. With a practiced glance, one could tell how much it cost, how well it was cared for, how good a lawn had been coaxed into uncertain life, and how tastefully plants and shrubs had been set out."[26]

The reverence for property is especially strong, even if not everyone has much to show off. In 1972 Democratic presidential candidate George McGovern made what he thought would be a surefire, popular promise to blue-collar rubber factory workers: as president he would seek to increase inheritance taxes so that the rich could bequeath less to their families and more to the government. To McGovern's amazement, he was roundly booed.[27]

In 1979, 26.1 million Americans, slightly more than one-tenth of the populace, were impoverished. By 1984 the figure had increased to 33.7 million, almost 15 percent.[28] The failure of so many to attain the American dream exposes its numerous falsehoods. In the Bruce Springsteen tune "The River," one of the characters wonders whether a dream was a lie if not fulfilled or whether it represented something worse? Throughout much of their history, Americans have consistently refused to confront such a haunting question, preferring to shoulder the blame themselves for having failed to live up to expectations. A quarter of a century ago a mechanic said:

I could have been a lot better off but through my own foolishness, I'm not. What causes poverty? Foolishness. When I came out of the service, my wife had saved a few dollars and I had a few bucks. I wanted to have a good time, I'm throwing money away like water. Believe me, had I used my head right, I could have had a house. I don't feel sorry for myself—what happened, happened, you know. Of course you pay for it.[29]

In 1986 an Iowa farmer facing foreclosure expressed a similar view: "My boys all made good. It's their old man who failed."[30]

Any attempt to limit the American dream meets with considerable resistance. Opportunity without constraints has been a recurrent pattern in our political thought. A 1940 *Fortune* poll found 74 percent rejected the idea that there "should be a law limiting the amount of money an individual is allowed to earn in a year."[31] Forty-one years later, the consensus held: 79 percent did not think that "there should be a top limit on incomes so that no one can earn more than $100,000 a year." Even those who earned less than $5,000 held that opinion.[32] A 1984 National Opinion Research Center survey found 71 percent believed that differences in social standing were acceptable because they resulted from "what people made out of the opportunities they had."[33]

Beneath such opinions is a faith that approaches fanaticism. Garry Wills wrote in 1978 that in the United States one must adopt the American dream "wholeheartedly, proclaim it, prove one's devotion to it."[34] He may have had in mind the House Committee on Un-American Activities, which was established during the hysteria about worldwide communist expansionism in 1945. For three decades the committee inquired into the public and private lives of suspected communists. Perhaps the most notable among the committee's many investigations was one led by freshman Congressman Richard Nixon in 1946. Nixon doggedly pursued Alger Hiss's ties to the Communist party, an inquiry that eventually resulted in Hiss's indictment and conviction for perjury. However, the committee's injudicious blacklisting of other Americans formed a stain on the witnesses and the committee itself that could not be removed. In 1975 the Committee on Un-American Activities was abolished on the grounds that it, too, was un-American.

The Committee on Un-American Activities illustrates the country's rigid enforcement of its political orthodoxy. Daniel Boorstin rhetorically asks, "Who would think of using the word 'unItalian' or 'unFrench' as we use the word un-American?"[35] As political scientist Louis Hartz once observed, "When one's ultimate values are accepted wherever one turns, the absolute language of self-evidence comes easily enough."[36] Indeed, our advancement of the "American Way of Life" has taken on missionary proportions. In the nineteenth century Herman Melville compared Americans to the biblical tribes of Israel, calling them "the peculiar chosen people . . . the Israel of our time."[37] A century later Ronald Reagan subscribed to a similar creationist view: "Think for a moment how special it is to be an American. Can we doubt that only a Divine Providence placed this land, this island of freedom, here as a refuge for all those people in the world who yearn to breathe free?"[38]

While Americans remain highly pluralistic regarding public expressions of unpopular views, their ideological zealotry about "the American way" places limits upon such speech. A majority say those with unconventional life styles should be restrained from using the classroom to promote their convictions: 54 percent maintain that "someone who is against churches and religion" should not be allowed to teach in a college or university; in the case of someone who believes "blacks are inferior," 55 percent; in the case of someone who advocates "doing away with elections and letting the military run the country," 58 percent; in the case of a communist, 53 percent. Only when asked about an "admitted homosexual" teacher did a majority, 53 percent, favor retention.[39]

These figures reflect an enduring pattern. Through the years Americans have been extremely reluctant to have public schools used as a platform for opposing ideologies. More than six decades ago a conference on immigrant education held the academic process responsible for ensuring the longevity of the American creed: "We believe in an Americanization which has for its end the making of good American citizens by developing in the mind of everyone who inhabits American soil an appreciation of the principles and practices of good American citizenship."[40] In 1987 the American Federation of Teachers reaffirmed this view, urging educators to abandon a "morally neutral" approach to teaching and affirm that "democracy is the worthiest form of human government ever conceived."[41]

A Puerile Conflict?

After traveling what was then the breadth of the United States in 1831 and 1832, and after having spoken to notables and ordinary citizens, the Frenchman Alexis de Tocqueville remarked, "All the domestic controversies of the Americans at first appear to a stranger to be incomprehensible or puerile, and he is at a loss whether to pity a people who take such arrant trifles in good earnest or to envy that happiness which enables a community to discuss them."[42] Tocqueville's observation was undoubtedly inspired by the relative ideological homogenity in the United States—especially when compared to his native land. No wonder that he found the young nation's political disputes almost quaint, even charming.

But as Tocqueville also noted, political scraps in the formerly British colonies were earnestly fought. Most were the result of an insufficient ideological underpinning. The Founding Fathers realized that freedom and liberty, the two ideas that "make America great," were not enough to build a nation. Writing in *The Federalist Papers*, James Madison observed, "Liberty is to faction what air is to fire."[43] He labeled the cacophony of interests (or to use his term "factions") as the source of all "instability, injustice, and confusion" introduced into public forums, which have been "the mortal diseases under which popular governments have everywhere perished."[44]

Liberty, in Madison's view, must have a suitable companion value to restrain its inevitable excesses. But which value? The Pledge of Allegiance speaks of "liberty and justice." Tocqueville himself paired liberty with several values: morality, law, the common good, and civic responsibility.

Each of liberty's potential mates seeks to restrain it. To pair liberty and morality, for example, implies that sexual mores must be confined to what constitutes "common decency." In ongoing polls conducted by the National Opinion Research Center over the past dozen years, 94 percent favor some limitations on the distribution of pornography; only 6 percent say there should be no restraints.[45] The marriage of liberty and civic responsibility also suggests that behavior must be circumscribed. The lawlessness depicted in Thomas Hobbes's "state of nature," wherein life was "solitary, poor, nasty, brutish, and short," suggested what could happen if there was liberty without civic responsibility.[46] Even a staunch democrat like Andrew Jackson acknowledged that "individuals must give up a share of liberty to preserve the rest."[47] Former *New York Times* columnist James Reston compares liberty without restraint to a "river without banks . . . It must be limited to be possessed."[48]

How do you limit liberty and still possess it? This is what divided Alexander Hamilton and Thomas Jefferson. Hamilton wanted liberty to be coupled with authority, so that economic interests (including his own) could be protected. Jefferson preferred that liberty be paired with local civic responsibility. It was on this basis that the enduring struggle between Hamiltonian Nationalism and Jeffersonian Democracy began.

Hamiltonian Nationalism envisions the United States as one "family," with a strong central government—especially an energetic executive—acting on its behalf. In 1791 Hamilton proclaimed:

Ideas of a contrariety of interests between the Northern and Southern regions of the Union, are in the main as unfounded as they are mischievous . . . Mutual wants constitute one of the strongest links of political connection . . . Suggestions of an opposite complexion are ever to be deplored, as unfriendly to the steady pursuit of one great common cause, and to the perfect harmony of all parts.[49]

Richard Henry Lee, author of the American resolution calling for independence from Great Britain, warned that Hamilton "calculated ultimately to make the states one consolidated government."[50] Jefferson was also wary of Hamilton's motives. Unlike Hamilton, Jefferson had a nearly limitless faith in the ordinary citizen. To a nation largely composed of farmers, he declared, "Those who labor in the earth are the chosen people of God, if ever He had a chosen people, whose breasts He has made the peculiar deposit for substantial and genuine virtue."[51] Jefferson's devotion to liberty made him distrust most attempts to restrain it, particularly those of government: "Were we directed from Washington when to sow, and when to reap, we should soon want bread."[52] In 1825 Jefferson warned of the expanding power of state government and wrote that the "salvation of the republic" rested on the regeneration and spread of the New England town meeting.[53] The best guarantee of liberty in Jefferson's view was the exclusion of the "invisible hand" of government. Americans, he said, would "surmount every difficulty by resolution and contrivance. Remote from all other aid we are obliged to invent and execute; to find means within ourselves and not lean on others."[54] Given the peculiar character of his compatriots, it was not surprising that Jefferson won the presidency in 1800.

By the time of Tocqueville's visit almost six decades after the revolt against George III, most citizens remained suspicious of central government. Tocqueville described them as having "acquired or retained sufficient education and fortune to satisfy their own wants. They owe nothing to any man, they expect nothing from any man; they acquire the habit of always considering themselves as standing alone, and they are apt to imagine that their whole destiny is in their own hands."[55]

For nearly two centuries the debate between Hamiltonian Nationalism and Jeffersonian Democracy has dominated U.S. politics. Republicans and Democrats have argued both sides of the issue, not always adhering to the same one. During the Civil War and the industrial era that followed, Republicans stood with Hamilton; Democrats claimed Jefferson as their own and promoted "states rights." Since the days of Franklin D. Roosevelt, Democrats have consistently aligned themselves with Hamilton, preferring to view the nation as a family. Mario Cuomo refers to the idea as "a fundamental of our history," adding: "The recognition that at the heart of the matter we are bound inextricably to one another; that the layoff of a steel worker in Buffalo is *our* problem; the pain and struggle of a handicapped mother in Houston is *our* struggle; the fight of a retired school teacher in Chicago to live in dignity is *our* fight."[56]

While Cuomo and the Democrats have reinvented Hamilton's vision, the Republicans have rearticulated Jeffersonian Democracy. Listen to Reagan: "Through lower taxes and smaller government, government has its ways of freeing people's spirits."[57] Reagan and his partisans view the country not as a family but as a collection of diverse communities for whom liberty means, in the words of former Supreme Court Justice Louis Brandeis, "the right to be let alone."[58]

Henry Steele Commager believes that since the nation's founding, the character of the American people has not changed greatly nor has the "nature of the principles of conduct, public and private, to which they subscribe."[59] Our values may be constant, but the circumstances in which they are applied are not. The whiff of civil war, the onset of a depression, or the ravages of inflation inevitably cause Americans to take stock of the situation, their expectations of government, and settle upon a course of action in a manner consistent with the American creed.

At critical junctures, Americans have oscillated from Hamiltonian Nationalism to Jeffersonian Democracy. The shift in public attitudes has usually been influenced by a dominant personality. Abraham Lincoln reasserted Hamilton's vision of a national family so as to save the Union. Three score and ten years later, Franklin Roosevelt chose Hamiltonian Nationalism to meet the Great Depression head on: "We have been extending to our national life the old principle of the community . . . [The] neighbors [now] are the people of the United States as a whole."[60] At other times Jeffersonian Democracy has been preferred. Reagan promised to restore the concept of neighborhood in 1980 by taking "government off the backs of the great people of this country" and turning "you loose again to do those things that I know you can do so well."[61]

Usually, however, citizens do not choose between Hamiltonian Nationalism and Jeffersonian Democracy but enjoy the fruits of both simultaneously. Walter Lippmann put it this way: "To be partisan . . . as between Jefferson and Hamilton is like arguing whether men or women are more necessary to the procreation of the race. Neither can live alone. Alone—that is, without the other—each is excessive and soon intolerable."[62] Nevertheless, Americans have tried at various intervals to live with one and not the other. The results have been less than satisfactory. Herbert Croly argued that Hamilton "perverted that national idea as much as Jefferson perverted the American democratic idea, and the proper relation of these two fundamental conceptions one to another cannot be completely understood until this double perversion is corrected."[63]

It is the inevitable perversion of Hamiltonian Nationalism and Jeffersonian Democracy that insures periodic swings from one to the other. As each prevails at one juncture or another, Americans experience a sense of return when the old battles start up again on new but seemingly familiar territory. Hamilton would be astonished to learn that his concept of a national family is being used to promote the interests of the have-nots, especially women and minorities. And Reagan's espousal of Jeffersonian Democracy is premised on a welfare state first erected by Roosevelt's New Deal. The circumstances may change, but the arguments always have a familiar ring.

High Priest, Chief Warrior

Several years after leaving the White House, Harry Truman described the presidency as "the most peculiar office in the world."[64] British scholar Harold Laski elaborated on Truman's statement, saying that the essence of the American presidency is "that it functions in an American environment, that it has been shaped by the forces of American history, that it must be judged by American criteria of its responses to American needs."[65]

One of the unusual requirements of the electorate is its insatiable need to reaffirm the American dream. This stems, no doubt, from the dream's inherent illogic. James Truslow Adams had this to say: "The American dream—the belief in the value of the common man, and the hope of opening every avenue of opportunity to him—was not a logical concept of thought. Like every great thought that has stirred and advanced humanity, it was a religious emotion, a great act of faith, a courageous leap into the unknown."[66]

In many respects the American dream has assumed religious trappings, with the president acting as a high priest. This is due, in part, to the voters' extraordinary expectations: the president is to make the American dream come true for them, just as it has come true for the president himself. Nixon understood this when, as a candidate in 1968, he spoke of his youthful aspirations:

I see [a] child tonight. He hears a train go by. At night he dreams of faraway places where he'd like to go. It seems like an impossible dream. But he is helped on his journey through life. A father who had to go to work before he finished the sixth grade sacrificed everything so his sons could go to college.

A gentle Quaker mother with a passionate concern for peace quietly wept when he went to war but she understood why he had to go.

A great teacher, a remarkable football coach, an inspirational minister encouraged him on his way. A courageous wife and loyal children stood by him in victory and also in defeat.

And in his chosen profession of politics, first there were scores, then hundreds, then thousands, and finally millions who worked for his success.

And tonight he stands before you, nominated for President of the United States of America.

You can see why I believe so deeply in the American dream.[67]

Republicans are not alone in pledging fealty to the American dream. In 1984 Democrat Walter Mondale was aggressively equalitarian when he selected the first woman to run for vice president on a major party ticket. He paid homage to the dream, reminding the convention delegates, "America is a future each generation must seek to enlarge . . . For the rest of my life, I want to talk with young people about their future. And whatever their race, whatever their religion, whatever their sex, I want to hear some of them say what I say, with joy and reverence tonight, 'I want to be President of the United States.'"[68]

Presidents embody the dreams of their fellow citizens in a way that no other public official can. Clinton Rossiter said, "The final greatness of the presidency lies in the truth that it is not just an office of incredible power but a breeding ground of indestructible myth."[69] Seeking reelection in the midst of a bloody civil war with victory not yet secured, Lincoln was depicted in several "popular life" biographies as an example of what a poor American boy can achieve if he wants "to climb the heights."[70]

Nothing much has changed since then. Log cabins have been replaced by middle-class ranch homes. But political hagiographers still stress a president's relatively humble beginnings, or deemphasize a president's more prosperous origins. This results from the expectation that the public persona of every chief magistrate must become a "living symbol," like the Statue of Liberty was to the immigrants, of the values and aspirations of the populace. Reagan is fond of reminding audiences of his early days as a lifeguard in Dixon, Illinois, earning fifteen dollars per week. Before Reagan became president, pollster Richard Wirthlin told him, "[By] symbolizing the past and future greatness of America and radiating inspirational confidence, a President can pull a nation together while directing its people toward fulfillment of the American dream."[71]

Presidents cannot simply pay homage to the American dream; they must reaffirm it by actions that enhance individual self-esteem and self-fulfillment. That task casts the president in a second great role: chief warrior in the struggle between Hamiltonian Nationalism and Jeffersonian Democracy. Traditionally, the presidency has been perceived as the principal catalyst for the engine of progress. Often that means a candidate for the office has to decide on the faction— Hamiltonian Nationalism or Jeffersonian Democracy—with which he chooses to identify. Hamilton understood this when he wrote: "Every vital question of state will be merged in the question, 'Who will be the next President?'"[72] A 1980 Decision/Making/Information survey conducted for the Reagan campaign found most still thought this was so: 76 percent rejected the idea that "it really doesn't matter who is elected President since things won't change much anyway."[73]

Before he entered politics, Woodrow Wilson remarked, "There can be no mistaking the fact that we have grown more and more inclined from generation to generation to look to the President as the unifying force in our complex system, the leader of both his party and of the nation." He added, "If he rightly interprets the national thought and boldly insists upon it, he is irresistible; and the country never feels the zest of action so much as when its President is of such insight and calibre. Its instinct is for unified action and it craves a single leader."[74]

By 1980 the craving for a leader who would act decisively became irresistible. As Herbert Croly would have predicted, Hamiltonian Nationalism had been perverted by Roosevelt's successors and Jeffersonian Democracy looked to be an alternative. Voters wanted a redefinition of the country's course. As Roosevelt once said, "All our great Presidents were leaders of thought at times when certain historic ideas in the life of the nation had to be clarified."[75] The electorate was demanding just such a clarification. The time had come for a change.

3

A TRANSFORMING ELECTION

Honk if you believe in anybody or anything!
—automobile bumper sticker, circa 1980

The atmosphere in the room was hot, tense, expectant. The high command of the Reagan for President team sat around a large table. Its members had met many times before—early in the morning, late at night, at all hours. Most had devoted the past six years or more to advancing Ronald Reagan's presidential ambitions. Now it had come down to this: the final strategy session prior to Tuesday's balloting. The public polls were only modestly encouraging. Louis Harris had Reagan ahead by 5 percentage points; George Gallup, 3; CBS News and the *New York Times*, 1. These findings reflected the view of many pundits that the Reagan-Carter contest would be close, that it might resemble the Kennedy-Nixon photo finish of 1960.

The final calibrations made by Reagan polltaker Richard B. Wirthlin showed a very different result: Reagan, 50.0 percent; Carter, 40.5; Anderson, 9.3. Wirthlin's electoral count also looked good, with the worst-case scenario giving Reagan 290 electors, 20 more than required for victory. Some of those seated at that table were nervous about the discrepancies between the polls, but Wirthlin was confident victory was at hand. Election night saw him vindicated: forty-four states and 489 electors had seen to it that Ronald Reagan would live up to his billing as "the next president of the United States." Political pundits were forced to answer a simple, compelling question: "What happened?"

Most focused on the "events" of 1980. Every presidential campaign leaves markers, and that year was no exception. There was Carter's clumsy attempt to quarantine challenger Edward M. Kennedy with the threat "I'll whip his ass." But Kennedy had already lost his way even before he started. In an interview with Roger Mudd the Massachusetts Democrat gave these inchoate reasons for wanting to move to 1600 Pennsylvania Avenue:

> Well, I'm—were I to make the—announcement . . . is because I have a great belief in this country, that it is—has more natural resources than any nation in the world . . . the greatest technology of any country in the world . . . the greatest political system in the world . . . And the energies and the resourcefulness of this nation, I think, should be focused on these problems in a way that brings a sense of restoration in this country by its people to . . . And I would basically feel that—that it's imperative for this country to either move forward, that it can't stand still, or otherwise it moves back.[1]

The Republican trail had its important markers, too. Most came in debates starring Reagan. At a gathering featuring the GOP hopefuls at a school gymnasium in Nashua, New Hampshire, Reagan grabbed the microphone when he learned that only George Bush would be allowed to participate, shouting, "I am paying for this microphone, Mr. Green [sic]!"[2] Reagan's statement, a borrowed line from actor Spencer Tracy's performance in the film *State of the Union*, resulted in a primary win that all but ended the contest for the nomination. Still, the most distinctive Republican marker was Reagan's parting jab at Carter: "Are you better off than you were four years ago?" In the few seconds it took to utter that remark came the rationale for ousting an incumbent president, only the second time since the close of World War II that that had happened.

To consider only these events is to miss a larger and more important story in American politics. Nearly two decades ago Samuel Lubell wrote that voting is analogous to "a river that rises in the past and empties into the future."[3] For presidential elections, a more appropriate analogy might be an ocean. The tidal wave that swept Reagan into office had its origins in the swirling sixties and seventies. It is not hard to remember the earlier waves that had pounded the electoral shores:

- November 22, 1963. John Kennedy, thirty-fourth president, is assassinated in Dallas.
- August 7, 1964. Congress passes the Gulf of Tonkin Resolution, a measure that Lyndon Johnson interprets as a declaration of war on North Vietnam.
- August 28, 1968. Hubert H. Humphrey receives the Democratic presidential nomination amid violence in the streets of Chicago.

- August 15, 1971. Richard Nixon imposes wage and price controls in an effort to contain the 4 percent inflation rate.
- June 17, 1972. Five men working for the Committee to Reelect the President burglarize the offices of the Democratic National Committee in the Watergate office complex.
- October 15, 1973. A mostly Arab group, the Organization of Petroleum Exporting Countries (OPEC), imposes its first oil embargo on the United States.
- August 9, 1974. Richard Nixon, thirty-seventh president, resigns in the face of certain impeachment and conviction by Congress.
- November 4, 1979. U.S. embassy personnel are seized and held hostage for 444 days in Teheran.
- October 24, 1980. The Bureau of Labor Statistics reports that the annual rate of inflation has jumped to 12.7 percent.

These waves, one after another, left voters emotionally exhausted and politically frustrated. From 1973 to 1980, fewer than 20 percent thought the country was on the "right track"; 75 percent believed it was in disarray.[4] Inflation was judged to be a primary cause of the chaos, according to a December 1979 Decision/Making/Information poll. A few typical responses: "Everything goes up except the wages"; "We're not going to have money for anything"; "Inflation will be the death of us all unless taken care of very soon"; "There's no way we can make it with inflation. Our crazy government is to blame."[5]

Inflation was just one of the discouraging phenomena. More disheartening were future prospects. For the first time, a substantial number of Americans began to question whether the quality of their lives and inevitably those of their children would be better. Suddenly, the American dream had become suspect. Patrick Caddell, Jimmy Carter's polltaker, was the first to spot the sea change. By late spring of 1979, he found most Americans believing they would be "worse off" five years hence than they were then.[6]

"Honk If You Believe in Anybody or Anything!"

In a turn-of-the-century work, *Success among the Nations*, Emil Reich wrote:

The Americans are filled with such an implicit and absolute confidence in their Union and in their future success, that any remark other than laudatory is unacceptable to the majority of them. We have had many opportunities of hearing public speakers in America cast doubts upon the very existence of God and of Providence, question the historic nature or veracity of the whole fabric of Christianity; but it has never been our fortune to catch the slightest whisper of doubt, the slightest want of faith, in the chief God of America—unlimited belief in the future of America.[7]

Seven decades later there were many doubting Thomases. A popular automobile bumper sticker advertised the national self-doubt: "Honk if you believe in anybody or anything!" Historian Oscar Handlin wrote of this apostasy to the American dream:

The idea that the future holds exciting and wonderful things to look forward to is pretty much washed up these days. Even during the Great Depression, there was a sense of hope that a better society of some sort, a new twentieth century society, would emerge. And even before the Civil War there was a tremendous excitement for the future. Those are really the only two precedents for this national mood, and yet there was hope and optimism even then.[8]

It seemed as though the country's foundations had crumbled and its structure was collapsing. Caught in the breakdown was the American family itself. A 1981 Decision/Making/Information poll found 68 percent believing "families are weaker now than they were several years ago." A plurality blamed a lowering of parental standards and sexual permissiveness.[9] One American tale could be used to illustrate the changing family scene. In the early 1940s an Illinois-born man emigrated to the "Promised Land"—California. He entered a burgeoning profession, marrying shortly thereafter. By the end of the decade things went sour. The marriage failed. The career he had embarked upon faltered. The children of a successful second marriage seemed to mock his and his wife's values. For a time during the 1960s one of them lived, unmarried, with a rock singer. Another dropped out of college and, for a time, became a writer for *Playboy* magazine.

Reagan's story may not be typical, but it does illuminate some of the phenomenal social and cultural changes over the past two decades—transformations that by 1980 had exacted their price. Consider:

- Two of three Americans said, "Everything changes so quickly these days that I often have trouble deciding which are the right rules to follow."

- A majority believed "we were better off in the old days when everyone knew just how they were expected to act."
- Seventy-one percent thought that "many things our parents stood for are going to ruin right before our eyes."
- Nearly eight in ten held that "what is lacking in the world today is the old kind of friendship that lasted for a lifetime."
- One in two agreed with the statement "I feel left out of things going on around me."[10]

The widespread sense of personal normlessness was coupled with the pervasive ridicule toward traditional values from those in positions of power. A 1980 study done for the Connecticut Mutual Life Insurance Company found values held by the nation's leaders—in business, the news media, government, science, education, and the law, among others—were considerably at odds with those shared by the public. For example, 71 percent of the general respondents believed that homosexuality was "morally wrong"; just 51 percent of those in business, 38 percent of those in the news media, 36 percent of government workers, 27 percent of scientists, and 30 percent of educators so believed. Sixty-five percent thought that abortion was "morally wrong;" fewer than half of those in business and only one-third of the media people, government workers, scientists, educators, and lawyers thought so. Lesbianism was condemned by 70 percent, but only 42 percent of the elites found such conduct abhorrent. Seventy-one percent also disapproved of sex before the age of sixteen; just 55 percent of the leaders disapproved. Smoking marijuana was classified as "morally wrong" by 57 percent of the general populace; only 48 percent of the business leaders, 28 percent of the news media, 26 percent of those in government, 21 percent of the scientists, 30 percent of the educators, and 19 percent of the lawyers objected to this practice. Divorce produced an even sharper division: slightly more than half the general public thought it should be "more difficult" to obtain, and only one-fifth of the elites surveyed thought so.[11]

A values gap between the governed and their governors had become one of the dominant features of American life. Just before the 1980 election, that gap widened into a veritable Grand Canyon. A 1979–1980 study found half of those who worked in the news media listed their religion as "none"; 54 percent labeled themselves "liberal"; 90 percent said a "woman has a right to decide on an abortion"; 80 percent favored "strong affirmative action for blacks"; 76 percent did not believe that "homosexuality is wrong"; 85 percent rejected the view that "homosexuals should not teach in the public schools"; 54 percent disavowed the notion that "adultery is wrong."[12] As differences widened between influentials and the masses, a fundamental political question was reopened: *Who should exercise authority?* According to studies conducted by S. Robert Lichter and Stanley Rothman, more than eight of ten leaders preferred that Hubert Humphrey, George McGovern, and Jimmy Carter do so in the presidential contests that spanned the years 1968 to 1976.[13] The public agreed, narrowly, in only one instance: Carter.

The dichotomy of opinion between the public and its leaders was reflected in an alienation from those institutions the elite occupied. One Pennsylvania woman maintained: "I feel so far from government. I feel like ordinary people are excluded from political power."[14] She was not alone. By 1980, the disassociation from government had grown to alarming proportions: 51 percent did *not* believe that "important national problems such as energy shortages, inflation, and crime could be solved through traditional American politics"; 50 percent did *not* believe that the vote was "the main thing that determines how the country is run"; 48 percent did *not* believe that "important decisions on public issues are best left in the hands of our leaders."[15] A malaise gripped the nation, one that questioned the legitimacy of American values and institutions.

Jimmy Carter's Malaise

In a surprise move the president of the United States took to the airwaves and admonished his fellow Americans to "snap . . . out of the self-doubt, the self-disparagement that saps our energy and erodes our confidence in ourselves."[16] So proclaimed Richard Nixon in that summer of our discontent, August 1971. That first "malaise speech" marked the beginning of numerous Oval Office exhortations, the essence of which was "If only we would believe in ourselves again!" Vietnam, Watergate, and a lackluster economy, however, muted the pep talks of Nixon and his appointed successor, Gerald Ford. By 1975, just 19 percent thought the country was on the "right track"; 71 percent believed it was headed in the wrong direction.[17] According to pollster Wirthlin, voters wanted a president who would "supplant disarray with order, mismanagement with management, and malaise with confidence."[18] It was in this context that Jimmy Carter launched his quest for the presidency.

A successful candidate defines and captures the issues of the times. That political maxim held in 1976. After Vietnam and Watergate, the electorate yearned for a reaffirmation of the values that constitute the American dream: liberty, family, patriotism, self-esteem, and self-realization. Carter understood that, often sounding more like a preacher than a politician:

We have lost some precious things that historically have bound our people and our government together. We feel the moral decay that has weakened the country; that it's crippled by a lack of goals and values and that our public officials have lost faith in us. . . . We want to have faith again. We want to be proud again. We just want the truth again![19]

Carter tried to exemplify the values of which he spoke. He proudly announced that he was a "born-again" Christian. Some of his advisers warned him not to advertise that fact, to which the Georgian succinctly retorted: "That's all right, it'll get me votes."[20]

The public had great difficulty taking Jimmy Carter's measure. In his campaign autobiography *Why Not the Best?*, Carter introduced himself this way: "I am a Southerner and an American. I am a farmer, an engineer, a father and a husband, a Christian, a politician and former governor, a planner, a businessman, a nuclear physicist, a naval officer, a canoeist, and, among other things, a lover of Bob Dylan's songs and Dylan Thomas' poetry."[21] No other aspirant, with the possible exception of Thomas Jefferson, could have checked so many occupation boxes on a White House job application. In the wee hours after the election, NBC News correspondent Edwin Newman observed that Carter had "spent twenty-three months in pursuit of the presidency . . . and he will embark on that presidency as little known as any man who has won that office in many, many years."[22] Still, the desire for a strong leader who would reaffirm the American dream was such that a narrow majority handed the reins of government to a relative unknown.

In 1976 Carter the man won the public's trust, and in 1977 Carter the president was perceived as capable of making the American dream more of a reality for many. By 1979, however, the pre-1976 funk had returned, and Carter's popularity fell from 75 percent at the start of his term to a dismal 39 percent.[23] Voters continued to view him as likeable, religious, moral, and trustworthy, but they were not convinced that these qualities were being translated into a strategy for successful governance.

During the 1960 presidential campaign, Eric Sevareid spoke of a "managerial revolution" that had come to politics. Nixon and Kennedy, he claimed, were sharp, ambitious, opportunistic, but devoid of strong convictions—unlike the young men of the thirties who "dreamt beautiful and foolish dreams about the perfectibility of man, cheered Roosevelt and adored the poor."[24]

In the ensuing two decades, Sevareid's managerial revolution was brought to completion within the Democratic party. The warmth and humanity of personal leadership became submerged. Rather than emphasizing common values, the Democrats, according to former Massachusetts Attorney General Francis X. Bellotti, "developed a whole class of technocrats, managers and statisticians to give us supporting data for our assumptions, to help us fine tune our solutions." The consequence: "Many of our political leaders gave away their power to make the decisions and lost their will to fight for the individual."[25]

The Carter administration exhibited all of the symptoms Bellotti described. It was both blessed and cursed with an extraordinary number of young, capable managers including special assistant Stuart Eizenstat, National Security Advisor Zbigniew Brzezinski, economist Barry Bosworth, adviser Anne Wexler, and former *Time* managing editor Hedley Donovan. Yet the sum of all that talent was less than its individual parts. After leaving the White House in 1978, former Carter speech writer James Fallows said, "In the two years in the government I had not one serious or impassioned discussion with a member of the senior staff about what all these countless government programs meant, which of them, if any, really worked, how the government might be changed. I think it must have been different in other days."[26] Fallows dubbed the Carter regime "the passionless presidency," claiming Carter was

still the detail man used to running his own warehouse, the perfectionist accustomed to thinking that to do a job right you must do it yourself. He would leave for a weekend at Camp David laden with thick briefing books, would pore over the budget tables to check the arithmetic, and, during his first six months in office would personally review all requests to use the White House tennis court.[27]

Not all of Carter's troubles stemmed from his engineer's bent for attending to detail. The U.S. polity operates best when the values and aspirations of its leaders are congruent with those of their followers. During Franklin Roosevelt's presidency and for a generation thereafter such a consensus existed. Its mainstay was FDR's rearticulation of Hamiltonian Nationalism.

Hamiltonian Nationalism remained popular long after Roosevelt's death because it was congruent with traditional American values and it worked. During the 1960 presidential campaign, historian and Kennedy confidant Arthur Schlesinger felt compelled to write a tract titled *Kennedy or Nixon: Does It Make Any Difference?*[28] Given the atmospherics of the Kennedy and Johnson years, any resurrection of Jeffersonian Democracy was viewed as a radical departure, as Barry Goldwater conceded: "Extremism in the defense of liberty is no vice. Moderation in the pursuit of justice is no virtue."[29]

Goldwater's unsuccessful resuscitation of Jeffersonian Democracy forced Republicans to reexamine his slogan "A Choice, Not An Echo." The Grand Old Party could recognize Hamiltonian Nationalism's grasp upon the majority, or it could adhere to orthodoxy and slowly wither away. The decision, made at its 1968 convention, was for less choice and more echo. That was achieved by awarding the nomination to that last unreconstructed New Dealer—Richard Nixon.

Whatever misgivings Nixon may have had about FDR's reconstruction of Hamiltonian Nationalism, they were well concealed in his actions as president. Attorney General John N. Mitchell set the motif for the Nixon era: "Watch what we do, not what we say." Among the administration's doings were the raising of Social Security benefits by 15 percent in 1969, 10 percent in 1971, and 20 percent in 1972.[30] New federal agencies were established, including the Environmental Protection Agency, the Occupational Safety and Health Administration, and the Consumer Product Safety Commission. A nationalization of all welfare programs was attempted, albeit unsuccessfully.[31] By 1972, for the first time in the post-World War II era, federal spending on income maintenance, health, and education exceeded defense expenditures. Declared Nixon, "We are all Keynesians now."[32]

Hamiltonian Nationalism did not go quite unchallenged. In 1968 third-party candidate George Wallace mounted an aggressive counterattack against what he saw as its excesses. He described the Washington bureaucracy as a bunch of "strutting pseudo-intellectuals" who were writing guidelines and telling communities that "they have not got sense enough to run their own schools and hospitals and local domestic institutions."³³ As if to prove Alexis de Tocqueville's point about the "puerile nature" of our domestic disputes, Wallace promised that if elected president, he would run over many employees in his government-issue limousine.

A more carefully reasoned critique came from Robert F. Kennedy. In *To Seek a Newer World* the former attorney general deplored the "loss of the sense of community" and the "suppression of individuality."³⁴ Much of Kennedy's remedy rested in Thomas Jefferson's vision of a participatory democracy, specifically in hundreds of neighborhood voluntary organizations.³⁵ Such self-help groups, in Kennedy's view, provided the necessary corrective lenses for Jefferson's vision of the United States, which had become "increasingly difficult [to see] in the face of the giant organizations and massive bureaucracies of the age."³⁶

The Wallace and Kennedy criticisms opened a decade-long reevaluation of Hamiltonian Nationalism's goals and methods. Subsequent events only intensified the scrutiny—the most unpopular war in American history, Vietnam; the worst scandal to afflict the presidency since Teapot Dome, Watergate; economic dislocations; and America held hostage, Iran. As each act unfolded, FDR's construct of Hamiltonian Nationalism became increasingly perverted as his successors, particularly Lyndon Johnson, enlarged upon it.

Johnson's Great Society took Hamiltonian Nationalism to unprecedented heights: Medicare for the elderly; Medicaid for the poor; food stamps for the hungry; legal assistance for the indigent; economic revitalization plans for distressed areas; research and care for victims of heart disease and cancer. Campaigning in 1964, Johnson gave this grand summation of his forthcoming governing strategy on a Providence, Rhode Island, street corner: "We're in favor of a lot of things and we're against mighty few."³⁷

The unintended by-product of Johnson's spending programs and prosecution of the Vietnam War without additional federal taxes was inflation. One measure of its ravages: a 1967 dollar would have purchased $3.37 worth of goods in 1913 when Ronald Reagan was a toddler; by 1981 the 1967 greenback was worth a mere 41 cents.³⁸ Public confidence that government could act as an equitable balance wheel—engaging in deficit spending when the economy was depressed, and restraining its expenditures in good times—was shaken.

That particular tenet of Keynesian economics was jettisoned by skyrocketing inflation and high unemployment.

Another perversion of FDR's Hamiltonian Nationalism manifested itself in the enlarged vision presidents had of their responsibilities. Hamilton's concept of federalism included a strong, purposeful leader who would articulate and fulfill the needs of the national community. "Energy in the Executive," he wrote, "is the leading character in the definition of good government."[39] Three decades after Roosevelt's death, energetic executives were no longer exerting their powers to secure majoritarian goals. Johnson single-handedly prosecuted the Vietnam War. Nixon sought refuge from prosecution for his handling of the Watergate affair. These failed presidencies allowed the electorate to compile a lengthy indictment against the federal bureaucracy that included the following particulars: it is engaging in activities that are illegitimate; it is controlled by a few large business and labor interests; and it fails to act appropriately, even when a popular consensus exists that some action should be taken.[40]

Sensing that the Democratic party's concept of Hamiltonian Nationalism was in trouble, Carter attempted to experiment. He established a new division at the Department of Housing and Urban Development, the Office of Neighborhood Voluntary Associations and Consumer Protection. He fought for and won deregulation of the airline and trucking industries. Carter explained, "Government cannot solve our problems. It can't set our goals. It cannot define our vision. Government cannot eliminate poverty or provide a bountiful economy."[41]

Carter's tinkering lacked coherence. By midterm the public portrait of Carter had some darker hues: 66 percent of a national sample said it was "hard to know where he stands"; 58 percent thought he "lacks strong leadership qualities"; 48 percent maintained he "offers unimaginative solutions to national problems."[42] James Fallows wrote, "Carter has not given us an *idea* to follow . . . Hubert Humphrey might have carried out Lyndon Johnson's domestic policies; Gerald Ford, the foreign policies of Richard Nixon. But no one could carry out the Carter program because Carter has resisted providing the overall guidelines that might explain what his program is."[43]

Not all of this was Carter's fault. One reason for the perceived lack of coherence is that some Democrats discerned a pattern to the

Carter approach and did not like what they saw. Rather than let him redesign what had taken years to build, many encouraged Edward M. Kennedy to challenge Carter. Special interest groups also attacked Carter at every turn. In a July 1979 assessment of his record, Carter was told that "the public acknowledged my intelligence and integrity, my ability to articulate problems and to devise good solutions to them, but doubted my capacity to follow through with a strong enough thrust to succeed."[44] These evaluations prompted him to give a reprise of Nixon's 1971 speech. In this second "malaise speech," Carter asserted:

What you see too often in Washington and elsewhere around the country is a system of government that seems incapable of action. You see a Congress twisted and pulled in every direction by hundreds of well-financed and powerful special interests. You see every extreme position defended to the last vote, almost to the last breath by one unyielding group or another. You often see a balanced and fair approach that demands sacrifice, a little sacrifice from everyone, abandoned like an orphan without support and without friends.[45]

Carter promised to find a way out of the crisis, but any attempt to redirect the Democratic party back to the future was going to be resisted by most members of the Democratic Congress and the interest groups that contributed so heavily to their campaigns. The 1980 Democratic platform reflected this struggle for the party's soul. Covering every conceivable issue from water rights to Puerto Rico, it promised in three successive paragraphs "to live within the limits of anticipated revenues," resist "drastic cuts in social programs which impose unfair burdens on . . . [those] who can least afford them," and dedicated the party "to operating our government more efficiently, and concentrating our efforts on eliminating waste, fraud, and abuse."[46]

As the Carter reelection campaign became mired in difficulties, the president conceded defeat to his party's Hamiltonian Nationalists. In the debate with Reagan, Carter emphasized his Rooseveltian roots:

We have made good progress. And there's no doubt in my mind that the commitment to unemployment compensation, the minimum wage, welfare, national health insurance, those kinds of commitments that have typified the Democratic party since ancient history in this country's political life are a very important element of the future.[47]

Although Carter was making overtures to his fellow Democrats, he was far from conceding defeat to Reagan. During the campaign, White House Chief of Staff Hamilton Jordan flatly stated: "The American people are not going to elect a seventy-year-old, right wing, ex-movie actor to be President."[48]

A Strategy of Values

From the outset he was heard to say, "I have premised my campaign for the Presidency on the single assumption that the American people are uneasy at the present drift in our national course, that they are disturbed by the relative decline in our vitality and in our prestige, and that, they have the will and the strength to start the United States moving again."[49] So said John Kennedy in 1960. Kennedy's premise held by the narrowest of margins. He attacked Dwight D. Eisenhower's "hidden-hand" management of domestic affairs,[50] the administration's clumsiness during the U-2 incident,[51] and a purported "missile gap" that gave an advantage to the Soviet Union.

Twenty years later Ronald Reagan echoed John Kennedy's themes. But unlike the Kennedy campaign of long ago, there was a sense that something more was wrong with the country than merely ineffectual leaders. In 1979 the Reagan campaign commissioned a poll inquiring about the values and aspirations of the electorate. Results indicated that Reagan backers regretted the loss of values in society, particularly those associated with the business ethics of hard work and high yield. Respondents preferred Carter to Reagan by a margin of 46 percent to 42 percent. But the Reagan-Carter battlelines were clear: respondents who had a high sense of service to country, were critical of most welfare programs, were antiunion, wanted to reduce the size of government, and were less likely to be pacifists were more strongly in support of Reagan.[52] It was from this perspective that Reagan launched what became known within the campaign as "a strategy of values." Its ingredients were vitriolic attacks on the Carter record and charges that the Carter policies eroded American family values. To shouts of approval from convention delegates, Reagan derided the Carter era: "Can anyone look at the record of this administration and say, 'Well done'? Can anyone compare the state of our economy when the Carter administration took office with where we are today and say, 'Keep up the good work'? Can anyone look at our reduced standing in the world today and say, 'Let's have four more years of this'?"[53] Even Patrick Caddell conceded that "there was no way we could survive if we allowed [the election] to become a referendum on the first three years of the Carter administration."[54]

The economy proved a sore spot for Carter. Running against Ford in 1976, Carter devised the "misery index," a figure arrived at by adding the rates of inflation and unemployment. In 1976, the misery index stood at 12.5 percent; by 1980, it was nearly 20 percent. Reagan cited the misery index repeatedly, arguing that the economist's dictionary should be amended as follows: "A recession is when your neighbor loses his job, a depression is when you lose your job, and a recovery is when Jimmy Carter loses his."[55]

The larger portion of the Reagan strategy, however, was a reiteration of traditional values. Accepting the Republican presidential nomination in 1980, Reagan proclaimed his party was "ready to build a new consensus with all those across the land who share a community of values embodied in these words: family, work, neighborhood, peace and freedom."[56] The party platform, drafted by Reagan loyalists, elaborated:

We will reemphasize those vital communities like the family, the neighborhood, the workplace, and others which are found at the center of our society between government and the individual. We will restore and strengthen their ability to solve problems in the places where people spend their daily lives and can turn to each other for support and help.[57]

Reagan was particularly well suited to carry this message to the electorate. For more than a decade such value-laden language had punctuated his rhetoric, as evidenced in a letter written while he was governor to a California constituent: "I am deeply concerned with the wave of hedonism—the humanist philosophy so prevalent today—and believe this nation must have a spiritual rebirth, a rededication to the moral precepts which guided us for so much of our past, and we must have such a rebirth very soon."[58]

Throughout the campaign Reagan returned to these themes, promising to embark on "an era of national renewal," one that "will revitalize the values of family, work, and neighborhood."[59] From these values sprang others that Reagan left unstated but were a subliminal part of his message—self-esteem, patriotism, self-realization, and religiosity. The values strategy communicated the Reagan campaign's faith in the American dream; talk of the dream's death was premature. Wirthlin advised Reagan, "The primary leadership function of the American president is to reaffirm constantly the country's highest purposes and the potential for individual efforts to alter the course of the future in a positive direction."[60]

Reagan's selling of traditional American values had two objectives: winning election to the presidency, and establishing a framework for governing thereafter. Achieving these dual goals was not going to be easy. Historically, the odds against defeating an incumbent president are very small indeed. Oddsmakers could hardly fail to notice a pattern since 1940 of one-party, eight-year control of the White House: 1940–1948, Democrats; 1952–1960, Republicans; 1960–1968, Democrats restored; 1968–1976, Republicans again. Only the second Truman administration (1948 to 1952) interrupted the cycle. Carter, of course, would not relinquish the Executive Mansion without a fight. Wirthlin wrote in a lengthy memo that "Jimmy Carter practices piranha politics—he eats his opponents alive."[61]

History aside, the partisan foundation from which Reagan would launch his quest also was shaky. Fifty-one percent of the voters called themselves Democrats; only 30 percent said they were Republicans, and 19 percent were independents. Moreover, a mere 8 percent considered themselves "strong Republicans," while 17 percent said they were "strong Democrats."[62] To win, Reagan had to get a massive majority of the Republican vote, large numbers of independents, and cut substantially into Carter's Democratic base. As the campaign began, he was warned that unseating Carter "will be extremely difficult, even unlikely."[63]

Although the Democrats were weaker, the party still held nearly half of the electorate, and Carter could be counted upon to appeal to the party's wavering constituencies. Ever since Roosevelt's death in 1945, troubled Democratic presidential candidates have asked the party faithful to "come home" to the party of FDR. John Kennedy reminded voters of the New Deal's unfinished business and promised to "get America moving again." Plagued by an unpopular war, Hubert Humphrey wrapped himself in the Democratic mantle of helping the "little guy" and pleaded with the rank and file to come home. Humphrey's strategy almost worked; what had appeared to be a near-certain Nixon landslide became a cliffhanger.

In trouble in 1980, Carter began to emulate Humphrey's 1968 tactics—he tried to make himself and the Democratic party one. It was quite an about-face from the outsider role Carter had played four years earlier, but the beleaguered Democrat had no alternative. One Carter television commercial showed the Democratic "Hall of Fame"—Roosevelt, Truman, and Kennedy—and reiterated the party's traditional concern for the "common man." But these tried-and-true tactics no longer worked. Carter had become, in Ambrose Bierce's famous phrase, "the greased pig in the field game of American politics."[64] And the field had become so chaotic that the old rules no longer applied. By 1980 most of the play-by-play commentators used the words "fragmentation," "disorder," and "disarray" to describe it.

Only by selling American values was some order established on the field. Four groups in particular were lining up in formation: southern whites, blue-collar ethnics, "born-again" Christians, and Roman Catholics. Of these, southern whites, blue-collars, and Catholics had once strongly supported the New Deal, but over the years their psyches had been jarred, as if subjected to a series of electric shock treatments. These "voters without memory" were ready for a leader who, in the face of widespread uncertainty and self-doubt, would restore their confidence in themselves and their institutions. The moment had arrived. The right man and the right message were at hand.

For more than two decades Reagan had decried the excesses of Hamiltonian Nationalism—first as a spokesman for General Electric, later as governor of California. On the "chicken and mashed potatoes circuit," he had castigated government's excesses: "Government tends to grow, government programs take on weight and momentum as public servants say, always with the best of intentions, 'What greater service we could render if we only had a little more money and a little more power.' But the truth is that outside of its legitimate function, government does nothing as well or as economically as the private sector of our economy."[65] With such rhetoric he had defeated California's last New Deal Democratic governor, Pat Brown, in the 1966 gubernatorial contest.

Ten years later the Reagan message was unchanged. Seeking the Republican presidential nomination unsuccessfully in 1976 Reagan charged, "Thousands of towns and neighborhoods have seen their peace disturbed by bureaucrats and social planners through busing, questionable education programs, and attacks on family unity."[66] On the eve of the 1980 balloting, he renewed his cry to slay the federal dragon: "Government has grown too large, too bureaucratic, too wasteful, too unresponsive, too uncaring to people and their problems." It was time, he said, to "embark on a new age of reform in the country."[67] Like Jefferson, it was by promising to weaken the federal government that Reagan won the right to control it.

Before that could happen, the Republican party would have to be remade into Reagan's spitting image. In a 1977 interview, Reagan criticized "some in our party who advocate . . . trying to be all things to all people."[68] By 1980, those Republicans who counseled "me-too" were gone. Taking down their "me-too" flag, Reagan hoisted a banner of "no pale pastels." The 1980 Republican platform declared, "For too many years, the political debate in America has been conducted in terms dictated by the Democrats. They believe that every time new problems arise beyond the power of men and women as individuals to solve, it becomes the duty of government to solve them." The GOP writers sounded a call to arms: "A defense of the individual against government was never more needed and we will continue to mount it." Its armament was a restoration of "the family, the neighborhood, the community, and the workplace as vital alternatives in our national life to ever-expanding federal power."[69] Four years later, after having been overwhelmingly re-elected to a second term as president, Reagan's view was unchanged: "A political party isn't a fraternity. It isn't something like the old school tie you wear. You band together in a political party because of certain beliefs of what government should be."[70]

The Republicans' attacks on Hamiltonian Nationalism and their promise of something different represented an attempt to alter the images of the two parties. Their efforts had an impact. Midway through the Reagan-Carter contest, Daniel Patrick Moynihan, a Democrat with sensitive political antennae, picked up some disturbing signals: "There is a movement to turn Republicans into Populists, a party of the people arrayed against the Democratic party of the state." He added, "Of a sudden, the GOP has become a party of ideas."[71]

The voters were ready to listen to any message that offered hope and strong leadership. At the same time they believed that the situation was far from desperate. According to surveys taken for the Reagan campaign, seven of ten agreed with the statement "a few good leaders could make this country better than all the laws and all the talk."[72] Seventy-four percent believed a competent president could keep prices from continually rising. An even larger majority,

77 percent, thought a competent president could balance the federal budget in five years.[73] Wirthlin advised that the campaign should "convey the clearest possible message that Reagan stands for leadership and control. The prevailing view in America is that no one is in control; the prevailing impression given by the White House is that no one can be in control; and the prevailing view abroad is that the will to be in control is gone."[74]

"A Choice, Not an Echo"

John Kennedy was fond of reminding his cabinet that "to govern is to choose."[75] In 1980 voters made one irrevocable choice best stated by Kennedy's brother, Ted: "No more hostages, no more high inflation, no more high interest rates, *no more Jimmy Carter*."[76] The voters' retrospective judgments about Carter were so harsh that he received the smallest percentage of any Democratic incumbent president seeking reelection. Moreover, the Democrats lost control of the Senate for the first time in fifteen elections. Party strategist Peter D. Hart believed that "voters saw the Democrats as ineffective stewards of the nation's affairs, whose underlying agenda related to the past rather than to the present or future, and whose approach lacked the balance necessary to keep America on an even keel."[77] The polls supported Hart's diagnosis. By election eve fewer than half those surveyed could name one positive aspect of another Carter term, whereas seven of ten could envision some positive results from a Reagan presidency.[78]

In making their choice, voters did more than rebuke Carter— they issued a challenge. They wanted Reagan to initiate major changes in government. Wirthlin advised the transition team: "The values the President-Elect described in his Detroit acceptance speech [of family, work, neighborhood, peace, and freedom] should now begin to be rearticulated as operational components of a new sense of civic duty for all Americans."[79]

Americans were optimistic that they had found the right man to lead the search for a new public philosophy. Louis Harris wrote that 66 percent of the respondents in a survey he conducted agreed with the statement "[Reagan] is no ordinary politician because he really wants to cut federal spending and cut back the federal bureaucracy."[80] Other surveys showed 61 percent believing that Reagan "has the strong leadership qualities the nation needs"; 71 percent, that he "offers the single best hope to reduce inflation";[81] 69 percent, that he "has a highly attractive personality and will inspire confidence in the White House";[82] 53 percent, that economic improvement or reduced inflation rates is "one good thing that will happen to American families" now that Reagan was president.[83]

Economist Alfred Marshall, in *The Principles of Economics*, penned the Latin phrase: *"Natura non facit saltum"* (Nature never leaps).[84] That phrase may describe nature's realm, but not the political one. In 1980 a surprisingly large numbers of voters leapt to Reagan— not because of issues per se, but in response to Reagan's "call to faith" in American values. According to one analyst, "It appears that our society is at a transition point, and that the public may be willing, under almost imperceptible influences, to throw its entire weight behind a leader who strikes the correct 'moral' or 'reaffirming' tone."[85] The next four years would test this thesis.

4

THE ENCORE

Don't let them do it!
—Walter Mondale, 5 November 1984

Walter Mondale stood up to address the multitude for the last time as the Democratic party's candidate for president in 1984. In just twenty-four hours the ballots would be counted and the campaign would be over. Mondale had been advised several days earlier by his campaign manager that the situation was serious.[1] Just how serious remained to be seen, but most Democrats were dreading the outcome. Party Chairman Charles Manatt predicted that Mondale would carry only four states.[2] Mondale kept telling his enormous audiences, "Polls don't vote; people vote"—all the while reassuring himself that these were not "loser's crowds."[3]

Mondale's audiences certainly did not look or feel like loser's crowds. Barry Goldwater's, in contrast, had been pitifully small in 1964; one day he had greeted more police officers than voters on the streets of Los Angeles.[4] George McGovern, another landslide loser, had to restrict his appearances to college campuses to ensure a large turnout. In each case the diminished numbers matched the relative handful of votes received.

Not so for Mondale. Thirty thousand cheered the former vice president in Corpus Christi.[5] Seventy-five thousand lined the streets of Chicago. Sixty thousand stood on the grass of Boston Common. A hundred thousand welcomed him in New York City. Many sensed that something important was about to end. Spurred by the enthusiasm of the crowds, "Fighting Fritz" clenched his fists and told them, "The choice is clear. If you let them make history, they'll turn your vote into a future you never wanted. Don't let them do it!"[6]

All year long Democrats and Republicans had argued that this election was going to be different. It was no Kennedy-Nixon race for best manager, but a struggle between two value systems and two different philosophies of governance. The opening lines of the party platforms set the stage. The Democrats proclaimed, "A fundamental choice awaits America—a choice between two futures."[7] For once, Republicans agreed: "This year, the American people will choose between two diametrically opposed visions of what America should be."[8]

The Reagan Revolution

The 1984 campaign commenced the moment Ronald Reagan took office in 1981. As soon as the inaugural festivities were completed, Jimmy Carter left to greet the newly freed hostages; Walter Mondale left for Minnesota to plot his political future; and Ronald Reagan entered the White House to embark on what he promised would be a "new beginning." Reagan was cognizant of the public desire for change and the immediate communication of it. A transition memo had advised:

How we begin will significantly determine how we govern. Certainly the people and the pundits will start asking whether the Reagan administration constitutes a juncture in American history when the role of the federal government was changed and a 'new beginning' was commenced along the lines of Mr. Reagan's approach to governance.[9]

The values Ronald Reagan resold in 1980 provided the framework for the new beginning. Its specific components were faith in the folk values of U.S. society that are largely responsible for sustaining its growth; leaders, both public and private, who must live up to the shared values of family, work, neighborhood, peace, and freedom; the encouragement of individual initiative; a belief that government should not perform functions better handled by individual citizens acting on their own behalf; a conviction that government's size and costs exceed what is reasonable and result in waste and extravagance; a belief that excessive government spending, taxation, and regulation were the primary causes of the nation's economic distress.[10]

Translating Reagan's values into laws was not going to be easy. Congressional barons and myriad interest groups sought to protect the status quo. The soon-to-be Office of Management and Budget Director David Stockman wrote an ominous-sounding memo after the election, "Avoiding a GOP Economic Dunkirk." He warned,

"If President Reagan does not lead a creatively orchestrated high-profile policy offensive based on revision of the fundamentals . . . the thin Senate Republican majority and the de facto conservative majority in the House will fragment and succumb to parochial 'fire fighting as usual' in response to specific conditions of constituency distress."[11]

Reagan proceeded to chart a new course. Speaking before a joint session of Congress, the freshly inaugurated president told legislators that "spending . . . must be limited to those functions which are the proper province of government. We can no longer afford things simply because we think of them."[12] On the day an assassin's bullet nearly claimed his life, Reagan reiterated his views to an audience of construction workers: "Government's first duty is to protect the people, not run their lives."[13] A 1982 administration report echoed the same theme: "Federal Government action should be reserved for those needed functions that only the national government can undertake."[14]

What were "those needed functions"? Clearly, defense was one. Reagan proposed, and Congress passed, the largest peace-time increase in the Pentagon's budget. The B-1 bomber, rejected by Carter, was back in business. Smaller and more mobile Midgetman missiles were proposed. Additional Trident submarines were built. The administration and Congress decided a six-hundred-ship Navy was required. Research began on the Strategic Defense Initiative, often called "Star Wars," a protection against incoming Soviet nuclear warheads. Reagan's five-year military budget was estimated at 1.7 *trillion* dollars.[15] Defense accounted for 27 percent of the federal budget, up from 23 percent in 1980.[16]

Johnson's Great Society was not within the "proper province of government."[17] Reagan, who had campaigned vigorously for the Republican ticket in 1964, now sought to overturn Goldwater's loss. Stockman called Johnson's Great Society programs "nonsense" and argued that "their cost should be zero";[18] Reagan eventually proposed a 60 percent reduction in funding. Among the more significant cuts were the Job Corps, 39 percent; child nutrition, 28 percent; financial aid for students, 16 percent; food stamps, 14 percent; Aid to Families with Dependent Children (AFDC), 14 percent; Supplemental Security Income (SSI), 11 percent.[19]

Regulatory agencies were also scaled back. Those that suffered the most were the Occupational Safety and Health Administration, a 22 percent cut; the Environmental Protection Agency, 21 percent;

the Equal Employment Opportunity Commission, 16 percent; the Civil Rights Commission, 16 percent.[20] Others were slated to be "zeroed-out," including the century-old Interstate Commerce Commission. Federal regulations were eased, as tracked by the *Federal Register*: in 1984 it contained 50,998 pages, a reduction of slightly more than 36,000 pages from four years earlier. Republicans applauded Reagan's reelection boast, "You ain't seen nothing yet!" Democrats shuddered at its significance in a second Reagan term.

Increased defense spending and reduced social services were accompanied by a substantial drop in federal taxes. In 1980 Reagan wholeheartedly approved of a Republican tax plan known as Kemp-Roth. Named after its legislative sponsors, Representative Jack Kemp and Senator William Roth, it proposed a 30 percent reduction in tax levies over a three-year period. Third-party candidate John Anderson had argued that the Reagan promises of tax cuts, massive defense expenditures, reductions in social programs, and a balanced budget could be accomplished only with blue smoke and mirrors.[21] Republican presidential candidate George Bush called it all "voodoo economics."

In the emotional aftermath of an unsuccessful assassination attempt, and with no Democratic alternative forthcoming, Congress, in House Speaker Tip O'Neill's words, was willing to "give Reagan a chance."[22] In August of 1981 Reagan signed into law the largest income tax reduction in history: 23 percent cut over three years. "Reaganomics" was born.

Reagan also embarked on a new relationship between the federal, state, and local governments. In 1981 he persuaded Congress to collapse fifty-six specific federal grants to the states into nine broader categories called "block grants." Financial accountability would be the responsibility of the state governments. Federal guidelines pertaining to other state programs would be collapsed from 318 pages to 11. Reagan's brand of Jeffersonian Democracy, which he dubbed "New Federalism," closely resembled the third president's views of the federal government's relationship with its constituents. Republican speech writers suddenly became fond of quoting Jefferson's admonition: "When all government, in little as in great things, shall be drawn to Washington as the center of all power, it will render powerless the checks provided of one government on another."[23] The operating principle of Reagan's New Federalism became "We should use the level of government closest to the community involved for all the public functions it can handle."[24]

Equally important was the development of what Reagan called "mediating institutions"—among them religious groups, unions, community and professional organizations, and volunteer groups such as neighborhood fire departments and crime prevention patrols. For too long these voluntary organizations had been supplanted by what Reagan called "puzzle palaces on the Potomac" that he claimed undermined traditional values and neighborhoods.

Reagan's rearticulation of Jeffersonian Democracy differed substantially from the Hamiltonian Nationalist model modified by Franklin Roosevelt and his successors. According to former American Enterprise Institute President William J. Baroody, Jr., the federal government "will no longer play the role it did in the 1960s and 1970s . . . While it will continue to provide for the truly needy, it will not be the inventive, imaginative problem-solver it tried to be in important areas of social welfare such as job training, education, transportation, and housing."[25] Baroody hastened to add that Roosevelt's New Deal would not "wither away."[26] In fact, Social Security and Medicare would continue to grow exponentially, but the emphasis was clearly shifting from the national capital to the local community.

Reagan's approach to governance was consonant with the values he had espoused in the 1980 campaign. Family, work, neighborhood, peace, and freedom were themes he returned to time and again as president. In his 1985 State of the Union Address, he said, "From thousands answering Peace Corps appeals to help boost food production in Africa, to millions volunteering time, corporations adopting schools, and communities pulling together to help the neediest among us at home, we have refound [sic] our values."[27] To Reagan, the "everyday heroes of American life" were the families and communities who espoused the values he cherished:

. . . parents who sacrifice long and hard so their children will know a better life than they've known; church and civic leaders who help to feed, clothe, nurse and teach the needy; millions who've made our nation and our nation's destiny so very special—unsung heroes who may not have realized their own dreams themselves but then who reinvest those dreams in their children. Don't let anyone tell you that America's best days are behind her, that the American spirit has been vanquished. We've seen it triumph too often in our own lives to stop believing in it now.[28]

On the stump in 1984 Reagan almost invariably included these lines in his pitch: "We're going forward with values that have never failed us when we lived up to them: dignity of work, love for family and neighborhood, faith in God, belief in peace through strength, and a commitment to protect the freedom which is our legacy as Americans."[29]

Reagan used the symbolism inherent in his office to reaffirm traditional values. After the U.S. military takeover of Grenada in 1983 Reagan issued more medals than there had been combatants, prompting "Doonesbury" cartoonist Garry Trudeau to lampoon the conquest as "the Pentagon's equivalent of the Special Olympics."[30] Most of the time, however, Reagan looked to ordinary Americans for examples of the values he cherished. Among his most effective uses of the bully pulpit were his State of the Union Addresses, a constitutional mandate each president has to recommend to the Congress "such Measures as he shall judge necessary and expedient." Instead of proposing new laws, Reagan introduced to his television audience those persons who exemplified the values he cherished. In his 1982 speech, for example, the Great Communicator hailed Lenny Skutnik, who had rescued several drowning passengers of an airplane that had crashed in the Potomac River. In 1984 he lauded Sergeant Stephen Trujillo, an Army medic who risked his life saving the wounded in Grenada. He also singled out Bruce Ritter, a Catholic priest whose Covenant House provides shelter for abused children, and Charles Carson, a pioneer in the field of computerized walking. In 1985 Reagan praised Jean Nguyen, a Vietnamese refugee who had graduated with honors from West Point, and Mother Hale, a Harlem resident who cares for drug-addicted infants. The following year he hailed the nation's youth, citing Richard Cavioli, a high school student whose science experiment was carried aboard the ill-fated Challenger; Tyrone Ford, a twelve-year-old music prodigy; Shelby Butler, a thirteen-year-old school crossing guard who rescued a classmate from an errant school bus; and Trevor Ferrell, a thirteen year old who helps the homeless. To Reagan, their stories were parables with a common theme: "For us, faith, work, family, neighborhood, freedom, and peace are not just words; they're expressions of what America means, definitions of what makes us a good and loving people."[31]

Democrats contended that Reagan's values, as interpreted by his Jeffersonian approach to governance, were anything but loving. To them, Reagan symbolized the dark side of the American character. In Mario Cuomo's words: "God helps those whom God has helped, and if He's left you out, who are we to presume on His will?"[32] The administration's cuts in food stamps, child care, and student loans were deplored as attempts to divide the nation into haves and have-nots. Democratic party advertisements maintained: "It isn't fair. It's Republican."

The 1984 campaign intensified. Mondale asserted that Reagan had divided the nation into "two Americas—the thin veneer of the rich, who are doing better and better, and the rest who are doing worse and worse."[33] Running mate Geraldine Ferraro echoed Mondale:

> If you're a defense contractor you received $2,000 for a 13-cent nut. But if you're an elderly woman living on the minimum Social Security benefit, you were told that $122 a month was too much and had to be cut.
>
> If you're an oil company, your friends in the government support oil drilling in wilderness lands and off our beautiful coasts. But if you are an average family living near a toxic dump, your children are menaced by dangerous chemicals.
>
> This administration says, if you're homeless, it's because you like it that way. If you're hungry, have some cheese. If you're unemployed, vote with your feet.[34]

Democratic consultant John Rendon used even harsher language to describe Reagan's policies: "Ronald Reagan's politics seek to be almost as divisive as Richard Nixon's Watergate was. Reagan brazenly sought to drive blacks into the Democratic camp and white, blue-collar ethnics into the Republican camp by placing his political interests above the best interests of this country. And I think that's abominable."[35]

The Republicans countered that the divine commandment to be a Good Samaritan depended on individual, not government, initiative. They believed that with neighbor helping neighbor, the United States would become (using John Winthrop's celebrated phrase) "a city upon a hill." Reagan was fond of quoting the Massachusetts Puritan, and Mondale was fond of paraphrasing Winthrop's conclusion: "We must rejoice together, mourn together, labor and suffer together. We must be knit together by a bond of love. So may it always be in America."[36] In that vein, Mondale pleaded with voters to "end this selfishness, this greed, this new championship of caring only for yourself."[37] Ferraro, too, made the case, saying the election was "a referendum on what kind of people we are."[38] If successful, Mondale and Ferraro promised to "redirect the moral compass of our country."[39]

Selling American Values: Mondale's Pitch

Meeting in San Francisco on a warm July day in 1984, the Democrats proudly proclaimed, "We are the Party of American values."[40] Values, especially flag and family, had become fashionable. Convention delegates waved hundreds of U.S. flags before the television cameras while the nation's families watched in their living rooms and heard Mondale declare his fealty to traditional American values, recalling his humble origins:

> I grew up in the farm towns of southern Minnesota. My Dad was a preacher and my Mom was a music teacher. We never had a dime, but we were rich in the values that are important. And I have carried those values with me ever since. They taught me to work hard, to stand on my own, to play by the rules, to tell the truth, to obey the law, to care for others, to love our country, and to cherish our faith.[41]

Throughout the campaign the former vice president stressed these values before those enormous crowds he attracted. People were often listless as Mondale derided Reagan's inattention to the details of the presidency, but when he spoke of his own and his party's values, they reacted enthusiastically: "When I talk about *values*, I can see it in their eyes."[42] Mondale promised to "reassert American values" as president.[43] It was as if he had taken Carter's 1976 script, added some of Reagan's lines from 1980, and fashioned it into something that suited him.

Mondale's recitation of values began early in 1984 and helped him to turn back a challenge from Gary Hart. Hart maintained that Reagan's philosophy amounted to substituting individual "kindness" for social justice.[44] The senator from Colorado believed the task for him and the country was to find "a vision for the future that incorporates the noblest values from America's past,"[45] and he depicted himself as the candidate of "new ideas." When Mondale chided Hart's proposals as lacking "beef," Hart's lame response was to advise Mondale to read his book *A New Democracy*.[46] Hart's real difficulty was not his' thinly sliced "beef," but his failure to organize his proposals into a value-oriented framework.

Mondale did not make that mistake. He continually urged his party to get back to basics. The Democratic platform, its content shaped by the Mondale forces, deemphasized specifics and stressed values. The party document so resembled the 1980 Republican one in this respect that Reaganites accused their opponents of "rhetorical pilfering."[47] Mondale ignored the charge and kept reminding his sizable crowds that this election "was about values."[48]

The choice of Geraldine Ferraro as a running mate was designed to add substance to the Mondale values strategy. For months, Mondale had been pressured by factions within the party to consider a woman for vice president. Addressing the National Organization for Women, he promised to "seriously consider" a woman for second place on the ticket. Mondale was told by a number of Democratic female officeholders that the choice would enhance his strength among women, thereby widening the "gender gap." But Mondale chose to cast his selection of Ferraro in a different light. In his telling, the Geraldine Ferraro Story is "an American classic— doing your work, earning your way, paying your dues, rising on merit."[49] Ferraro dutifully echoed him: "If you work hard, and play by the rules, you can earn your share of America's blessings. Those are the beliefs I learned from my parents. And those are the values I taught my students as a teacher in New York City."[50] Ferraro's feminism was coupled with a faith in the American dream that, with enough hard work and determination, individual effort can lead to success.

Foremost in the Mondale-Ferraro values pitch was the idea that the United States was akin to a "family." That concept, a particularly Hamiltonian one, was well suited to Democrats. Mario Cuomo, who often spoke of the "Family of New York State," came to the convention armed with this metaphor to address the Family of America:

We believe in a single fundamental idea that describes better than most textbooks and any speech what a proper government should be. The idea of family. Mutuality. The sharing of benefits and burdens for the good of all. Feeling one another's pain. Sharing one another's blessings. Reasonably, honestly, fairly—without respect to race, or sex, or geography, or political affiliation.[51]

This Democratic credo contrasted sharply with Reagan's emphasis on neighborhood. Both Reagan and Mondale were raised in small towns, and each evoked vivid images of their upbringing. But from these similar experiences came different visions. Reagan saw the United States as a collection of small-town Dixons, each a family unto itself. Mondale saw his hometown of Elmore, Minnesota, as part of something much larger: "My America is a community, a family, where we care for each other."[52] Such a perspective allowed the Democratic nominee to shape a governing strategy that was as coherent as Reagan's, yet sharply different.

Mondale first arrived in the nation's capital in 1965, already a committed Hamiltonian Nationalist, to complete the unexpired term of his political mentor, Senator Hubert Humphrey, who had just become vice president. He was elected in his own right one year later. In 1973 he told Elizabeth Drew, "There are so many human problems in the midst of our wealth that we need a country that cares and a Government that tries."[53]

Through the years, Mondale's compassion for the individual and his belief that the federal government should "try" to help remained undiminished. The Democratic party platform, shaped by the Mondale forces, reflected his conviction: "We believe in the dignity of the individual, and the enormous potential of collective action."[54] The "collective action" proposed included job training programs for the unemployed, more money for education, and a rebuilding of the nation's infrastructure. The platform concluded, "Our Party must be a vehicle for realizing the hopes, the aspirations, and the dreams of the people of this country."[55]

Democrats, in general, were not so much interested in individual empowerment as in *group* empowerment. At Howard University in June 1965, Lyndon Johnson had declared that equal opportunity was "not enough." The remedy for racial discrimination was blanket equalitarianism: "We seek . . . not just equality as a right and a theory but equality as a fact and equality as a result."[56]

Johnson's "equality as a result" transformed the perception of the nation previously held by many Democratic leaders. Hamilton's "family" was no longer a collection of some 230 million individuals free of competing group or regional interests. Now, Democrats preferred to characterize the populace as a patchwork of different races and groups. Nearly twenty years after Johnson's Howard University speech, Jesse Jackson was still sounding its theme:

America is not like a blanket—one piece of unbroken cloth, the same color, the same texture, the same size. America is more like a quilt—many patches, many pieces, many colors, many sizes all woven and held together by a common thread. The white, the Hispanic, the Black, the Arab, the Jew, the woman, the Native American, the small farmer, the business person, the environmentalist, the peace activist, the young, the old, the lesbian, the gay, and the disabled make up the American quilt.[57]

The Democrats sought to sew more patches onto the American

quilt. Lacking the clout of a Democratic president, having been shut out in four of the last five contests, they opted to open their presidential nominating process to women, blacks, and the young. However, instead of empowering them as individuals, the party recognized them as separate groups. By 1984 the Democrats had become "caucus-happy," freely extending their benediction to the Lesbian/Gay caucus, an Asian/Pacific caucus, the Black caucus, the Women's caucus, the Liberal/Progressive caucus, the Business/ Professional caucus, and the Hispanic caucus. Each was given a designated number of seats on the Democratic National Committee. Other groups petitioned for representation; these included Native Americans, farmers, supporters of Israel, the disabled, and a collection of male WASPs who audaciously called themselves the All-American caucus.[58]

Not every petitioner won the Democrats' blessing, but eventually some were so extraordinarily successful that *their* imprimatur—not that of the party leadership—became more important to those seeking the nomination. The bestowal of the National Education Association's (NEA) blessing upon Carter in 1980 established the pattern. At the convention that year the largest single bloc was the 464 delegates who were members of the NEA. These delegates were committed to the Carter cause mostly for one reason: in 1976 he had promised to create a Department of Education, and he had kept that promise.

By 1984 the NEA strategy was being copied by other groups, who saw the Democratic party's nomination process as a vehicle for achieving their goals. Many backed Mondale, the candidate they had known the longest and liked best. Notable among these was the AFL-CIO, which broke with tradition and endorsed a candidate before the convention. Others followed, including the National Organization for Women (NOW) and, again, the NEA. Each exacted a price. To the membership of the AFL-CIO, it was a Mondale promise to impose a tariff on imported goods, particularly automobiles and steel; NOW's was a Mondale promise to consider a female vice president, along with the obligatory promise to work for the Equal Rights Amendment to the Constitution. NEA's was a Mondale promise of more federal dollars for education. One New Hampshire man in a 1987 interview mocked the Democrats' tendency to placate these interests: "There was a program for everyone. If you were an elephant trainer, there was something for an elephant trainer in retirement. [This] came to a screeching halt with the conservative approach of the Reagan administration."[59]

Republicans also have interest groups making demands upon them. But they have been far more skilled than the Democrats in responding to these—usually behind closed doors. The Republican party hierarchy is keenly aware after the Mondale experience that public concessions to special interests are particularly unsavory in a television age. Television singles out individuals, not groups. Reagan, more than any other president, understood this and played "National Host" to the continuing saga. The word "hero" was a frequent Reagan appellation. Those who landed in Normandy, the marines who died in Beirut, servicemen killed in Grenada, Oliver North, or the sailors lost on the frigate U.S.S. *Stark*—all were heroes to Reagan. In 1982 he said the nation's families were heroes.[60] A year later he called the nation's mothers "quiet, everyday heroes."[61] Finally, seeking reelection in 1984, Reagan called us all "the real heroes of American democracy, . . . magnificent as we pulled the Nation through our long night of our national calamity."[62] It is almost as if television provided the Great Communicator with the technology that gave coherence to his governing strategy of individual empowerment.

Mondale had a different conception of his audience, viewing it more like a quilt in need of mending. The threads a president needed, he seemed to think, were to be purchased from the interest groups and their leaders. According to Mondale, the preeminent task of the chief executive was to "make us a community and keep us a community."[63] If to do so meant making a few promises to those who clamored the loudest, so be it. That once may have been (and still is, no doubt) an important presidential function, but it doesn't play well on television. Many cheered the selection of Ferraro as a vice presidential candidate, but it lost some of its luster when Judy Goldsmith, president of NOW, was shown applauding the choice in her hotel suite. Roger Ailes, one of the foremost experts on the political uses of television, declared that the move, instead of making Mondale appear to be bold and decisive, made him look as though he was caving in to the demands of women's groups.[64] After the election Mondale blamed his loss on his inability to master the art of television. Seen from this perspective, he was right.

The Mondale approach contrasted sharply with the most telegenic of Democrats: John Kennedy. Kennedy was the first president to understand television's importance, and he intuitively knew what would register positively in the nation's living rooms. For instance, in his speech accepting the Democratic presidential nomination in 1960 he declared, "The new frontier of which I speak is not a set of promises—it is a set of challenges. It sums up not what I intend to offer the American people, but what I intend to *ask* of them."[65] That speech, and the debates with Nixon that followed, did play well in most front parlors, and accounted as much as anything for Kennedy's razor-thin victory.

Kennedy celebrated the individual during his presidency—especially when he lauded John Glenn and the other Mercury astronauts for their singular achievements. In the Carter administration it was groups, not individuals, that received most of the kudos. Carter feted the victorious U.S. hockey team after the 1980 Winter Olympics, singling out no one for meritorious praise. He prayed daily for the safety of all the U.S. hostages in Teheran. Only rarely did Carter single out an individual.

What the Democrats did celebrate, time and again, was the patchwork quilt analogy devised by Johnson and reprised by Mondale and Jackson. It had become so thoroughly ingrained in the minds of the party hierarchy that to view the United States as a collection of individuals became equated with selfishness. In his first debate with Reagan, Mondale declared, "I don't think this nation is composed of people who care only for themselves."[66]

Thus, the Democrats had an especially hard time overcoming the power of the Great Communicator. Mario Cuomo likened him to a "salesman" and urged voters to separate Reagan from the "product." Yet, when it came to celebrating the individual or devising a strategy for governing the country, they hedged. Mondale reasserted FDR's Hamiltonian Nationalism, but he also alluded to a "new realism": "We know that government must be as well-managed as it is well-meaning." Mondale vowed to cut federal spending, reminding his listeners of Truman's comment: "A President has to be able to say yes and no—but mostly no." In that vein he pointed with pride to the Democratic platform, noting that there were "no defense cuts that weaken our security . . . no business taxes that weaken our economy . . . no laundry lists that raid our Treasury."[67]

Reagan ridiculed Mondale's "new realism," calling it the old liberalism in disguise: "They will place higher and higher taxes on small businesses, on family farms, and on other working families so that government may once again grow at the people's expense." He accused the Democratic leadership of "trying to change colors" at their convention, adding: "We won't and no matter how hard they tried, our opponents didn't in San Francisco."[68]

The Republicans portrayed themselves as being in tune with traditional values. Announcing for a second term, Reagan said, "We've begun to restore great American values—the dignity of work, the warmth of family, the strength of neighborhood, and the nourishment of human freedom."[69]

If Reagan thought he was in sync with these folk values, it followed for him that the Democrats were hopelessly out of sync. Addressing the Republican National Convention, the U.S. Ambassador to the United Nations, Jeane Kirkpatrick (then a Democrat), dubbed Mondale and his partisans "San Francisco Democrats"—a mutant strain of FDR's New Dealers whose values were no longer those of the Democrats of old. According to her, the Democrats were not giving sustenance to the American dream but instead were "blaming America first."[70]

Reagan, for his part, continued to call on the American dream. In his stump speech he appealed to Democrats, urging those who had supported Roosevelt, Truman, and Kennedy to "walk with us down that new path of hope and opportunity, and together we can and will lift America up to meet our greatest days."[71]

The Encore

During his final days of political exile at his Texas ranch, Lyndon Johnson frequently expressed surprise at the outcome of the 1972 presidential election. Not so much that Nixon had defeated McGovern, for Johnson's receptive political antennae had detected those signals months before. Rather it was the size of the Nixon margin that caught him off guard: forty-nine states and 60.7 percent of the popular vote. Johnson often remarked to intimates that even Alfred Landon—"*who was a Republican for Chrissake*"—had carried *two* states. Said Johnson of McGovern, "I didn't know they *made* presidential candidates that dumb."[72]

Six weeks after the 1972 ballots were counted, Johnson was dead. Had the wily Texan lived another dozen years, he might have been astounded that yet another Democrat would be so overwhelmed by a Republican. Walter Mondale, like McGovern, won only one of the fifty states and garnered just 40.6 percent of the vote. In fact, Reagan's forty-nine state sweep exceeded the *combined* number of states Democratic candidates carried in the last five presidential elections.

One factor that considerably aided in Reagan's reelection was the success of his "riverboat gamble," to use Howard Baker's phrase. In a daring move, one that could easily have come back to haunt him, Reagan asked voters in 1980, "Are you better off than you were four years ago?"[73] The "Initial Actions Project," an unpublished 1981 transitional document, acknowledged the risk: "Ultimately our success rides on whether things by 1984 'have changed for the better,' when more Americans, one hopes, will answer the question, 'Are you better off now than you were four years ago?' with a resounding 'Yes!' If so, our mandate will have been met."[74] By 1984 most Americans could answer in the affirmative: 49 percent thought their financial situation had improved since 1980; only 20 percent believed they were worse off. Of those who thought their wallets had grown fatter, 84 percent voted for Reagan. Of those who thought their wallets were slimmer, 85 percent voted for Mondale.[75] Moreover, three-fourths of the Reagan voters believed he would "handle the economy so that there will be no recession during the next four years"; only one-fourth of the Mondale voters agreed.[76]

A healthy economy made it difficult for Mondale to coalesce a sizable negative vote. Richard Wirthlin, repeating in 1984 his role as a Reagan strategist, maintained that sustained economic prosperity blunted the Democrats' "fairness" arguments: "Growth is the best alternative we can offer to the Democrats' state-welfarisms."[77] And by 1984 the economy had grown dramatically: inflation had fallen from the stratospheric high of 12.4 percent to 4.1 percent; interest rates had dropped from 21.5 percent to 12 percent; unemployment hovered at 7 percent, but this was a dramatic improvement from the 10 percent mark of the 1982 recession.

The day before the election it was all but over. While Mondale was addressing his last campaign rally in Los Angeles, the confident Reagan strategists gathered to assess the probable outcome. Wirthlin forecast a Reagan win with 59 percent of the vote and forty-nine states. Election night saw the projections on target: 58.8 percent of the vote to Mondale's 40.6 percent, and Reagan winning every state except Minnesota. The 525 electoral votes for Reagan constituted the largest total ever accumulated by a presidential candidate.[78] Even at the micro level the Reagan victory was momentous: 2,755 Reagan counties to 321 for Mondale.[79]

Equally impressive was Reagan's "stretch factor." In nearly every jurisdiction, he had exceeded his 1980 tally, sometimes by significant margins. The overall total improved by 8 percentage points, but that figure masked enormous shifts. Among voters aged eighteen to twenty-four, Reagan added 16 percentage points;[80] among white born-again Christians, 17 points;[81] those earning between $12,500 and $34,999, 13 points;[82] among whites, 11 points.[83]

Mondale, on the other hand, was unable to stretch Carter's 1980 total. He registered improvements only among a handful: Jews, 7 percent; blacks, 2 percent; and, predictably, the unemployed, 8 percent. Mondale held his own with Hispanics and Democrats, among whom Reagan's "stretch factor" shrank to zero. Finally, Mondale scored well among unmarried females, winning 52 percent of their votes—Ferraro undoubtedly contributed to this improvement.[84]

Mondale's gains among Jews, blacks, the unemployed, and unmarried females were overshadowed by the breadth and depth of the Reagan win. Nixon believes that Mondale's loss heralds the end of an era, one that began with the election of Franklin Roosevelt in 1932:

The Democrats face a traumatic dilemma. In 1972, they could excuse McGovern's loss by the fact that he was not a mainstream Democrat. This year, they had an establishment Democrat, Mondale, campaigning on traditional Democratic issues and appealing to the old Democratic coalition of minorities, labor, the disadvantaged, etc., which proved unbeatable for Roosevelt, Truman, and Johnson. What this election demonstrates is that there just aren't enough voters in those groups to make a majority.[85]

Reagan also enjoyed a significant advantage in the warm feelings many had for him. On a scale ranging from zero to 100, voters were asked to take the temperature of the two men. Reagan's was 67.4 degrees, with 62 percent of the voters having extremely warm feelings for him and 19 percent with very cold feelings. Mondale's mean temperature registered a much cooler 56.0 degrees, with 41 percent having very warm feelings for him and 30 percent having cold feelings.[86]

More important than personality, however, was voter judgment as to which candidate could best tackle the important tasks of the presidency. Seventy-two percent of the voters thought Reagan was "effective in getting things done"; 69 percent said he "has the strong leadership qualities this country needs"; 64 percent thought he was "in touch and in charge"; 63 percent maintained he would "deal with the problems of the future effectively and boldly"; 52 percent believed he would "better prepare the world for a lasting peace." Only when it came to the perception of which candidate "cares and is concerned about people" was Mondale chosen over Reagan: 44 percent to 37 percent.[87]

But the Reagan landslide differed in one important respect from the two that preceded it. In 1972 and 1980 the winner's total was buoyed by a large negative vote. In 1972, 15 percent voted against McGovern; 15 percent against Nixon. In 1980, 17 percent of the voters were against Carter; 16 percent against Reagan. In 1984 the negative vote was comparatively small: just 8 percent said they voted against Mondale; 18 percent against Reagan.[88] Overall, 71 percent of the voters voted *for* one of the two presidential candidates. Half of the Reagan voters said they were for him; 21 percent of the Mondale voters said they were for him. Positive reasons given for a Reagan vote were on-the-job performance, issue positions, leadership, personality, ideology, and party affiliation. Of the pro-Mondale voters, most mentioned his stance on the issues, leadership, ideology, party affiliation, and personality.[89]

Analyzing the election results, Wirthlin wrote, "By comparing the issues voters consider most important in determining their vote with indications of who voters felt would provide the leadership and ability to best handle those issues, the 1984 election can clearly be construed as a referendum on Reagan's first term. Just as clearly, the dynamic of the vote decision indicates the electorate's overwhelming approval of his leadership and policies."[90]

Underlying the statistics was the fact that voters were choosing between two very different value constructs. Accepting renomination, Reagan had declared, "America is presented with the clearest political choice of half a century."[91] Mondale had in essence agreed: "This fall's election will be a high stakes election. There's more than a dime's worth of difference this time. This is deep and profound."[92]

Mondale's point was underscored by two women from opposite corners of the country. Lora A. Potter, a twenty-four-year-old Rhode Island teacher, explained why she supported Mondale: "Reagan is the big reason, his total uncaring attitude about anyone in the lower income brackets. He's cutting the many social services to the point where people who need them aren't getting them." Janet Patterson, a twenty-four-year-old from Mississippi, disagreed: "Reagan represents the American ideals that are most important to me, the true American spirit. That means that America always stands strong as a leader nation, that you can believe in your nation."[93] The explanations emphasize different value constructs. To Potter, making the American dream a reality to the dispossessed conjured visions of Franklin Roosevelt. Patterson, on the other hand, responded affirmatively to Reagan's recitation of the values of family, neighborhood, work, peace, and freedom—the "American ideals," as she called them. In this election two men dominated: Franklin Roosevelt and Ronald Reagan. And with defeat of Roosevelt's Hamiltonian Nationalism came a new party system, one that reflected the changed values.

5

THE PARTIES: US AGAINST THEM

Kid only wants to know . . . Are you on my side? Tell him!
—Speech writer Peter Tauber to Gary Hart, 23 April 1987

On his first day as national chairman of the democratic party in 1985, Paul Kirk received a large bouquet of flowers from his friend Paul Sarbanes, U.S. senator from Maryland. Kirk was pleased until he glanced at the enclosed card, which read, "Rest in Peace." He placed an angry call to the Baltimore florist who had delivered the flowers. The man was profusely apologetic, saying a grievous mistake had been made. It seems that at a Greek Orthodox cemetery somewhere in Maryland there was a large floral arrangement on a fresh grave with a card that read, "Congratulations. You have a tough job ahead. Best of luck from your new position. Paul Sarbanes."[1]

Some might say that misplaced bouquet is one sardonic indicator, among many, that the Democratic party "ain't what it used to be." Franklin Roosevelt's New Deal coalition, which enabled the Democrats to win seven of the nine presidential elections from 1932 to 1964, no longer commands a majority. Since 1968 only Jimmy Carter has managed to win the biggest prize in U.S. politics, the presidency. Accepting the party nod in 1976, Carter touted his role as an outsider, making the boast: "I have never met a Democratic President."[2]

The Democratic party's relative absence from the Executive Mansion prompted presidential aspirant Patricia Schroeder to remark ruefully, "There are three things the Democratic party must do to win the White House." She added, "Unfortunately, no one knows what they are."[3] Historian Arthur Schlesinger argues that the ebbing of the Democrats' fortunes is cyclical,[4] but ABC News anchor Peter Jennings believes that "the golden Democratic age of FDR will not soon come again."[5] Mondale polltaker Peter Hart says, "The data show that the days of Democratic dominance are over,"[6] adding in a subsequent interview, "I don't see enough consternation about this within the party."[7]

Yet, although Republicans have been spectacularly successful in obtaining leases to 1600 Pennsylvania Avenue, they have not translated that into majority status. In 1984 only fourteen freshmen were added to their already diminished ranks in the House of Representatives, and the party actually lost two U.S. Senate seats. Consequently, the Reagan landslide stands in sharp contrast with the Roosevelt avalanche of 1936. Roosevelt, like Reagan, carried nearly every state.[8] Unlike Reagan, he managed to help his ticket-mates along the way: 333 seats in the House and 75 in the Senate. These majorities were so huge that some of the new Democratic members had to sit on the Republican side of the aisles.

The message of 1936 was clear: a party realignment had taken place, one that created an enduring Democratic majority. Deciphering the electoral tea leaves of 1984 is much harder, for the results are littered with contradictions. Reagan won nearly everything in sight, but ornery voters in state after state refused to endorse fully either the Democratic or Republican slates. In Nebraska voters gave Reagan 71 percent of their ballots but rejected the Republican senatorial candidate, giving the Democrat nearly *twice* as many votes as Mondale. New Jersey voters awarded Reagan 60 percent of their ballots, but the Republican senatorial candidate polled *even fewer* votes than Mondale. Nationwide, 44 percent of the congressional districts selected a presidential candidate of one party and a congressional candidate of another. As the dichotomous results poured in, the discordant notes between a Republican White House and a Democratic House of Representatives grew louder. Of the presidents reelected since George Washington in 1792, Reagan faced the largest number of opposition party members in the lower chamber (table 1).

The prospect of yet another Democratic majority in the House of Representatives prompted Republican Minority Leader Bob Michel to lash out at his party's triumphantly reelected president: "Ronald Reagan really never . . . joined that issue of what it really means to have those [Republican] numbers in the House . . . Here the son of a buck ended up with 59 percent and brings in just fourteen seats."[9]

Frustrations mounted as election night turned into the morning

TABLE I

Reelected Presidents with Opposite-Party Control of the U.S. House of Representatives, 1792–1984

Year	Party and president	Opposite party, seat margin
1792	Federalist, Washington	Democratic-Republican, 9-seat margin
1916	Democrat, Wilson	Republican, 6-seat margin
1956	Republican, Eisenhower	Democratic, 33-seat margin
1972	Republican, Nixon	Democratic, 53-seat margin
1984	Republican, Reagan	Democratic, 71-seat margin

Source: ABC News, *The '84 Vote* (New York: American Broadcasting Company, 1985), 336.

after. Massachusetts conservative Republican Ray Shamie, after watching Reagan win his state while he himself was losing his Senate race to liberal Democrat John Kerry, told reporters, "Why would somebody vote for President Reagan and then vote for John Kerry? It doesn't make any sense."[10]

Some years ago the Marxist writer Antonio Gramsci had this to say: "The crisis consists precisely in the fact that the old is dying and the new cannot be born; in this interregnum a great variety of morbid symptoms occurs."[11] Something similar is happening in the 1980s. At mid-decade, the New Deal coalition is moribund. Some elements linger on, but the old loyalties no longer contain enough life to tug at the bulk of the electorate. At the same time, the Republicans do not have enough pull to command a majority. Surveys taken for the Reagan White House by pollster Richard Wirthlin show that during the 1986 preelection cycle (January to June) Democrats averaged 42 percent of the voters; Republicans, 39 percent. For the first time since the 1930s, Democrats and Republicans have reached a strategic "balance of power." *Washington Post* political reporter Thomas B. Edsall says, "Out of the 1986 election, there is a widely shared view, to which I subscribe, that Democrats and Republicans are at rough parity in the electorate, that both parties at the moment are minority parties."[12] Democratic pollster Paul Maslin says the skirmishes between Democrats and Republicans resemble "trench warfare."[13]

A parity party system has emerged, one filled with the "morbid symptoms" described by Gramsci. The ongoing rearrangement of partisan loyalties does not fit the realignment paradigm of political scientists—a model constructed with the 1936 election in mind. The conditions that culminated in the political changes of the 1930s were *sui generis*. The altered states of the 1980s have produced their own peculiar anomalies. There is no realignment in the traditional sense, but a new party system that retains the values enunciated by Roosevelt while grafting onto itself those articulated by Reagan.

Passions, Politics, and Values

Before Gary Hart's fall from grace, there was a revealing moment in the half-life of his 1988 presidential campaign. In late April 1987 Hart arrived in Raleigh, South Carolina, to speak at St. Augustine's College, one of the many black colleges in the South. As he entered the student union, speech writer Peter Tauber noticed prominently displayed portraits of Martin Luther King, Jr., and Malcolm X. Next to these was a Jesse Jackson poster. Tauber advised Hart to juxtapose Malcolm X's rage against racial discrimination and King's nonviolent protests.

Hart evoked a positive response from his mostly black audience until one of the students asked, "What do you feel about the persistence of racism and the declining status of the black man?" To Tauber, the query was a perfect lead-in to his suggested closing about the need to insure liberty and justice for all. He slipped Hart a note that read, "Kid only wants to know how you feel; are you on my side? Tell him!" Instead, Hart recited some cold, dry statistics from his proposed Defense Education Act of 1986 and then left town.[14]

Hart's failure to practice the politics of passion sets him apart from most political leaders. In fact, Hart is something of a historical oddity in this regard. Ever since the founding of the republic, party leaders have appealed to American passions, urging voters to "become one of us." The Federalist party, for example, advocated ratification of the Constitution by mimicking the opening words of its preamble: "We, the people."

Not much has changed in two centuries. Today, membership in

the political parties constitutes something more than a signature on a voter registration form. It is a declaration that the registrant is "one of us."[15] Historically, the most successful political leaders have been those who have aroused our passions by appealing to our deeply held values. Roosevelt, for instance, formed a Democratic majority based upon the idea of "fair play" for the "common man."

Roosevelt's emphasis on fairness, compassion, and self-esteem created new passions. Voters either loved or hated him; there was no middle ground. To those who, in Roosevelt's words, were "ill-nourished, ill-clad, ill-housed," the patrician from upstate New York was "one of us." To those who were more well-to-do, he was a traitor who had deserted his class to become "one of them." Conferring with advisers about his upcoming bid for reelection in 1936, Roosevelt said, "There's one issue in this campaign. It's myself, and people must either be for me or against me."[16]

Party coalitions are not formed solely on the basis of economic necessity. Roosevelt's famed collection of New Deal supporters is a case in point. To be sure, the have-nots moved en masse to FDR in 1932, partly because they adjudged Herbert Hoover to be an ineffective leader whose economic policies were not working. In fact, during the campaign, Candidate Roosevelt attacked Hoover's billion-dollar deficits, promising to cut expenditures by 25 percent until the ledgers were balanced. President Roosevelt later explained that his increases in federal spending came from agencies whose goal was to reduce unemployment, and that he had kept his promise to reduce *normal* government expenses.[17]

Roosevelt need not have bothered to explain this unkept promise because the policies he set in motion aroused passions like none before. He articulated a set of values that were congruent with the circumstances of the Great Depression. Enhancing self-esteem through employment served to make the American dream a reality for many. His New Deal created jobs: the Civilian Conservation Corps put people to work in the first federal environmental program; the National Youth Administration offered assorted jobs to young men who would otherwise be unemployed; the Public Works Administration, Works Progress Administration, and other government-sponsored programs gave those willing to work a fresh start. And for those too old to work, Social Security insured their dignity in their retirement years.

Widespread economic deprivation and FDR's willingness to use the tools of the federal government to alleviate it, provided a bonding agent that held his disparate coalition of have-nots together. And commonly shared values were another bonding agent. By emphasizing fairness, compassion, and self-esteem, Roosevelt bound many Americans to the Democratic party long after their subsistence needs had been fulfilled. Thus, Roosevelt redefined the American sense of "us" versus "them." Accepting renomination in 1936, Roosevelt maintained that he was using the instruments of government to empower the "common man" (translation: "us") while taking power away from the "economic royalists" (translation: "them") who sought to preserve the status quo: "These economic royalists complain that we seek to overthrow the institutions of America. What they really complain of is that we seek to take away their power."[18] A story related to Roosevelt highlighted the struggle between "us" and "them" that was being ever more indelibly etched in voters' minds. Many New York subway riders began their day traveling to work wearing Roosevelt pins. But as they neared Wall Street, most removed the pins and put on Landon badges to appease their bosses.[19]

Roosevelt loved this tale because of the passions it raised that were ensuring his reelection. At a campaign rally in Madison Square Garden a few days before the balloting, he continued to practice the politics of emotion: "Never before in all our history have those forces been so united against one candidate as they stand today. They are unanimous in their *hate* for me and I welcome their hatred." He concluded, "I should like to have it said of my first Administration that in it the forces of selfishness and of lust for power met their match. I should like to have it said of my second Administration that *in it these forces met their master*."[20] Roosevelt biographer James MacGregor Burns described the audience response as a "raucous, almost animal-like roar [that] burst from the crowd, died away, and then rose again in wave after wave."[21] Thenceforth, the Roosevelt script called for Democrats to be cast in the "good guy" role as the "party that cares more about people like me," and for Republicans forever to be the "bad guys," demonized as the "party of privilege."

Republicans sputtered, "But I *am* one of you!" Campaigning for the GOP ticket in 1932, Calvin Coolidge declared: "The charge is made that the Republican party does not show solicitude for the common run of people but is interested only in promoting the interests of a few favored individuals and corporations . . . All this is a question of method . . . We have advocated strengthening the position of the employer that he might pay better wages to his employees."[22]

As the years passed, Republican candidates—if they wanted to win—had to accept the New Deal while characterizing themselves as of "the common run of people." In his 1946 race for Congress Richard Nixon ran on a platform of "practical liberalism."[23] In an upset, he defeated Democrat Jerry Voorhis and thus launched a long and checkered political career.

Even a generation after Roosevelt likened the Democrats to the "common man" and Republicans to "economic royalists," these mental pictures persisted.[24] A 1951 Gallup poll found that most people would tell a new voter that the Democratic party stood for the "working man" and that the Republican party promoted the "privileged few."[25]

Other Gallup surveys added texture to that portrait. A 1946 poll gave the Democrats a better than two-to-one lead as "the party best able to keep wages high."[26] A plurality maintained in 1948 that the GOP was "run by a few big businessmen."[27] Finally, a majority surveyed in 1955 believed that Republicans best served the interests of "professional and business groups" while the Democrats were more concerned about "skilled" and "unskilled" workers.[28] These images lingered because most Americans credited the New Deal programs with their new found middle-class status.

Images of a "common man" Democrat and "country club" Republican endure. Recalling his modest origins, Reagan told a 1986 rally, "Believe me, there are plenty in the other party who find the fact that this Republican was born to ordinary working people— they find that kind of hard to take." That recollection prompted him to add, "I've always wondered why it is—the Democrats call supporters of the Republican party fat cats, but their own contributors are called public-spirited philanthropists."[29]

Too often analysts of the American psyche emphasize its pragmatic nature—namely, the calculations voters make when figuring, "Am I better off than I was two, or four, or six years ago?" Economic judgments, of course, do constitute an important component of the electoral calculus, as Reagan's wins in 1980 and 1984 clearly demonstrate. But such decisions, often clinically made, are not particularly long-lasting. Political leaders, like Franklin Roosevelt, who base their actions less on economics and more on appeals to the soul are those who make long-term changes in our political system.

John Kennedy understood this. A few days before his assassination, he wrote to political scientist Clinton Rossiter, whose book on the presidency he had just read. Rossiter believed that the essence of the office rested in the enormous burden placed upon each of its occupants, and hence began his book with a quotation from *Macbeth*: "Methought I heard a voice cry 'Sleep no more!'" Kennedy thought other Shakespearian lines were even more apropos. In *King Henry IV,* Part 1, Glendower boasts, "I can call spirits from the vasty deep," and Hotspur replies,

> Why, so can I, or so can any man;
> But will they come when you do call for them?[30]

Kennedy, like Roosevelt, knew how to appeal to the passionate side of American politics—the "vasty deep"—by communicating that he was one of us, even though he had little in common with us. In many ways Kennedy's opponent, Nixon, was more "like us." The son of a small grocery store owner, Nixon had scratched and clawed his way to the top of American politics. During his early years he had worked to support his wife and two daughters, but Kennedy had never worked a day in his life. Although Kennedy had little in common with ordinary, everyday people, he was viewed as empathizing with them. Witness Kennedy's passage to the presidency on the streets of Manhattan in the 1960 campaign, as chronicled by president-watcher Theodore H. White:

One remembers being in a Kennedy crowd and suddenly sensing far off on the edge of it a ripple of pressure beginning, and the ripple, which always started at the back, would grow like a wave, surging forward as it gathered strength, until it would squeeze the front rank of the crowd against the wooden barricade, and the barricade would begin to splinter; then the police would rush to reinforce the barricade, shove back, start a counter-ripple, and thousands of bodies would, helplessly but ecstatically, be locked in the rhythmic back and forth rocking.[31]

Even while Kennedy basked in the approval of those gathered in the streets, he could look up and see the business tycoons on the upper stories of Wall Street's "Fortune 500" corporations making obscene gestures at him. When United States Steel later defied federal guidelines and raised its prices, Kennedy denounced the businessmen, calling them "sons of bitches."

In the late 1960s, Roosevelt's definitions of "us" and "them" began to lose their relevance. Campaigning for the presidency in 1968, Hubert Humphrey tried to arouse voter passions by reminding the "little guys" that he, like Roosevelt, could be found championing their cause while Nixon and the Republicans were still the same old "economic royalists" FDR denounced nearly three decades before:

Our Republican friends have fought every piece of social legislation that has benefited this country, they have fought against social security, they have been against all forms of federal aid to education, they have been against Medicare for our senior citizens. They have been against minimum wages . . . You just name it, and I'll guarantee you that you will have found a majority of them in Congress against it.[32]

Switching, Humphrey became "one of us": "The Democrats have been responsible for every piece of constructive legislation that has passed [Congress] in these last thirty-five years."[33] Next, back to Nixon as "one of them":

When did you start to get so progressive, Mr. Nixon? All your life you stood there and resisted and fought. You called my party the party of treason—and he did. He fought Harry Truman. He fought Roosevelt. He fought Kennedy and Stevenson. He fought Lyndon Johnson. And he fought me . . . Mr. Republican is saying he's a friend of the workingman. Now that's news for you, I'll guarantee you that—if he is a friend of the workingman, Scrooge is Santa Claus.[34]

Humphrey concluded by pleading for votes on Election Day, so that together he and his listeners could defeat Nixon. Unfortunately for Humphrey, the passions aroused by the Vietnam War submerged those he tried so hard to resurrect.

The Democratic party's nod to George McGovern four years later saw an even more dramatic alteration of the Rooseveltian pictures of "us" versus "them." McGovern appealed to the nation's youth, many of whom resided on college campuses. His empathy with the young was evident time and again in the affection shown as he spoke on the college greens.

To many older voters, such college students were, to use the description imputed to Nixon, "bums."[35] They belonged to the "counterculture," shorthand for "them." Counterculturists subscribed to a set of values fundamentally at odds with those of the "silent majority." Stereotypes involved excesses of all sorts, especially drugs and sex. Nixon supporters depicted McGovern as the "AAA candidate," favoring amnesty for Vietnam draft dodgers, *a*cid (LSD), and *a*bortion on demand. With the exception of abortion, none of these positions reflected McGovern's actual views. But that did not matter. At the few Nixon rallies held in 1972, those who came were segregated into the "clean cut" and the "bums" who backed McGovern.

This new picture of "us" and "them" was becoming more deeply etched in voters' minds. Because McGovern was one of "them," his defeat was inevitable. Mario Cuomo said that McGovern drove away the middle-class worker, who "felt alienated by a new Democratic party which he thought neither understood nor related to him."[36]

Carter's nomination in 1976 gave the Democrats a welcome respite from the new etchings of "us" and "them." Carter inundated voters with numerous cues that suggested he really was "like us." To born-again Christians, he was a member of the fold; likewise for farmers and white southerners. At a Carter rally in Hartford, one sign read, "Three Who Make America Great: Jesus Christ, John Countryman, and Jimmy Carter." But by 1980 Carter's assertions had worn thin, even though he tried to depict himself as following in the footsteps of Roosevelt, Truman, and Kennedy.

Carter's inability to portray himself believably as "one of us" stemmed not so much from his personal failings, as from the fact that the mental pictures of "us" and "them" were now completely redrawn. Democrats were seen no longer as promoters of individual self-esteem and empowerment for the "common man" but as the tax collectors for the welfare state, defenders of a status quo that stifled rather than promoted opportunity. Republicans denounced in unison the "tax and spend, tax and spend" policies of Democratic administrations. One member of the Democratic National Committee, in a moment of pique, defected to the Republicans in 1985, saying, "The Democratic party has drifted far to the left of the mainstream of American thoughts and needs. America's great middle class of working men and women has been abandoned by the Democratic party, its values ignored and even opposed."[37]

Republicans it seemed to many, were becoming more "like us," acting to bring about widespread economic growth and prosperity. Stumping for Republican candidates in 1986, Reagan declared: "You see today, we Republicans are demonstrating to the nation that the GOP is the true party of opportunity, the party of all Americans—women and men, black and white—who believe that individual enterprise, not big government is the true source of prosperity and freedom."[38] Other Republicans emulated Reagan saying that they, too, were acting on behalf of the ordinary American. Alfonse D'Amato of New York, running for the U.S. Senate in 1980, labeled himself a "fighter for the forgotten middle class." Republican polltaker Lance Tarrance believes that it is these changed images that have given his party the best chance of making the American dream come true:

For thirty years, the Republican party tried to win on the issues of economic redistribution. We lost. So we've created a whole different territory called new growth and the future. Reagan is the symbolic leader of that trend. He is capturing the imagination of people who are now saying, "I may not want to be another shopkeeper like my Dad. I may want to do something else in Phoenix instead." The Democrats are protecting the status quo. I find this fascinating because heretofore the Republicans have been status quo and establishment-oriented and the Democrats have been pro-change. It is reversed today.[39]

A Republican Restoration

An apocryphal tale is told among Irish Americans of a Mrs. O'Reilly being driven to the polls one election day by her son, James. Mrs. O'Reilly, who is seventy years old, has always sided with Democratic candidates. James, who is forty-five and has obtained some financial success, votes Democratic more often than not but, sometimes, will vote Republican. James asks his mother how she plans to vote and is given the predictable reply: "Straight Democratic."

"Mom," says a frustrated son, "If Jesus Christ came back to earth and ran as a Republican, you'd vote against Him."

"Hush!" replies Mrs. O'Reilly. "Why should He change His party after all these years?"[40]

Mrs. O'Reilly's loyalty illustrates the difficulty party leaders have had trying to alter partisan commitments. Only by recruiting new voters, or by persuading the already persuaded to switch, can they shift the balance. If the near-impossible is to happen, it begins with new frames of reference by which the parties are judged, new definitions of "us" and "them."

In the years following Roosevelt's death, Democrats were often chosen by public opinion respondents as the party better equipped to handle most major issues. According to Gallup polls taken from

1956 to 1980, the public selected the GOP only four times when asked which party could better handle the most important problem facing the country, and only twice as the party better able to keep the nation prosperous.

During the Reagan years these judgments underwent a reversal. A November 1984 CBS News/*New York Times* poll found 31 percent saying they had had a better opinion of the Republicans than they did four years earlier; only 7 percent said their view of the Democrats had improved.[41] Polls taken for ABC News and the *Washington Post* that year also showed opinions in transition. In January voters still favored the Democrats by 42 percent to 37 percent as the party better able to handle the country's most important problem, but by July the parties were tied. In September the GOP forged ahead 49 percent to 39 percent. By election day the Republicans had a comfortable lead of 56 percent to 44 percent.[42]

On other critical aspects of party performance the Republicans have begun to match the Democrats. Polls taken in 1986 by George Gallup, Louis Harris, Daniel Yankelovich, and CBS News and the *New York Times* showed them averaging 13-point leads as "the party of prosperity." In fact, the GOP margin in the Gallup poll was the largest in the thirty-five-year history of the organization. A previously unpublished 1986 postelection survey done for the White House by presidential pollster Richard Wirthlin showed 53 percent saying the United States was "better off" than it was in 1980; 47 percent thought things were worse. Moreover, 59 percent believed their personal finances had improved; only 41 percent thought they had deteriorated.[43]

These performance-oriented questions reveal a crucial element in determining party identification. White House data show that of those who believe the nation is better off under Reagan, 50 percent are Republican, 30 percent Democratic, and 20 percent independent. Of those who say they are more prosperous, 47 percent are Republican, 35 percent Democratic, and 18 percent independent.[44]

Other polls give the GOP a significant lead in handling other important problems. Louis Harris shows the Republicans with a whopping 31-point lead as the party that would restore the nation's defenses.[45] A Yankelovich poll gives them a 17-point advantage as the party better able to handle our relations with the Soviet Union.[46] Another unpublished 1986 survey taken by presidential pollster Wirthlin shows the Republicans with a 14-point advantage on "reducing unemployment," a 15-point lead on "cutting drug usage," a 13-point margin on "controlling inflation," and a 5-point edge on "balancing the federal budget."[47] Democratic and Republican pollsters agree on the enormity of the change. Paul Maslin, a Democrat, writes: "These are historic gains for a party that has been traditionally viewed as wedded to established interests, isolationist, and the cause of the Depression."[48] Lance Tarrance, a Republican, concurs:

For the first time, voters see legitimate dichotomies between the two parties on issues that mean a lot: taxes, family values, and defense. The Democratic party played the tax issue wrong. They have never been strong on defense, and the Republicans recaptured some ground they lost in the 1930s on the issue of economic growth. The Democrats suddenly may be down three-to-nothing in long term forces.[49]

Still, Democrats retain their historic advantages on the "fairness issues." Of the 22 percent in a 1984 ABC News exit poll who cited "fairness" as the nation's most important problem, 90 percent voted for Mondale.[50] Most polls continue to favor the Democrats on issues having to do with redistributing scarce resources. A 1985 Yankelovich survey gave them a 40-point lead when respondents were asked which party was better at "helping the poor."[51] Polls taken in 1986 show the Democrats with a 29-point edge on "handling the problems of farmers";[52] a 23-point advantage on "increasing the rights of women and minorities";[53] a 20-point lead on "giving women better breaks on jobs, pay, and opportunities";[54] and a 17-point plurality on "protecting the environment."[55]

The extensive polling done by Wirthlin for the Reagan White House also show the "fairness issues" continuing to work to the Democrats' advantage. In 1986, Franklin Roosevelt's party held an unbeatable 36-point lead as better able to handle Social Security; a 24-point advantage on "maintaining the quality of the environment; and an 8-point edge on "improving the quality of high school graduates." But the same poll also shows that by a 29-point margin Democrats were perceived as "too often favoring give-away programs."[56] Democrat Peter Hart acknowledges the voters' standing commitment to his party on the "fairness issues," but warns that that is not enough: "The Democratic party must provide a vision . . . that goes beyond just economic redistribution. We must address the question of economic growth. We have done it so well in so many states and yet we have done it so poorly in national presidential elections."[57]

TABLE 2

Changes in Party Identification, 1980–1987

Party identification	May 1980[a]	November 1986 to January 1987[b]	Change
Strong Republican	8%	13%	+5%
Weak Republican	14	13	−1
Independent, leaning Republican	8	11	+3
Independent	19	17	−2
Independent, leaning Democrat	9	11	+2
Weak Democrat	25	15	−10
Strong Democrat	17	20	+3

Note: Text of question: "In politics today, do you usually think of yourself as a Republican, a Democrat, an Independent, or what?"

[a] Decision/Making/Information, survey for the Reagan for President Campaign, May 1980. Those surveyed total 1,620.

[b] Decision/Making/Information, merged data from studies done for the Republican National Committee, November 5, 1986, to January 29, 1987. Those surveyed total 17,700.

These altered perceptions have caused nearly 35 million Americans to switch party allegiance. In June of 1980 Democratic supporters outnumbered Republicans, 51 percent to 28 percent. By September 1984 the gap had closed significantly: Democrats, 48 percent; Republicans, 41 percent. In the afterglow of Reagan's re-election, the GOP took the lead 43 percent to 42 percent. Throughout 1985 and 1986 the Democrats maintained slim leads of 1 to 5 percentage points. Election Day 1986 found the Democrats at 44 percent, the Republicans at 39 percent.[58]

The GOP lost ground in the aftermath of the Iran-Contra affair. Surveys conducted for the White House by Wirthlin in late August 1987 show the Republicans 7 percentage points behind the Democrats in terms of party allegiance.[59] Nevertheless, the overall result is a considerable shift in party identifcation since 1980—a change that has largely favored the Republican party (table 2).

Polltaker Robert Teeter maintains that GOP candidates "can use the name Republican [in their campaigns] for the first time in my political life."[60] Previously, Republicans had avoided calling attention to their party label for fear of losing potential supporters. When

Republican John Volpe ran for governor of Massachusetts in 1960, he used the alliterative slogan "Vote the man, Vote Volpe" to counter the appeal of John Kennedy at the head of the Democratic ticket. Volpe narrowly defeated his Democratic opponent, while Kennedy swamped Nixon. Years later the word *Republican* was still shunned by many of that party. Former Rhode Island Republican State Chairman Don Roch, a salesman and a former state legislator, explained why Republicans shied away from too close an association with the party:

I am a salesman. I know how to sell. I know what I can't sell. When I first ran for election . . . , I had to sell Don Roch. That was enough. That was all the people could take. [Yet] . . . I lost. In 1970, I ran for the state Senate. I ran once again selling Don Roch. The third week before the election I added the tag "Republican." Now, if I've sold Don Roch, they can accept the word *Republican*. It's the soft sell.[61]

By 1974 the Grand Old Party seemed to be evolving from a full-fledged minority toward a half-party—unable to compete effectively in important electoral contests and forfeiting others to the opposition. Republican supporters numbered little more than one in four, while Democratic backers numbered nearly one in two. The electorate—especially after the Watergate fiasco—was skeptical about the Republican party's future. When asked at that time how the GOP would fare in the next five presidential elections, nearly a third of those questioned believed it would win none or just one.[62] It has won two of the three contests held thus far.

Even many Republicans thought the party was over. A 1974 Market Opinion Research poll found only a handful selecting the Republicans as better able to handle the nation's mounting woes: 8 percent said it would do the better job of reducing unemployment; 12 percent, that it would better control inflation; 19 percent, that it would better hold down taxes; an equal number, that it would better control government spending.[63] The party, it seemed, was following the same road to oblivion travelled by the Whig party a century before.

Thus, the current Republican numbers represent a startling comeback from near extinction. Confidential polling done for the White House by Richard Wirthlin shows that in 1987 the GOP registered a 9-point lead over the Democrats among voters aged seventeen to twenty-four, contrasted with a 12-point deficit in 1980. Similarly, a 1980 deficit among college graduates has become an 11-point lead.[64]

Among self-described conservatives the Republicans were behind in 1980, 50 percent to 35 percent; six years into the Reagan presidency, they had a 13-point advantage. Protestants preferred the Democrats in 1980 by 15 points; by 1986, they preferred the Republicans by 11 points.[65]

Even those who continued to side with the Democrats did so in diminished numbers. For example, in 1980 the Democrats remained the party of choice among Roman Catholics, 54 percent to 26 percent. By 1986 Catholic Democrats had shrunk to 48 percent and Republicans had grown to 34 percent. These numbers suggest that the apocryphal Mrs. O'Reilly continued in the "faith" but her son James may have embraced heresy. In the states that make up the outer South, Democrats retained their historic leads in 1980: 58 percent for the "yellow dog Democrats" to 25 percent for the Republicans. Six years later the Democratic advantage had been reduced by two-thirds: 45 percent to 34 percent.[66]

Much of this party movement reflected responses to contrasting value structures. Blacks, divorced and separated men and women, and single heads of households still adhere strongly to Roosevelt's sense of "fair play" and associate the Democrats with this value. These voters continue to view the Republicans unfavorably, saying, "They don't care about people like me." That perception is largely shaped by their relative position as have-nots in U.S. society.

Others have responded more positively to the values Reagan has been selling and have moved briskly to the GOP. Of all the electoral changes that have taken place during the Reagan presidency, the two that are potentially the most long-lasting are the moves of white southerners and the very young to the Republican party.

A New South

In late 1985 three dozen southern Democrats arrived at the White House for a meeting with Reagan. They came to renounce their party and pledge allegiance to the Republicans. One senior presidential aide described the session as a "naturalization ceremony."[67] That meeting represents in microcosm the demise of what was once the "solid South." After the Civil War white southerners routinely rejected Lincoln's party in favor of the Democratic party. Beginning in the 1960s, however, they moved away from the Democrats, first by rejecting their presidential spokesmen, and then by electing some

Republicans to state offices. Now, polltaker Hart says that once-Democratic faithful in the Old Confederacy are becoming "born again."[68]

The exodus continues, although not in the dramatic numbers of 1984. The change is clearly evident in presidential contests where the results have been "no contest" for some time. Since 1968 *no* Democrat has won majority support from southern whites. In 1984 Mondale received a dismal 29 percent, nearly the same percentage Hoover received in 1932. Even Georgian Jimmy Carter, the first white southerner to win a presidential nomination since 1848, twice lost the Confederates—in 1976 to Gerald Ford, a northerner, and in 1980 to Reagan, a westerner.[69] Paul Maslin ruefully concedes, "I don't think there is anybody in the South today who would say that even if a southern Democrat were nominated for the presidency [in 1988], the Democrats could count on winning more than four or five states, at most, of the eleven states of the Old Confederacy."[70]

As white southerners became accustomed to choosing Republicans for president, allegiance to the Democrats began to flag. During the 1984 campaign Peter Hart detected signs of the rapidly eroding Democratic base. A December 1983 Hart poll of white voters in Alabama found 53 percent saying they were still Democrats; just 24 percent called themselves Republicans. On Election Day nearly a year later, the Democratic ranks were reduced to 29 percent and the Republican ranks had swelled to 41 percent.[71] In a chance encounter on a Washington street corner, Democrat Hart asked Republican Wirthlin if he had noticed any changes in party identification. Wirthlin nodded. Hart said later, "I knew exactly what he was thinking. We were picking it up, too."[72]

Change was the order of the day, not only in Alabama but throughout the South. Texas polls from 1972 to the winter of 1983–84 showed the percentage of Lone Star Democrats off 14 points while the Republicans gained 11 points. Then, in the first ten months of 1984, Democrats lost an additional 12 percent while Republicans added another 6 percent—movement nearly as great as that which had occurred in the previous dozen years combined.[73]

The sweep of southern party change extended to the nonpresidential contests of 1984. According to exit polls conducted by ABC News, 59 percent of southern whites backed Republican candidates for Congress.[74] Of the fourteen freshman Republicans elected in 1984, half came from Texas and North Carolina.

The Texas and North Carolina returns represented a ten-strike for Republicans. In Texas the GOP added six new members to its congressional contingent—four replaced incumbent Democrats. Moreover, the party kept its U.S. Senate seat when Democrat-turned-Republican Phil Gramm easily bested Democrat Lloyd Doggett. Texas Republicans also added sixteen new members to the state House of Representatives, bringing their total to fifty-five seats in the one-hundred-fifty member body.

The most impressive Republican gains in the South were at the bottom of the ticket, races where party identification counts most and candidate identification least. These include contests for the posts of sheriff, judge, assessor, surveyor, and railroad commissioner, among others—the "stuff" of which political parties are made.

Since the end of Reconstruction in the South, courthouse politics had had an unwritten rule: No Republican need apply. In 1978 that rule held; the GOP was shut out of all sixty-eight elected Dallas County judgeships. The rule fell in 1984 when Republicans won fifty-eight Dallas County judgeships. After the balloting three Democratic judges switched to the GOP. The same story can be told of Houston. After having been wholly shut out, the GOP won two-thirds of the judgeships there in 1984. Lyndon Johnson's press secretary, George Christian, says that in Texas it is now "socially acceptable to be a Republican"[75]—an important new rule of etiquette since no Democrat in this century has won the White House without also winning Texas.

North Carolina has also seen impressive Republican gains. In the most expensive, most controversial, and most highly watched Senate race of 1984, Republican Jesse Helms easily defeated Democrat James Hunt, 52 percent to 48 percent. Peter Hart blames Hunt's defeat on dwindling Democratic ranks. "Jesse Helms was doing just about as well as he always does with Republicans. There were just more of them. Jim Hunt was doing just about as well as he does with Democrats. But there were fewer of them."[76]

Republicans also added four new members to the North Carolina congressional delegation, elected the first Republican governor since Reconstruction, and doubled their representation in the state legislature. Any one of these accomplishments would have represented a major victory in years gone by, but their simultaneous occurrence kindled Republican hopes of becoming the South's majority party.

Polltaker Hart says that when it comes to a potential southern realignment, the GOP may not be just whistling "Dixie": "I have no doubt that there is a major realignment taking place in the South. And if you look at state legislatures and mayors . . . what you see five years from now is going to be very, very different. There are going to be a lot more Republicans."[77]

At first glance the 1986 election returns from the South do not lend much credence to Hart's prophesy. Nearly every southern Republican U.S. senator who rode the 1980 Reagan tidal wave to victory crash landed in 1986: Jeremiah Denton in Alabama; Mack Mattingly in Georgia; Paula Hawkins in Florida. Another Reagan Republican, John East of North Carolina, committed suicide and his putative successor, James Broyhill, was cast aside in favor of Terry Sanford. The GOP had high hopes in Louisiana when long-time Democratic Senator Russell Long announced his retirement, but Republican Henson Moore lost to Democrat John Breaux. Only Republicans from the border states of Oklahoma and Missouri survived the Democratic onslaught.

To be sure, the GOP did make some gains. For the first time since Reconstruction, Republicans were elected governors of Alabama and South Carolina. Texas Republican William Clements and Democrat Mark White added a new chapter to their family feud: in 1982 White took the governorship away from Clements; four years later Clements won it back. Florida also saw election of a GOP governor, a Hispanic who derived considerable support from that state's solidly Republican Cuban émigrés.

Equally important, the Republicans held their own in the southern legislatures, especially in Texas, where they actually gained one seat in the state House of Representatives. Moreover, the GOP won some important local contests in the Lone Star State. All but two of the fifty-six judges in Dallas are Republicans, and in Houston, for the first time, more than half the local officials are Republicans. Still, for those who had had visions of the Republican party as the South's new majority, the 1986 elections were bitterly disappointing.

A closer look at the figures shows the depths of the Republican inroads into areas of previous Democratic strength. In the governor's races the GOP won 73 percent white support in Alabama, 65 percent in South Carolina, 55 percent in Texas, 54 percent in Florida and Oklahoma, and 48 percent in Tennessee. In the Senate races

that the Republicans *lost*, white southerners mostly stayed with the
GOP: Alabama's whites gave 63 percent of their votes to the Republican candidate; Louisiana, 61 percent; Oklahoma, 57 percent;
North Carolina, 56 percent; Georgia, 54 percent; Florida, 46 percent.[78] In each case, Democrats won because of overwhelming black
support. Alabama's blacks cast 94 percent of their ballots for the
Democratic candidate and only 6 percent for the Republican. Blacks
in North Carolina voted 94 percent Democratic; in Louisiana, 92
percent; in Georgia, 87 percent. Only in Oklahoma did the Republican incumbent capture a significant share of the black vote: 29
percent.[79]

Southern gubernatorial races produced much the same phenomena. In Alabama the Republican won, thanks to 73 percent backing
from white voters. Alabama's blacks stuck with the Democrat, giving him 97 percent of their votes. In Texas the Republican candidate
won with 55 percent white support, but blacks there gave the
Democrat 93 percent support. Tennessee's gubernatorial candidates
had similar experiences. In South Carolina the successful Republican received 65 percent of the white vote and a minuscule 4 percent
of the black vote.[80]

Long-time political reporter Sander Vanocur calls the issue of
race "the dirty little secret of American politics."[81] Nowhere is that
more apparent than in the South, where it results in a political
standoff. The Republicans can win significant backing from large
numbers of whites, but cannot augment that with anything more
than a handful of black votes. Democrats win overwhelming majorities from blacks, but obtain less white support than before. The
result is that both parties are now minorities in the South. Neither
can lay claim to a durable majority to ensure it of victory in the
important political contests.

A New GOP Generation

If anything has given Republicans great encouragement during
the Reagan era, it is the support they have received from first-time
voters. In 1984 Reagan won 66 percent of the ballots cast by those
aged eighteen to twenty-four, an increase of 20 points over 1980.[82]
A CBS News exit poll also showed 54 percent of the young supporting the GOP's 1984 congressional candidates.[83]

In 1980 the Democrats were the party of choice among the nation's youth: 42 percent for the Democrats, 30 percent for the Republicans.[84] This is as it had been since the 1930s, when first-time voters sided with Franklin Roosevelt and eventually cast their lot with the Democrats, while older voters—who had come of age during the 1920s and before—remained Republican. By 1987 the generational trends had reversed: voters aged seventeen to twenty-four preferred Republicans over Democrats, 46 percent to 37 percent. The Democratic advantage was greatest among older voters, especially those who came of age politically during the New Deal. Today Democrats have their largest leads among those aged fifty-five to sixty-four: 21 points. Those sixty-five and older back the Democrats by a 17-point margin.[85]

The first indications of a more youthful Republican party occurred in 1981. Pollster Wirthlin saw an emerging new voter who was "looking at this President, the Republican party, and the issues through very different eyes than their older brothers and sisters."[86] Wirthlin's Democratic counterpart, Patrick Caddell, warned in a 1984 memo that the Democrats were sending the wrong message to the young: "What I fear is that the signals have been that the party is anti-change, anti-growth, anti-participation, and primarily concerned with restoring the New Deal agenda and the primacy of the New Deal coalition members." He continued:

What is certain is that the party has been relatively indifferent to the problem. While the Republicans have consciously been targeting and appealing to these voters since 1981, the Democratic establishment has acted as though they were nonexistent. No efforts have been taken to reach them. To be absolutely harsh about it, the party has been busy trying to put Humpty Dumpty together again.[87]

Another glue making the nation's youth stick to the GOP is the "association game" all voters play with the parties. A southern man, whose allegiance to the Democrats was wavering, called attention to the importance of party leadership. Described as a "swing Democrat," he supported Reagan in 1984. In a 1987 interview, he said, "I think the Republican party has more conservative views . . . and I think the South is more conservative than are the liberal Kennedys . . . and [when] I think [about] the Democratic party, for some reason, I can't help but think of the Kennedys."[88] Nationwide, 54 percent in one poll linked the Republican party with Reagan; 46 percent connected the Democratic party with John Kennedy. Fewer than 10 percent associated the Democratic party with a current spokesperson.[89] Such associations have a significant impact upon the very young. First-time voters (and voters-to-be), simply because of their youth, have fewer and different memories. Persons who turned eighteen in 1987 were born during Richard Nixon's first year as president. Watergate occurred when those teenagers were toddlers. Mark Siegel observes that such voters do not associate the Democrats with the pantheon of presidents whose initials are the only source of identification most of the rest of us need: FDR, JFK, LBJ. Siegel argues that, instead, the nation's youth "identify the Democratic party with Jimmy Carter and the Republican party with Ronald Reagan."[90] When the terms of these two chief executives are juxtaposed, young voters vastly prefer Reagan.

Another bonding agent is Reagan's proficiency at rewriting the party scripts. Consider that eighteen year olds, prior to Reagan's presidency, never knew a time when government seemed to work, unlike their elders who remember the New Deal, Fair Deal, New Frontier, Great Society, and other government-aid packages that provided invaluable assistance. When Roosevelt sought reelection in 1936, anonymous voices from the multitudes gathered to greet him cried out, "He gave me a job!" or "He saved my home!"[91] Reminders by Democrats to today's young that FDR rescued their grandparents from destitution seem terribly antiquated and irrelevant.

A survey conducted in January 1985 uncovered a reservoir of cynicism directed at FDR's most enduring legacy, Social Security. Nationwide, there was an even division of opinion as to whether or not Social Security would still exist when the respondent retired. But among those aged eighteen to thirty, two-thirds thought the system would be defunct.[92] Merrie Zucker, a twenty-year-old bank teller, expressed the resentment of many young toward the program: "I can't believe how much . . . Social Security takes [from my paycheck] every week . . . I'm trying to make a start in life and the retired people just take their chunk of my check. I'm not going to see one cent of that money when I get old. There won't be any Social Security . . . I'm just giving that money away."[93] To most Democrats, Social Security remains the crowning achievement of the New Deal. To many newly enfranchised Republicans, it is just one more example of the federal government gone awry.

Not only are the old memories discounted, but FDR's portraits of "us" and "them" are now reversed among the young. In the depression, fewer than 6 percent of those aged twenty-five to twenty-nine were college graduates; the rest held blue-collar jobs or were looking for work. College was a luxury only the well-to-do could afford. By 1984, 22 percent of this age group held college degrees; most did not labor in factories but, rather, at white-collar occupations. As a consequence of this cultural inversion, those who several generations ago might have joined Roosevelt in denouncing the "economic royalists" now aspire to join them. Obtaining membership in a local country club or otherwise enjoying the finer things of life is something to be admired—not faulted.

Parity, American Style

While the two parties exist in near parity, it is of a very strange sort. The Republicans have won four of the last five presidential contests, but are still far short of majority status. As far as the presidency is concerned, a changing electoral college map should favor the GOP. Demographers believe that the 1990 census will find the heavily Democratic industrial Northeast and Midwest giving even more ground to the South and West. One estimate has New York, Illinois, Michigan, Ohio, and Pennsylvania losing two electoral votes each as a result of reapportionment.[94] The big winners appear to be California, Florida, and Texas with a potential aggregate gain of ten electoral votes. These votes would probably add to Republican totals in the electoral college. California has sided with the GOP in the past five presidential elections; Florida and Texas, in four of the last five. Overall, current estimates suggest a total of twelve to fifteen electoral votes will flow from the Northeast and Midwest to the South and West. That would follow a shift of seventeen votes westward after the 1980 census.[95] The ongoing stacking of the electoral college against the Democrats is neatly illustrated by this example: If the 1960 presidential election were to be rerun in 1992—with Kennedy and Nixon winning the same states—Kennedy would still prevail, but with an electoral margin of just nine votes.[96]

The Republicans, though, will continue to have great difficulty translating their presidential victories into legislative ones. Congressional Republicans, with an eye on the future, have formed the "1992 Club." They believe the new electoral college could transform the balance of power from Democratic superiority into a more competitive situation, perhaps even a Republican majority. Demographer John A. Morgan asserts that at mid-decade the Democrats were already overrepresented in the House of Representatives by twenty-three seats.[97] Still, achieving a Republican majority in the House, even by 1992, appears very unlikely.   One reason is that over the years voters have added another "check and balance" to those already included in the Constitution. Sixty-nine percent believe that it is almost always best for the country when the White House is controlled by one party and Congress by the other—an opinion confirmed in 1986, with the Democrats placed in charge of one end of Pennsylvania Avenue while the Republicans reigned at the other end.[98]

State results show a similar paradox. Sixty-two percent of Californians opted to return Republican Governor George Deukmejian to Sacramento, but only 49 percent wanted to send Republican Ed Zschau to the U.S. Senate. In Illinois, 57 percent decided to send Republican Governor James Thompson back to Springfield for a record fourth term, but 65 percent backed Democrat Alan Dixon for a second term as U.S. senator. New York's "selective majority" sided with Mario Cuomo by an unprecedented margin; at the very next line on the ballot, 57 percent went with Republican senatorial candidate Alfonse D'Amato; then voters turned around to support a Democrat for attorney general; next they backed the Republican comptroller; that was followed by a quick two-step in which, more often than not, they decided to support a Republican for the state senate and a Democrat for state assembly. Brookings Institution scholar A. James Reichley says, "Most voters now appear to regard themselves as political consumers, selecting between parties as they might shop at rival department stores."[99]

Clearly there is selective purchasing. Nowhere is that more apparent than in state capitals. In 1952, 83 percent of the states had unified party control, with one party in charge of both the executive and legislative branches. Today, only 41 percent have one-party government.[100]

Of late the Republicans have done very well in state governorships, currently holding twenty-four of the fifty. But the Democrats continue to outshine the GOP in congressional and state legislative contests. Nixon explains: "The reason presidential coattails are no longer effective is that the House of Representatives in recent years has become a club for the preservation of incumbents, be they

Democrats or Republicans."[101] The facts support Nixon. Of the 264 Democrats seeking reinstatement in 1984, 250 were successful; of the 149 Republicans, 146 were successful. Democratic incumbents fared even better in 1986; only one failed to win reinstatement. Six Republicans were denied another term.

Several explanations have been offered for Democratic successes in legislative races. Most focus on institutional factors: money, staff, and gerrymandering. The proliferation of political action committees (PACs), which act as the money arms of interest groups, has helped to keep congressional coffers full. In a single decade (1974–84), PACs grew from 608 to 4,009, an increase of 559 percent. Like gamblers at a racetrack window, most PAC leaders prefer the candidate favored to "win," not the one favored to "place." Incumbent House members in 1986 out-PACed their challengers by nearly six to one.[102]

The bureaucratization of Congress has also furthered the primary aim of most incumbents: reelection. Between 1967 and 1980 the personal staff allocated to each House member grew by 114 percent; in the Senate, by 145 percent.[103] In 1981 the average staff size for a House member was fifteen; of a senator, thirty-one.[104] Most have become a kind of permanent campaign staff—answering mail, acting as ombudsmen, and serving as the "eyes and ears" of the legislator.

Gerrymandering has also acted to prevent the placement of Democratic incumbents on an endangered species list. The redrawing of congressional districts in California is a classic example: in 1984 GOP candidates received 51 percent of the votes yet won just 40 percent of the seats. The skewed outcome was the result of a redistricting engineered by the late Democratic congressman, Philip Burton, and ratified in 1981 by the then-Democratic governor and state legislature.

Many Republicans like to blame these institutional factors for their party's relatively poor showings in legislative battles. Equally salient, however, are the contrasting perceptions voters have of the two parties. As election results and survey data make clear, the electorate prefers Republicans when it comes to presidential and gubernatorial issues such as ensuring economic growth, controlling government spending, and providing a strong national defense. Democrats, however, are favored on the legislative issues such as maintaining Social Security benefits, providing assistance to the poor, and ensuring the rights of women and minorities.

"Redistributive politics" help the Democrats considerably in legislative races when voters ask the primal question: "What have you done for me lately?" But redistributive politics play poorly in presidential contests. For example, among those who agreed with the statement "I will do financially better under Reagan, but feel Mondale programs will be fairer to all people," 71 percent supported Reagan.[105] Another survey gave Mondale large leads of 32 and 18 points when respondents were asked which of the two candidates could help the poor and protect the environment. But the same poll gave Reagan margins of 30 and 24 points on handling inflation and reducing taxes.[106] *New York Times* columnist Tom Wicker holds that the Democrats have become a *"party of access* in which the voiceless find a voice" while the Republicans "maintain enough coherence and unity to become a *party of government."*[107]

Stalemated Passions

Reviewing the 1986 election returns, journalist Thomas B. Edsall concluded, "By any standard the political balance of power is extremely fluid, and the equilibrium between Democrats and Republicans could tip in either direction at any time."[108] In the wake of the Iran-Contra affair, the Democrats have gained ground. A January 1987 ABC News/*Washington Post* poll shows them favored as the party "best able to deal with the main problems facing the country" by a margin of 46 percent to 38 percent, a reversal of the percentages recorded just four months earlier.[109] A Gallup poll taken in January 1987 showed both parties nearly dead even on the all-important issue of managing the nation's economy: 38 percent preferred the Republicans; 37 percent selected the Democrats. The slender Republican lead contrasts sharply with the overwhelming advantage held in a Gallup poll in March 1986, when the GOP held a 51 percent to 33 percent edge—the first time a majority selected the Republicans since Gallup began asking this question in 1951.[110]

The Reagan years have witnessed a wholesale transformation in the partisan composition of the electorate, as the data show. In part, this is a result of changed economic conditions, with the voters crediting the Reagan administration's policies for the relatively low inflation and their overall financial well-being. Economics, then, has been an important bonding agent in bringing the Republican party to a position of parity with the Democrats.

But Ronald Reagan's use of traditional American values has also served to glue disparate elements of the American electorate to the Republican party. A Gallup poll conducted in mid-1987 for the Times Mirror Company shows the result of Reagan's politics of values. In more than 4,000 personal interviews, the poll takers developed eleven voter typologies based on answers to seventy-two questions concerning politics, religion, moral attitudes, tolerance of dissent, and foreign policy.[111] Two of these were solidly Republican, enterprisers and moralists[112]; two others leaned toward the GOP, upbeats and disaffecteds.[113] Five groups favored the Democrats: New Dealers, '60s Democrats, seculars, the passive poor, and the partisan poor.[114] (Two other groups had no definite partisan leanings: bystanders and followers.[115])

The values espoused by these cohorts were often at odds, irrespective of party. Enterprisers and moralists, the most committed Republicans, formed distinct value clusters. The enterprisers, affluent and well-educated white males, were strongly probusiness and antigovernment but held generally more liberal views on the social issues. Moralists were mostly white, middle-aged and middle-income voters whose faithful included large numbers of southerners and born-again Christians. Unlike the enterprisers, they were somewhat more progovernment, favoring increased social spending except when targeted to minorities. But this group took extremely conservative positions on the social and cultural issues (table 3). Upbeats and disaffecteds, two groups that Reagan added to the GOP coalition, also occupied different value clusters. Upbeats were young, optimistic, socially tolerant voters, 86 percent of whom sided with Reagan in 1984. Disaffecteds were exact polar opposites: alienated, pessimistic, skeptical of big government and big business. Of these voters, 81 percent sided with Reagan in 1984.

Two of the most Democratic groups, the New Dealers and the '60s Democrats, also contained incredibly large fissures. The New Dealers, older voters whose life experiences were shaped by the depression and the New Deal, favored social spending except when it was aimed specifically at minority groups. They were also the most religious (usually Catholic), holding conservative views on the social issues. This set them apart from the '60s Democrats, who favored all forms of social spending, even that meant specifically for minorities. The '60s Democrats, whose life experiences were shaped by the Vietnam War, the civil rights movement, and the political

TABLE 3

Values and the Intraparty Divisions

Issue	Enter-prisers	Moralists	'60s Democrats	New Dealers	Total
Books containing dangerous ideas should be banned from public school libraries	28%	77%	10%	74%	51%
School boards have the right to fire teachers who are homosexuals	50	78	14	69	52
AIDS might be God's punishment for immoral behavior	36	61	15	56	44
Women should return to a traditional role in society	16	47	5	47	30
Laws should be changed to make it more difficult for a woman to get an abortion	40	60	26	54	41

Source: Gallup Organization for the Times Mirror Company, April 25–May 10, 1987. Reprinted in *U.S. News and World Report,* October 12, 1987, 33.

assassinations of that turbulent decade, had considerably more liberal views on the social issues (table 3).

Ronald Reagan's wooing into the Republican party of voters who are at loggerheads with one another is testimony to his ability to hold much of the electorate spellbound. Despite their differences, enterprisers, moralists, upbeats, and disaffecteds now say of the Republicans: "They're like us!" Meanwhile, other disparate groups— some remnants of FDR's New Deal coalition; another, a by-product of the '60s counterculture—say of the Democrats: "They're like us!" Given their internal inconsistencies, each of these groups could desert its respective political party at any time. The Republican coalition could easily crumble after Reagan leaves the presidency. On the other hand the Democratic pieces, which have remained disassembled in four of the last five presidential elections, might be put together once more. Events and personalities largely will determine the outcome.

Internal party contradictions are nothing new in American politics. The New Deal coalition was sharply divided between North and South on the issue of civil rights for blacks. Yet it remained intact for nearly four decades. Thus the differing value clusters within the Reagan coalition may continue to coexist uneasily for the indefinite future. Still, the internal disputes that characterize each party create the conditions for considerable electoral instability. Norman Ornstein, one of the authors of the Gallup/Times Mirror study, said: "The struggle to put the political pieces together in both parties will endure for many election years to come. The era of electoral fragmentation may be here to stay."[116]

Ronald Reagan's use of the politics of values has created new definitions of "us" and "them" for many Americans. But, unlike Franklin Roosevelt, he has not been able to transform the GOP into a majority. The parity party system he has created points to years of trench warfare between Republicans and Democrats, as each seeks to exploit the values contradictions within the opposition.

6

ECHOES IN THE
MARKETPLACE

Born in the U.S.A.!
—Bruce Springsteen, 1984

Ronald Reagan's salesmanship has had consequences that reach far beyond the presidency itself. Each president generally mirrors and amplifies the dominant values of the populace. So, too, do those who produce television programs, movies, records, and books. Reagan's rearticulation of traditional values—especially family, work, neighborhood, self-esteem, and self-realization—has met with strong acceptance from political consumers and consumers of all forms of entertainment. The success of rock superstar Bruce Springsteen provides a dramatic illustration of how a president's selling of himself by means of folk values can influence the entertainment industry.

Springsteen had been making the musical rounds for nearly a decade before he burst onto the record charts in the summer of 1984 with "Born in the U.S.A." After the song came wafting over Top-40 radio stations, thousands flocked to hear the artist. When it was announced that Springsteen would play in Washington D.C.'s Capitol Center, telephone lines there became jammed. On performance night capital subway cars were so crowded that many waiting for them were left stranded at the stations. At the concert itself, thousands waved American flags when Springsteen launched into his anthem "Born in the U.S.A."[1]

There by special invitation was *Washington Post* columnist George F. Will. It turned out that the wife of Springsteen's drummer was a fan of "This Week with David Brinkley," the Sunday interview program on which Will was a regular. The conservative Republican's attendance was, so far as anyone could figure, a first.[2]

Although Will had to leave at intermission (he had to arise early the next day to tape the Brinkley show), he managed to interview two of Springsteen's admirers. One, a male, when asked what he liked about him said: "He sings about faith and traditional values."

His girlfriend rejoined: "And cars and girls."

Said he: "No, no, it's about community and roots and family."

She: "And cars and girls."[3]

A few days later Will wrote an article lauding Springsteen as a "blue-collar troubadour": "Today 'values' are all the rage, with political candidates claiming to have backgrounds stuffed full of them. Springsteen's fans say his message affirms the right values. Certainly his manner does." Will confessed that he did not have "a clue about Springsteen's politics, if any," but observed that flags are hoisted at his concerts "while he sings songs about hard times." Will opined that Springsteen "is no whiner;" rather his recitation of the troubles that beset the characters he creates "always seems punctuated by a grand, cheerful affirmation: 'Born in the U.S.A.'"[4]

In addition to lauding Springsteen in print, Will saw an opportunity to help his friend Ronald Reagan. After the concert he contacted Michael Deaver's office at the White House and relayed what happened at the show—the flag-waving, the singing of what Will called Springsteen's "Internationale,"[5] "Born in the U.S.A."—and suggested that the singer be contacted about a possible endorsement of Reagan. Springsteen, who hails from New Jersey, was an especially popular native son. And, as Will was undoubtedly aware, the president would be making a campaign stop there in a few days.

Deaver's staff did not know anyone in the Springsteen entourage, but they did have an ally who worked with the producers of his Washington performance. Contact was made, and Springsteen was informed of Reagan's eagerness to have him appear at the rally and make an endorsement. Springsteen sent word through the grapevine politely, but firmly, declining.

That did not stop Reagan, however. In the small, rural hamlet of Hammonton, New Jersey, he spoke as usual of his reverence for family and neighborhood, this time adding: "America's future rests in a thousand dreams inside your hearts. It rests in the message of hope in songs of a man so many young Americans admire—New Jersey's own, Bruce Springsteen. And helping you make those dreams come true is what this job of mine is all about."[6]

The *Christian Science Monitor* noted that Reagan's allusion to Springsteen marked the first time a popular singer had been recruited by a president of the United States as a character reference.[7] Skeptical reporters asked Reagan what his favorite Springsteen song was. He could not think of one, but the very next day the White House announced it was "Born to Run."[8] That prompted wisecracks from several quarters. Johnny Carson joked, "If you believe that, I've got a couple of tickets to the Mondale-Ferraro inaugural ball I'd like to sell you."[9] Walter Mondale chimed in: "Bruce Springsteen may have been born to run, but he wasn't born yesterday."[10] The Democratic candidate claimed that the singer had already endorsed him, not Reagan. Later, Mondale had to issue a retraction when Springsteen, a registered independent, said, "I find it very difficult to relate to the whole electoral system as it stands."[11]

If Will, Reagan, and Mondale were confused, it was no wonder. Springsteen's "Internationale," "Born in the U.S.A.," was the title song to an album whose cover showed a masterful use of symbolism. Against a background of the U.S. flag was a close-up of Springsteen's buttocks clothed in faded jeans, one pocket worn and the other stuffed with a red baseball cap. (Springsteen's comment on that: "We took a lot of different types of pictures, and in the end, the picture of my *ass* looked better than the picture of my *face*, so that's what went on the cover.")[12] Springsteen later said with some accuracy, "The flag is a very powerful image, and when you set that stuff loose, you don't know what's gonna be done with it."[13]

What was "done with it" was astonishing. The public flocked to buy the record. By the end of 1984, sales totalled five million dollars. Chrysler Board Chairman Lee Iacocca got wind of the album's popularity and offered Springsteen twelve million dollars to sing "Born in the U.S.A." in his television commercials.[14] When Springsteen refused, Iacocca settled for a copycat tune, "The Pride Is Back."

When an attentive ear is cocked to the Springsteen album, it is obvious that his characters are not wrapped in the flag but in a magnificent desolation. In the title song, a Vietnam veteran is unable to find a job at the local oil refinery. He describes his brother, another Vietnam-scarred combatant, as "all gone." Another tune depicts life on a prison chain gang. Another tells of two "good-time Joes" heading South to look for work—one is arrested; the other moves on. Yet another lyric has a husband and wife talking about leaving home because they cannot find steady employment. If, as

Reagan stated, his job was "making dreams come true," then Springsteen's lyrics chronicle a litany of presidential failures.

Ironically, one of Springsteen's heroes, folksinger Woody Guthrie, had to cope with the misinterpretation of his most famous song nearly a half-century before. In 1940 Guthrie fashioned a composition he originally titled "God Blessed America," a blistering rebuttal to Irving Berlin's "God Bless America." Guthrie, who had travelled about the country early in the year, was disturbed by the Berlin song—both by the radio air time it received and the message it contained. After some tinkering, Guthrie retitled his song "This Land Is Your Land." Among the long-forgotten verses were these lines:

> As I went walking, I saw a sign there
> And on the sign it said "No Trespassing."
> But on the other side, it didn't say nothing—
> That side was made for you and me.
>
> In the shadow of the steeple I saw my people
> By the relief office I seen my people—
> As they stood there hungry, I stood there asking
> Is this land made for you and me?

Guthrie's message to the dispossessed—"This is your land, too!"—became lost in patriotic fervor. The song has been frequently suggested as a replacement for "The Star Spangled Banner." That never happened, but it did become the advertising jingle for United Airlines and the Ford Motor Company.[15] In 1966, after the Department of Interior cited Guthrie as a troubadour for the Pacific Northwest, and the Bonneville Power Authority named a substation after him, a friend of his said, "They're taking a revolutionary and turning him into a conservationist."[16]

Forty years later history repeated itself in the person of Bruce Springsteen. The singer was described by Martin Nolan of the *Boston Globe* as "the Ronald Reagan of rock."[17] But Springsteen was no friend of the president's. During a concert the night following Reagan's 1980 win, Springsteen introduced an original composition, "Badlands," by saying, "I don't know what you thought about what happened last night. But I thought it was pretty terrifying."[18] In 1982 Springsteen released the album "Nebraska," which articulated a miserable existence in the nation's heartland. A critic called it "the most complete and probably the most convincing statement of resistance and refusal that Ronald Reagan's U.S.A. has yet elicited from any artist or politician."[19]

It was inevitable that Springsteen would try to counter Reagan's implication that he and the president were one, even if they were not together on the campaign trail. At a performance in Pittsburgh, at the confluence of the Allegheny and Monongahela rivers, Springsteen spoke in Cuomo-like terms:

There's something really dangerous happening to us out there. We're slowly getting split up into two different Americas. Things are gettin' taken away from people that need them and given to people that don't need them, and there's a promise getting broken. In the beginning the idea was that we all live here in a little bit like a family, where the strong can help the weak ones, the rich can help the poor ones. I don't think the American dream was that everybody was going to make it or that everybody was going to make a billion dollars, but it was that everybody was going to have an opportunity and the chance to live a life with some decency and some dignity and a chance for some self-respect. So, I know you gotta be feelin' the pinch down here where the rivers meet.[20]

When he concluded, a harmonica sounded the poignant opening notes to "The River" and the audience erupted into applause. At the composition's coda the singer shouted, "That was for Local 1397 [a steelworkers union] rank and file."[21]

The cultural confusion surrounding Bruce Springsteen went beyond U.S. shores. In 1985 the artist went on a concert tour of Europe. There he was greeted by thousands of fans, many of whom had sewn the emblems of their native lands together with the American flag and waved them whenever "Born in the U.S.A." was played. In Gothenburg, Sweden, 120,000 seats were sold in ten minutes. One million would-be British concertgoers applied for 100,000 spaces. And in Ireland, 100,000 loyalists jammed Slane Castle outside Dublin for an evening performance.[22] The infusion of patriotism and pride, however mistaken, was not Springsteen's message but America's.

America is a cultural behemoth. Its entertainers, writers, musicians, and artists dominate markets as far-ranging as Bangor and Bangkok. Jeffrey Simpson, a columnist for the Toronto *Globe and*

Mail, once described our preeminent cultural position by picturing its inversion:

> Imagine a movie-lover in St. Louis who checked the local paper and discovered that 97 percent of the films showing in his city were foreign. Or how about a book-lover in San Francisco who found that in every city store foreign authors had written 75 percent of the titles and that American books were consigned to an inconspicuous display quaintly called "Americana."
>
> Try to picture the vast record stores of New York filled with three foreign records for every American one. Think about watching television in Phoenix and finding three out of every four programs made, not in the United States, but somewhere else. Consider the possibility that in Chicago three out of every four publications sold were foreign.[23]

Concluded Simpson, "This is what cultural life is like for Canadians."[24]

Canada's proximity, of course, accounts for some of its neighbor's influence. But motion picture industry executive Jack Valenti tells of walking the streets in far-away Moscow with Kirk Douglas. As several passersby gazed intently at the pair, one approached and said haltingly, "You Kirk Doooglas." Another greeted the actor with tears streaming down his cheeks, giving the impression that he had found a long-lost brother.[25]

The arm of U.S. culture extends even further. In October 1985 Kenya's nomadic Masai gathered at the foot of one of that country's remote volcanoes for a tribal ceremony. Young warriors' heads were shaved; an ox was slaughtered; and at the edge of the encampment a concessionaire sold Coca-Cola. Said the executive in charge of Kenyan distribution of the soft drink, "There is a perceived way of life embedded in each bottle of Coke. Coke is modern, with it."[26] In another part of the globe a young Czechoslovakian concurred: "Coke equals America. America equals freedom."[27]

The messages that emanate from U.S. culture resonate throughout the world. Charlton Heston said, "American film exports the American dream which is achievable, not a fantasy. What film has done to the developing world is to change its sense of possibility."[28] Charles Z. Wick, a former talent agent and director of the United States Information Agency during the Reagan years, remarked, "I would hope that American pop culture would penetrate into other societies, acting as a pilot parachute for the rest of American values."[29]

Obviously, any change in American values has an enormous impact, not only in the United States but worldwide. If Americans were pessimists after Watergate, people in both Peoria and Prague saw it. *New York Times* reporter Aljean Harmetz says that Jack Nicholson "with his shark smile and anti-hero ways was a perfect star for Watergate and the cynical years that followed."[30] If Americans were optimists during the Reagan years, the upbeat mood was shown in movie houses from Montreal to Manila. "Top Gun," which earned more than $177 million for Twentieth Century-Fox, reflected the I-can-do-anything attitude. A studio executive declared that the appeal of the movie's lead, Tom Cruise, rests in "a return to traditional values."[31]

Signs of cultural change in the U.S. are carefully monitored. Among the most watchful are the political consultants, whose marketing techniques often mirror those used to sell soft drinks, cars, or the proverbial bar of soap. Democratic polltaker Patrick Caddell pays close attention to Springsteen's lyrics, as well as those of another rock-and-roll singer whose stage name is "Sting." According to Caddell a baby-boomer is someone who knows the song Jo Beth Williams played on the piano in the opening funeral scene of the movie *The Big Chill*. (Answer: The Rolling Stones' 1969 hit, "You Can't Always Get What You Want.")[32]

Political consultants not only echo trends in the marketplace but often help to establish them. Shortly after the 1980 Reagan landslide, the top three U.S. automobile executives conferred with presidential pollster Richard Wirthlin. Concerned about the declining sales of their cars in favor of Japanese models, they were thinking of a possible combined advertising campaign that would spur sales. Wirthlin told them that patriotism was a value that should form a portion of their pitch: "Buy an American car because it is smart, and it happens to be patriotic." One said, "No thanks." Another, "I cannot go along with the ads unless we all agree." The third said, "Sign me up this afternoon."[33]

Of the "big three" it was Lee Iacocca who was sold on the value of patriotism in advertising. During the 1984 campaign, Reagan proclaimed, "America is back." After Reagan's overwhelming win, the Chrysler slogan became "The pride is back."

The linkage between political consulting and the marketplace is stronger than most realize. In 1985 Caddell's firm had the Coca-Cola account. After Caddell miscalculated public reaction to the introduction of "New Coke" in place of Coca-Cola's standard formula, the company took its business to Wirthlin's firm. Today commercial accounts represent the fastest growing component of the Wirthlin Group. In 1986 sales totaled $10.4 million, a larger amount than that amassed by the Gallup organization.[34]

As the 1988 presidential campaign draws near, political consultants—both Democratic and Republican—are closely monitoring the country's cultural heartbeat. George Bush Campaign Manager Lee Atwater conducts some of his research at Florida's "Disney World," a Washington, D.C., YMCA, and a Manhattan nightclub that plays 1960s music. Atwater touts his candidate as the youthful choice: "I don't think anyone is more plugged into baby-boomers than George Bush and his wife." He adds that Bush's children in 1988 will range in age from twenty-eight to forty-one. Democratic consultant Bob Squier cracks, "I'd like to be a fly on the wall when Lee Atwater explains heavy metal to George Bush."[35]

The Times, They Are A-Changin'

In 1968 Joe McGinniss wrote an expose of the Nixon campaign's advertising strategy titled *The Selling of the President 1968*.[36] Should there be a sequel, *The Selling of the President 1988* would have to account for a revolution in the economic and political marketplaces. Consider: Nearly twenty years ago Beatle John Lennon was singing a tune called "Revolution." Student demonstrators in Paris were successfully ousting Charles de Gaulle from power,[37] while in the United States protestors against the Vietnam War were marching in the streets. Now the song is used as a jingle on television commercials for Nike athletic sneakers. Company spokesman Kevin Brown says the ad "wouldn't have worked" a decade ago, but "'Revolution' can be interpreted differently today"—meaning the overthrow not of an unpopular government, but a revolution in public attitudes toward physical fitness.[38]

Another sign of the times is the changing patterns in circulation of men's magazines. Two decades ago more American boys came of age than at any other time in history. Subscribers to *Playboy* in 1972 totaled seven million; circulation now is slightly more than three million.[39] Other indicators tell of the bunny's slowed hop: corporate profits fell from $19.3 million in 1981 to $2.5 million just six years later.[40] Advertising pages shrank 17 percent in the same period.[41] *Playboy*, it seemed, was undergoing a mid-life crisis.

Changing demographic patterns accounted for only a portion of *Playboy*'s woes. Attacks on the magazine came from several quarters, including the attorney general's office. Edwin Meese fought to have it removed from drugstore racks, where it was often within easy reach of children. A commission appointed by the nation's chief law enforcement officer gave warning of action unless stores voluntarily removed *Playboy* and other similar publications such as *Penthouse*, *Hustler*, and *Playgirl* from their shelves. Many complied—including the 7-Eleven chain—prompting *Playboy* to feature a "Girls from 7-Eleven" layout in one issue.

Fundamentalists applauded the Reagan administration's actions, but the political threat *Playboy* and the other "skin magazines" faced came not so much from Meese or the born-again Christians as from the altered values of Americans generally. Similarly, the wives of U.S. Senator Albert Gore and Treasury Secretary James Baker launched a campaign to expunge sexual innuendo from rock music lyrics.

The Meese-Gore-Baker efforts were not hatched in a smoke-filled room. Instead, they reflected the celebration of family values that began in the early 1980s. Karlyn Keene, managing editor of *Public Opinion*, observed that the celebration of the family has become the norm on television: "The Diors have married and have had a child. Charlie, the independent Revlon woman, is rumored to be getting engaged."[42]

Sex, particularly promiscuous sex, is no longer condoned. Female rock singer Madonna sings about keeping her out-of-wedlock baby and marrying her boyfriend in "Papa, Don't Preach." Male vocalist Huey Lewis proclaims it is "Hip To Be Square." The AIDS epidemic encouraged this move toward monogamy, but the trend was in place long before the virus left central Africa. Beginning with its June 1987 issue, *Playboy* featured fewer nudes and more articles on issues and ideas along with advice on fashion, cooking, driving, and vacationing.[43]

Clearly, presidents do not make the times, they reflect them. When some members of Congress began to talk of a tax increase, Reagan promised a veto using Clint Eastwood's famous movie line: "Go ahead. Make my day!" On another occasion when discussing the military budget, Reagan likened the uniforms to "Pentagon wardrobe."[44]

Presidents, especially Reagan, do more than lift an occasional phrase from a movie. They mirror a national mood that is often captured in film or on record. During World War II, American culture reflected the preoccupation with the war effort. The most popular songs in 1942 were "Praise the Lord and Pass the Ammunition," "The Fuehrer's Face," and "You're a Sap, Mr. Jap." Theatre marquees boasted titles such as *Wake Island*, *Atlantic Convoy*, *One of Our Aircraft Is Missing*, *Torpedo Boat*, *Remember Pearl Harbor*, and *Flying Tigers*. Even advertisements signaled the nation's war mentality. Munsingwear's advertisements of undergarments for women pictured a WAC saying, "Don't tell me bulges are patriotic." Sergeant's Flea Powder showed "Old Sarge" exclaiming, "Sighted flea— killed same." Best-sellers included John Scott's *Duel for Europe*, Ethel Vance's *Reprisal*, and Herbert Agar's *A Time for Greatness*.[45]

The premise of these works was that the United States was the most blessed land on earth, and its people were exceptional. In his last inaugural address Franklin Roosevelt declared that God had given the American people "stout hearts and strong arms with which to strike mighty blows for freedom and truth." Roosevelt added that the nation was possessed with a "faith which has become the hopes of all peoples in an anguished world."[46]

By 1979 Americans had become part of an "anguished world." Jimmy Carter gave his malaise speech; in it he said he felt the nation's "pain"—mirroring the national funk.[47] During the last two years of his administration, the most popular movies were *Coming Home* and *The Deerhunter*, each a bitter denunciation of the Vietnam War and the government that prosecuted it. In the bookstores Bob Woodward and Carl Bernstein's *The Final Days*, an unflattering account of the Nixon presidency, was a best-seller. Other books emulated Carter's predilection for self-examination, particularly Gail Sheehy's *Passages* and Alex Haley's *Roots*. Still others were filled with foreboding about the future; foremost among these was Howard J. Ruff's 1979 best-seller, *How to Prosper During the Coming Bad Years*.[48]

Today the marketplace echoes the mood of another time—the 1950s. In the summer of 1987 Annette Funicello, aged forty-four, and Frankie Avalon, aged forty-six, headlined theatre marquees in *Back to the Beach*, a sequel to the "beach-blanket" movies they made decades before. The cast of "The Andy Griffith Show" was reunited in a made-for-television movie, as were the surviving actors of the "Perry Mason" series. And the stranded passengers on "Gilligan's Island" were finally rescued in a highly rated sequel.

No one is more sensitive to the power of film than Reagan. ABC News anchor Peter Jennings says that Reagan has always "brought his past forward, forward, forward with him."[49] The themes of heroism, faith, and patriotism liberally season the presidential rhetoric. There are equally heavy doses of these in the movies Reagan made when he was an actor. In the touchstone 1940 film *Knute Rockne—All American*, Reagan as George Gipp says of his coach, "He's given us something they don't teach in schools. Something clean and strong inside. Not just courage, but a right way of living none of us will ever forget."[50] A year later in *King's Row*—a title derived from a fictional village that was "a good place to live"— Reagan took the part of a playboy who found himself penniless when his fortune vanished with an absconding bank officer. At the film's conclusion Reagan's legs are amputated by a self-righteous surgeon who disapproved of the playboy's life-style. Upon awakening Reagan delivers his famous line, "Where's the rest of me?" *King's Row* reflects the values espoused by the New Deal. The "common man" is shown in combat with the conniving "economic royalists" whom Roosevelt denounced—a plethora of bad guys taking away their money and political power.[51]

For more than a decade Reagan's movies continued to evoke New Deal-like themes. The 1951 film *Bedtime for Bonzo* features Reagan as a psychology professor who was engaged to marry the dean's daughter, that is, until the dean learns that the professor's father was a hardened criminal. Says Reagan, "Given a decent start in life, my father would have gone as far in the right direction as he went in the wrong one." To prove it, he adopts a chimpanzee and tries to rear him as a human child. Bonzo, the chimp, often makes Reagan look every bit as crooked as his jailbird father, but in the final scenes Bonzo shows the very altruism Reagan has been trying to instill—proving Reagan innocent and the New Deal triumphant.[52]

Reagan's subsequent films reflected his growing conservatism. In *Hellcats of the Navy*, the only movie he made with his wife Nancy, Reagan shows no remorse at killing enemy and friendly soldiers alike. In one scene he leaves a crewman for dead, supposedly to ensure the safety of all. The dead sailor, however, had been a rival for Nancy's love.[53]

The themes of heroism, patriotism, and family that form so many of Reagan's movie and political lines have become a ubiquitous hallmark. Heroism, especially the depiction of ordinary men and women succeeding against the odds, is the order of the day. *Indiana Jones and the Temple of Doom* depicts a pistol-toting Harrison Ford overcoming the odds against an evil empire. The *Star Wars* films show an embattled Luke Skywalker and his companions (including Ford, again) waging war against Darth Vader. The advertisement for *Ghostbusters* reads, "They're here to save the world."⁵⁴ Clint Eastwood pummels ne'er-do-wells of every sort in his *Dirty Harry* movies.

Optimism is also regnant. In *Back to the Future* Michael J. Fox, a.k.a. Marty McFly, returns to the year 1955. The film is filled with delicious irony. In one scene Marty is asked by his mentor, Doc Brown, who the president of the United States is in 1985. When Marty answers, "Ronald Reagan," Brown retorts, "And I suppose Jerry Lewis is Vice-President?" Before travelling three decades backward in time, McFly's parents are the antithesis of the American dream. Lorraine is an alcoholic, and George is a none-too-successful, white-collar employee whose supervisor is his former high school tormentor, Biff. When Marty returns to 1985—after having made some changes in the past—his parents are living the dream fulfilled. Lorraine is a more wholesome character, and George is a very successful science fiction writer. Their surroundings are beautiful, and their healthy financial picture is depicted in their leisurely return from a Saturday morning at the golf course.

Marty literally falls down at the sight, particularly in one scene where his father gives his nettlesome high school friend, Biff, orders to wash the car (Biff has been demoted to car washer). Three times— in the past, present, and future—the characters remind one another of the adage: "If you put your mind to it, you can accomplish anything." As to the future, old Doc Brown, the inventor of the time machine, says: "Where we're going, we don't need roads." (Reagan quoted this line in his 1986 State of the Union Address.)⁵⁵

The man who best exemplifies the new mood is not Reagan— although he comes close—but auto magnate Lee Iacocca. To borrow a slogan from the army's television advertisements, he is a good illustration of the "be-all-you-can-be" American. In 1985 Iacocca received more than eleven million dollars as chairman of the board of the Chrysler Corporation—number thirteen on the "Fortune 500" list. Often called the country's "first corporate folk hero," this son of Italian immigrants began life in humble Allentown, Pennsylvania. He did not attend college—no money for that sort of luxury—but started a career as a car salesman. Iacocca's ability to sell was so great that he attracted the attention of Henry Ford II, who had him transferred to company headquarters in Detroit. There Iacocca was involved in designing Ford's most successful car, the Mustang. From that triumph he went on to become president of the company, but was later fired by Ford and demoted to an insignificant office that he described as "little more than a small cubicle with a desk and telephone."[56] Iacocca's motto, given to him by his wife, was "Don't get mad; get even."[57] Adhering to that adage, the ex-Ford president moved to more spacious quarters at the Chrysler Corporation, where he was installed as its chief executive.

Iacocca came to Chrysler at a time when, due to poor management and the popularity of Japanese imported cars, the company was floundering on the edge of bankruptcy. It took a controversial loan guarantee from the federal government—an action supported by the Carter administration and opposed by Reagan—to keep creditors away from the door. But it was Iacocca who ultimately saved the company from foreclosure. He went on television pitching Chrysler's new line of cars. Like Reagan, Iacocca could sell just about anything to anybody.

Iacocca's commercials gained him new visibility, and from that platform he wrote an autobiography, with William Novak, appropriately titled *Iacocca*. It became the largest-selling nonfiction book ever, remaining on the *New York Times* list for nearly two years. More than five million copies are in print. In the book Iacocca detailed his rise to the top. Robert Lacey, author of *Ford: The Men and the Machine*, writes that Iacocca's account of his departure from Ford was a far more complex tale than the one Iacocca tells. Lacey quotes one of Iacocca's colleagues at Ford as saying, "He had grown lazy, self-indulgent."[58]

The public persona of Lee Iacocca, however, is far different from the private one described by Lacey. Separating fact from fiction mattered little, as Lacey points out when explaining the auto magnate's ascent into mythology:

It was only right that he should become a folk hero. His cars were not always that good, but people bought them because he told them to. You could trust him. A lot of ordinary men and women felt they could identify with his blunt, no-nonsense ways . . . He became a national personality. Highly paid aides helped craft his columns for the newspapers, and when a ghostwriter helped the hero produce what passed for the truth about his life, mixed in with his thoughts on the state of the nation and some simplistic nostrums about how readers could duplicate his business success, it naturally produced a runaway best-seller. It was small wonder people started talking about him for the presidency.[59]

As for the dingy office that Iacocca said propelled him to Chrysler, it was a good three hundred square feet of floor space (not counting the outer office used by his secretary), complete with a large teak desk, a three-cushion sofa and chair, and a long, low table graced by a stylish brass lamp with cream shade.[60] Actually, the office had been previously used by the retired chairman of the board of the Ford Motor Company, Ernest R. Breech. But, as in the case of George Gipp, what passes for reality is unimportant.

Lee Iacocca, the myth, and Lee Iacocca, the reality, are one in the public's mind—in much the same way that "the Gipper" and Ronald Reagan were once inseparable. According to Gallup polls taken in 1985, Iacocca was the man most respected in the United States after Reagan and Pope John Paul II. Ordinary folks still write him at the rate of five hundred letters a day. Many relate their personal stories of how they, like him, are making the American dream a reality.

Iacocca's success has spawned a series of life stories, each of which depicts its hero-subject's overcoming nearly impossible obstacles to live the American dream. Air Force General Chuck Yeager overcomes death-defying odds in his best-selling *Yeager*; Frank Sinatra defies everyone in Kitty Kelley's *His Way*; Armand Hammer chronicles his rise to the top in the business world in *Hammer*; Betty Davis tells her tale in *This n' That*.

Some of the "I-can-do-it" feeling engendered by Iacocca has been carried to excess—starting with the Chrysler board chairman himself. Iacocca launched his company's 1987 advertising campaign by leasing Texas Stadium where "America's team," the Dallas Cowboys, play. In the presence of the Cowboys and their cheerleaders, he introduced Chrysler's new models. The emphasis on glitz is duplicated by pop singer Madonna. At concerts as she warbles the tune "Material Girl," she pulls wads of fake banknotes from the top of her dress and tosses them to the audience.[61] Tina Turner, another rock star, has made a comeback with a song entitled "What's Love Got To Do With It?" Ben Stein writes that on television's "Miami Vice" mankind is often mocked, and materialism is glorified: "In the world of Crocket and Tubbs [the two principal characters], man's spirit cannot be trusted, but a black Ferrari can. The camera worships it, lovingly laves it with its lens, bathes it in adoration."[62] "Miami Vice," however, remains something of an exception. With the 1980s has come the glorification of the family on television, led by the most popular program in the medium's short history, "The Cosby Show."

"The Cosby Show": Father (and Mother) Knows Best

Since its inception in the fall of 1984, "The Cosby Show" has had a firm grip on first place in television's A.C. Nielsen ratings. When Heathcliff and Clair Huxtable (Bill Cosby and Phylicia Rashad) take to the airwaves, some sixty-three million Americans are watching.[63] What they see are a very successful husband and wife—he's an obstetrician; she's a lawyer—and their five well-behaved, highly motivated children. The cast embodies much of the American dream. Heathcliff and Clair attend art auctions, making regular purchases, but they emphasize something more than materialism. They have the certitude that they are living better than their parents (who don't seem to be doing too badly, either), and that their children's lives will be even more comfortable than their own. In an interview, Cosby claimed, "My point is that this is an American family—an *American* family—and if you want to live like they do, and you're willing to work, the opportunity is there."[64]

Richard Zoglin writes, "Like Ronald Reagan, another entertainer with a warm, fatherly image who peaked relatively late in life, Cosby purveys a message of optimism and traditional family values."[65] Each episode of "The Cosby Show" uses the trivia of everyday family life to reaffirm folk values. In one, Heathcliff Huxtable purchases a used car for his oldest daughter; in another, one of the Huxtable children tries to explain away a bad grade. The Huxtable children espouse their parents' values, sometimes ad nauseam. In one episode, for example, a friend of thirteen-year-old Vanessa lights a cigarette in the Huxtable home, violating a parental rule. Each child chastised the girl, with eight-year-old Rudy sounding "like an ad for the American Cancer Society."[66]

Even the decor on the program is used to convey a subtle message. According to Cosby, he and the show's producers carefully selected the paintings that adorn the set. Most are portraits of black Americans by black Americans. Says Cosby: "When you look at the art work, there is a positive feeling, an up feeling. You don't see down-trodden, negative I-can't-do-I-won't-do. You see people with heads up. That's the symbolism. That's the strength."[67]

Americans, of course, realize that the Huxtable's are an idealized version of family life in the United States. Today the family is beset by many troubling issues: drugs, divorce, premarital sex, and teen-age pregnancy are just a few of these. According to Anne Roiphe, co-author of *Your Child's Mind*, these problems make for loyal viewers: "'The [Cosby] Show' demonstrates what Americans wish the world was like. This is what is missing in our lives—the strong support of a family."[68]

Cosby echoes the American longing for traditional family values in real life. His book, *Fatherhood*, sold more than 2.6 million copies and spent more than a year on the best-seller list. A second book, *Time Flies*, has advance orders of 1.75 million copies.[69] What gives a comedian, who received a Ph.D. in education from the University of Massachusetts, much expertise in parenting or aging is a mystery. But the character of Heathcliff Huxtable lends authenticity to Cos-by's pronouncements—as, once again, man and myth merge.

So many other programs have emulated "The Cosby Show" that the industry has concocted the term *warmedies*—signifying warm, family comedies—to describe them.[70] One of the warmedies is "Family Ties." Like "The Cosby Show," it projects a close-knit family, much like those of the 1950s pictured in "Father Knows Best," "Leave It to Beaver," and "The Adventures of Ozzie and Harriet." While the show reflects the values of its precursors, there is one difference: Alex P. Keaton, the oldest boy, played by Michael J. Fox, is an ardent Republican who fits the category "enterpriser" described in chapter 5. In one episode he is shown as a child carrying his school lunchbox with a picture of Richard Nixon on its cover. Alex always defends Reagan and castigates government, much to the annoyance of his parents, who are "'60s Democrats."

Another program that emphasizes family values but uses a differ-ent format is "Wheel of Fortune." The game show, a variation of the children's game "hangman," usually has three happily married contestants. Host Pat Sajak often allows each one a wave to his or her children or to some other relative. Something of a sensation is hostess Vanna White. This lovely young woman projects an image of wholesomeness, despite the fact that she has been featured nearly nude in *Playboy*. The public, however, continues to view her and

Sajak as "one of us." "Wheel of Fortune" wins its time slot in nearly every market and has earned millions for creator Merv Griffin.

"Gus Witherspoon," the salt-of-the-earth grandfather on the NBC warmedie "Our House," says, "Family may be an old-fashioned word. Well, I'm a little old-fashioned myself."[71] Most would agree. American Enterprise Institute scholar Michael Novak tells of how his children once obliged him to watch in sequence "The Cosby Show," "Family Ties," and "Cheers":

These were episodes with a remarkable treatment of classic family values. The humor is directed against the sorts of values that were common in the 1960s and 1970s. In fact, that was the explicit theme of one of the episodes— a friend of the family from the Berkeley days drops in on the family. The humor was delicious, understanding, and sympathetic. Those with traditional values could get the feeling—at least temporarily—of being in on the jokes rather than being the butt of them.[72]

Other programs, not usually thought of as keepers of traditional values, are cleaning up their acts. In the police drama "Cagney and Lacey," Cagney's former lovers have included David, a civil liberties lawyer; Lars, a ski bum; Ted, a paraplegic; Dory, a fellow police officer; and Ross, a journalist. Currently, Cagney has become a one-man woman, partly because of the AIDS epidemic but also as a consequence of the return to the more conservative values regarding fidelity and commitment. According to the show's creator, it is "no longer credible to write plots that include a lot of casual sex."[73] On "Dynasty," a homosexual character was made heterosexual and celibate. "Dallas" has tracked the pitfalls of the Ewing clan, including the "resurrection" and remarriage of Bobby and Pam. George Dessart, the head of television programming at CBS, says of the altered plots, "For a lot of reasons marriage is back in style. It's partly because of AIDS and herpes, but it also reflects some thinking about the nature of commitment and traditional values."[74] Terry Louise Fisher, one of the originators of "L.A. Law," agrees: "I think the sexual revolution is over. We may be heading for a new repression, a new 'Father Knows Best' era."[75]

Concurrent with the ascendancy of family values is the different treatment accorded authority figures on television. The Huxtable children on "The Cosby Show" disobey their parents from time to time, but they never question parental discipline or ridicule their parents. This is a monumental change from the 1970s, when authority figures were mocked on television. "All in the Family" established the pattern. Michael Stivik, Archie Bunker's son-in-law, ridiculed Archie, the government, religion, and every other vestige of authority. Archie would retort by calling Michael a "meathead." Archie, meanwhile, was filled with his own dislikes. His political hero, "Richard E. Nixon," was to be admired because he was the antithesis of the establishment created by Franklin Roosevelt. Bunker, in fact, opened the show by singing, "Mister we could use a man like Herbert Hoover again." Wife Edith was also ridiculed each time she tried to exert authority, and Archie stuck her with the moniker "dingbat."

"M*A*S*H" also derided authority, at least in its early years. Lieutenant Colonel Henry Blake, the commander of the surgical hospital, was a compassionate buffoon. Major Frank Burns was a buffoon without compassion. Another major, Margaret Houlihan, went by the nickname "Hot Lips." Meanwhile, that pervasive symbol of authority, the army, could do nothing right. Each of its representatives was either drunk, or incompetent, or both. The characters provided the perfect foils for the aptly named "Hawkeye Pierce," "Trapper-John McIntyre," and "B. J. Honeycutt."

In its later episodes, however, attitudes toward authority changed. Henry Blake died, and his successor, Colonel Sherman Potter, commanded respect. Frank Burns was replaced by Charles Emerson Winchester III, who argued with Hawkeye, and even got the better of him sometimes—all the while receiving the respect accorded his rank of major. Margaret Houlihan did not leave the cast; instead, her character was transformed from a caricature of promiscuity into a mature woman cooperating with, and earning the admiration of, the nursing staff. And Corporal Maxwell Klinger exchanged his women's dresses for army fatigues and became the unit's company clerk.[76]

The Reagan Presidency and American Culture

The resurrection of the authoritative hero, suggests polltaker Wirthlin, is one reason for young voters' preference for Reagan in 1984: "When we examined the importance of authority figures— that is, the need to hold someone in a position of freely given authority—young voters ranked very high. They viewed Reagan as an authoritative figure, not as an authoritarian figure."[77] Respect for authority seems to be so great that even a popular cartoonist like Garry Trudeau, whose "Doonesbury" strip has taken readers on a tour of a void called "Reagan's Brain" among other irreverences, finds his material relegated to the editorial page.

The new mind-set regarding authority figures in television and in politics has produced its own kind of historical revisionism. *New York Times* theater critic Vincent Canby writes that the Vietnam War and the violent public aversion to it "now appears to have been so effectively rewritten—at least by hugely popular movies like *Rambo* and *Missing in Action*—that a defeat has been turned into a victory."[78] In *Hamburger Hill*, a 1987 film about the 101st Airborne Division's struggle to take Hill 937 in Vietnam's Ashau Valley, a soldier received a letter from his stateside girlfriend saying that their relationship was over because the war that he is fighting is "immoral." The movie also shows a television news reporter informing the soldiers that "Senator Kennedy says you don't have a chance."[79] The Vietnam War certainly has not been forgotten, Canby notes, but it has been "accommodated as an unpleasantness with a happy ending."[80]

In such a manner, Ronald Reagan's use of American values both reflects and designs American popular culture. Family, work, neighborhood, and authority are rediscovered themes in entertainment, from "Leave It to Beaver" (which has returned for yet another run) to "The Cosby Show." In all of this, Reagan is as much a creator of the climate in which these shows work so successfully as are any of their producers, performers, or network scheduling czars. From bookstore to playhouse, the values Reagan has so repeatedly espoused seem firmly ensconced, for now, in the nation's culture.

7

A SENSE OF RETURN

Until humans can solve their philosophical problems, they're condemned to
solve their political problems over and over and over again. It's a cruel,
repetitious bore.
—Tom Robbins, *Even Cowgirls Get the Blues*

In 1986 voters in France went to the polls to choose a new prime
minister. That election was an especially important one. For five
unprecedented years the Socialists had held the post. Now they
were facing their most serious challenge to date as rejuvenated
conservatives called for a rollback of socialism, the return of national
industries to the private sector, a reduction of tax rates and government spending, and a return to free-market solutions. The French
had a word for the conservative agenda—and it is a French word—
Reaganism.[1]

Reaganism, as defined by the French conservatives, has triumphed
at the polling places in much of the Western world. Its progenitor,
Ronald Reagan, has carried a total of ninety-three states and 1,014
electoral votes in two presidential elections. In Canada the conservatives were swept into power in 1984, marking the first time since
1963 they have managed to seize the reins of government for a
prolonged period.[2] The leader of the United Kingdom's Conservative party, Margaret Thatcher, won a third term as prime minister
in 1987, becoming that country's first person to win majorities in
three consecutive Parliaments. West Germany has a conservative
chancellor in Helmut Kohl. And in that 1986 contest, France was
added to the growing list of conservative governments.

Reaganism has been enormously popular with many electorates,
as the election returns in West Germany, France, the U.K., and the
United States indicate. But is it a temporary reaction to the malaise
that gripped many of the Western nations during the 1970s? Some,

like Walter Mondale, view Reaganism as mostly ephemeral: "It's not substance, it's positioning and selling. It's not policy, it's polling. It's market surveys, it's film-making, it's using the skills of Hollywood to lead the country."[3] Others find Reaganism's predilection for free enterprise nostrums increasingly unsatisfactory. A New Hampshire woman who does volunteer work in a soup kitchen says, "You wouldn't believe the mothers we get [here] with babies and with children. Their husbands don't have jobs. One family was sleeping in a car . . . I think we are a generous nation, . . . but I don't understand how this kind of thing can be going on in this country. It disturbs me."[4] Many agree. A 1986 Harris survey finds 41 percent believing that "the federal government should use its powers more vigorously to promote the well-being of all segments of the people"—an increase of 11 percentage points in four years.[5]

Others believe Reaganism will have longer-lasting powers. Stuart Eizenstat, a domestic adviser to Jimmy Carter, points to the burrowing deep within the federal establishment of the Reaganites: "Any Administration in the future—Democrat or Republican—will have to face a bureaucracy considerably shifted to the right, and very consciously so."[6] Presidential scholar Hugh Heclo sees Reaganism's longevity stemming from a different lifeblood: "Just as liberalism made it all right to talk about sex, Reaganism made it all right to talk about patriotism, work requirements and family values, parochial allegiances, moral purpose and, yes, imposing middle-class values on others." Heclo adds, "Reaganism has a future because Americans want to talk about these things in politics."[7]

Look to the Left

The future of Reaganism is secure not because there are right-wing radicals boring into the nooks and crannies of the federal bureaucracy but thanks to its relative acceptance by the political *Left*. Consider:

• Upon assuming the chairmanship of the Senate Labor and Human Resources Committee in 1987, Edward Kennedy renewed his twenty-year campaign for congressional enactment of a national health insurance policy. Instead of a costly federal program, however, Kennedy proposed that *private* health insurers provide minimum benefits to policyholders.[8]

- Jane Fonda's husband, California State Assemblyman Tom Hayden, addressed an "open letter" to fellow Democrats in 1986 calling for a reimposition of the death penalty and restraints on state spending. Says Hayden, "Do you want the Democratic Party to be a principled party, or a majority party? I see no point in seeking to be a minority party."[9]
- The West German Green party platform of 1983 decried the excessive bureaucratization of government that "thwarts citizens from taking initiatives for themselves." The Greens demanded establishment of "democratically controllable self-administration close to the citizens" and the "thorough-going decentralization and simplification of units of administration."[10]

Ronald Reagan and the Left have little in common except this: each is calling the nation to experience "a sense of return" to the Jeffersonian concept of community, using the values of family, work, peace, freedom, self-esteem, and self-realization to achieve their diverse political ends.

The nuclear freeze movement of 1982 provides an excellent illustration of the return to community. In many New England town meetings held that year consideration of a "mutually verifiable freeze" on the production of nuclear weapons in the United States and the Soviet Union was added onto local agendas that called for votes on purchasing new snowplows, road repairs, and school budgets. The movement that began in the small New England villages eventually reached into larger metropolitan areas. Four thousand people took part in eleven "neighborhood" meetings in New York City to debate the issue. One Yale professor said the gatherings reminded him of "Jeffersonian democracy in action."[11]

Another illustration of the return to community came in August 1984 when sixty-two men and women met in St. Paul, Minnesota, to establish a U.S. variant of the West German Green party. The native Greens tossed about concepts like "beyond left and right," "connectedness with earth," "global awareness," "neighborliness," "empowerment," "roots," and "community." One West Coast activist said he imagined shopping centers where clerks would sometimes tell people they *shouldn't* buy things.[12]

Other examples abound. In Amherst, Massachusetts, Democratic party activists agreed in 1985 to collect signatures for a "Pledge of Resistance," a document calling for an end to the stationing of nuclear weapons in the Bay State. In upstate New York concerned citizens banded together to form the Central American Peace Project, a "teach-in" designed to focus local concerns regarding the Reagan administration's policies in Central America.

Each of these groups is at odds with established Reagan doctrine. Yet every one has attempted to emulate Reagan by using traditional values to promote its ends: reverence for neighborhood, inveighing against centralized government, the necessity for peace, the warmth of family.

The Green party of West Germany was the first to devise the slogan "Think globally, act locally." Although most Americans reject the Greens' critique of their society, their motto meets with overwhelming acceptance. "Live Aid," the global rock concert organized in 1985 by British musician Bob Geldof to alleviate hunger in Africa, and "Hands Across America," a rock-and-roll revival in 1986 to rally local communities to the cause of abolishing hunger at home, struck deeply embedded emotions in the American psyche, feelings that extend back to the birth of the nation. The liberal penchant to "do good"—as evidenced by efforts like "Live Aid" and "Hands Across America"—is no longer viewed through the rose-colored glasses of a burgeoning federal government but through the prism of the neighborhood. The rebirth of localism did not start with Ronald Reagan but had its beginnings in Lyndon Johnson's Great Society.

The Politics of Consensus

The "politics of consensus" culminated during Lyndon Johnson's campaign in 1964 against Barry Goldwater.[13] That year Johnson's political support extended from conservative U.S. Senator Richard Russell of Georgia to black activist James Farmer; from union boss Walter Reuther to auto magnate Henry Ford II; from Republicans in Vermont to Democrats in southwest Texas. In more of a consensual act than a majoritarian one, 61.1 percent of the voters confirmed Johnson as their president. But the electorate was engaged in something more than a plebiscite on Johnson the man; they also provided a mandate to Johnson the philosopher. A strong, active presidency—with the states and localities yielding considerable authority to the federal government—had become acceptable to everyone except Goldwater and a few "extremists." One of the exceptions was movie actor Ronald Reagan. Sounding like a prophet of doom,

Reagan stumped the countryside for Goldwater, warning, "Either we accept the responsibilities for our own destiny, or we abandon the American Revolution and confess that an intellectual belief in a far-distant capital can plan our lives for us better than we. Already the hour is late."[14]

Few voters shared Reagan's sense of urgency. An overwhelming majority believed that the federal establishment was in full accord with the principles established by the Founding Fathers. As they saw it, government was promoting the economic well-being of the "common man," thereby enhancing the average citizen's freedoms and liberties. Presidential assistant Eric Goldman suggested that Johnson's 1964 State of the Union Address include the sentence: "Today, in a very real sense, we are all liberals, we are all conservatives—and we are moving toward a new American consensus."[15]

Johnson did not use Goldman's words, but he did heed Goldman's advice in 1965, paraphrasing Thomas Jefferson in that year's State of the Union Address: "We have achieved a unity of interest among our people that is unmatched in the history of freedom."[16] Two weeks later, taking the oath of office for the first time as an elected president, Johnson spoke of a "new American consensus" that would allow the country to "achieve progress without strife" and "change without hatred."[17]

Johnson's "politics of consensus" was forged during the Great Depression, which saw the ebbing of political authority away from the states to the federal government. In 1933 Luther Gulick, a noted student of public administration, declared, "The American state is finished. I do not predict that the states will go, but affirm that they have gone."[18] Two decades later one of Gulick's disciples, Leonard D. White, confirmed the diagnosis: "If present trends continue for another quarter-century, the states may be left hollow shells, operating primarily as field districts of federal departments."[19]

The Democratic party did not mourn the relative demise of the states. Its 1936 platform writers paraphrased the Declaration of Independence by proclaiming several "self-evident truths," including,

that this three-year recovery in all the basic values of life and the re-establishment of the American way of living has been brought about by humanizing the policies of the Federal Government as they affect the personal, financial, industrial and agricultural well-being of the American people.[20]

To the Democrats gathered to nominate Franklin Roosevelt for a second time, it was also "self-evident" that pressing national problems such as "drought, dust storms, floods, minimum wages, maximum hours, child labor and working conditions in industry, monopolistic and unfair business practices cannot be handled by forty-eight separate State Legislatures, forty-eight separate State administrations and forty-eight separate State courts."[21] The remedy, as prescribed by "Dr. New Deal," was simple: "Transactions and activities which inevitably overflow State boundaries call for both State and Federal treatment."[22] Roosevelt's Supreme Court packing scheme of 1937 was vaguely foreshadowed when the platform warned that should it become necessary, the Constitution would be amended to allow the federal government to act in the best interests of "the family and the home."[23]

Republicans vigorously protested. Their 1936 platform spoke in apoplectic tones:

America is in peril. The welfare of American men and women and the future of our youth are at stake. We dedicate ourselves to the preservation of their political liberty, their individual opportunity and their character as free citizens, which today for the first time are threatened by government itself.[24]

They denounced the "vast multitude of new offices" and the "centralized bureaucracy" from which "swarms of inspectors" swooped over the countryside "to harass our people."[25] The bill of particulars against the "New Deal administration" included: presidential usurpation of the powers of Congress; a flaunting of the integrity and authority of the Supreme Court; flagrant violations of the rights and liberties of American citizens; the taking unto itself by the federal government of the rights reserved to the states and the people; and the frightful waste and extravagance of federal spending.[26] Pledging to maintain local self-government, free enterprise, and private competition, the Republicans declared that 1936 was a different kind of an election—a battle that "cannot be waged on the traditional differences between the Republican and Democratic parties."[27]

The overwhelming defeat of GOP presidential nominee Alfred Landon in 1936 silenced much of the conservative critique against the resurgent federal government. Not until World War II concluded was the call to arms sounded again when sociologist Robert

Nisbet deplored the depersonalization of human relationships and the withering away of community.[28] Others maintained that big government, big business, and big labor were replacing what Edmund Burke called "the inns and resting places of the human spirit": local churches, schools, shops, neighborhoods, and families.[29]

Voters did not agree. For all the imploring of the conservatives, most remained obdurate in believing that the New Deal programs had worked. Roosevelt biographer James MacGregor Burns argues that every president after FDR sought to enhance the average citizen's clout.[30] Harry Truman's Marshall Plan and Point Four Program brought an American version of the New Deal to the nations devastated by World War II. Dwight Eisenhower signed the first major civil rights legislation since the Civil War. John Kennedy's New Frontier extended the idea of the "common man" to those in Third World countries through such initiatives as the Peace Corps.

But it was Lyndon Johnson who sought to bring more "outcasts" into the political and economic mainstream than had any of his Democratic predecessors save Roosevelt. After the 1964 election returns were in, he was advised by Goldman: "Consensus [politics] can . . . be an active, dynamic, rolling credo. [It] can be a springboard."[31] Johnson forged ahead with his Great Society. At his insistence Congress passed the Civil Rights Acts of 1964, the Voting Rights Act of 1965, a highway beautification program (a special project of Lady Bird Johnson), a food stamp program, and the Model Cities program. Congress also created the Office of Economic Opportunity, the Department of Housing and Urban Development, and the Department of Transportation to administer the new programs.

Richard Nixon, despite attempting to dismantle his predecessor's War on Poverty, largely continued the Johnson initiatives. He signed into law the Occupational Safety and Health Act of 1970, and the Clean Air and Water Acts of 1971, and added the Environmental Protection Agency to the growing multitude of federal agencies. He also imposed wage and price controls in an attempt to bring down a spiraling inflation rate. Faced with an economy sliding into a recession, a Democratic Congress earmarked $250 million in 1974 for a massive job creation program approved by Gerald Ford.[32] Jimmy Carter sought to enlarge federal authority through the creation of the Department of Energy while at the same time satisfying the National Education Association by establishing a Department of Education.

The courts added their own modifications to the federal compact. After the Supreme Court reversed itself on the New Deal in 1938, many federal judges threw away theretofore self-imposed restraints and engaged in an unprecedented degree of activism. For example: a district court judge in 1974 seized control of Boston's segregated schools; an Alabama judge laid down a long list of administrative regulations to be observed in the operation of that state's largest mental hospital;[33] and a federal district court in New Orleans directed that city jails provide certain medical and dental services, construct a new hospital, provide more and better recreational facilities, and limit the number of inmates in the main facility.[34] One constitutional scholar, concerned about such extraordinary judicial interference in executive functions, termed this "government by judiciary."[35] Taken together, these actions—presidential, congressional, and judicial—restructured the Founding Fathers' original concept of federalism.

As the federal contract was being rewritten, the citizen view of government also changed. It had its beginnings in the midst of a bloody Civil War when Abraham Lincoln proclaimed that the Union's government was "of the people, by the people, and for the people."[36] This was a major departure from the Founders' notion that envisioned the House of Representatives as "the people's" only agent in Washington.

As the bureaucracy expanded—first as a matter of necessity to combat the Great Depression, then as a matter of choice after the World War II—Americans came to view the *entire* federal government as their own. Voters changed from being ratifiers to proprietors, watching over political leaders in much the same way that a board of directors oversees the chief executive officer of a large corporation. Like the corporate financiers of Wall Street, the electorate focused not on details or excuses but results. A New Hampshire man put it this way: "All we're looking for is straight talk. Straight answers, no wishy-washy stuff, no dodging the question."[37]

When it comes to the presidency, voters have strong proprietary feelings. A series of in-depth interviews conducted by a Washington-based think tank confirms this. One woman compared the presidential selection process to submitting a job application: "Every time I've applied for a job, I've had to produce a resume and fill out a job application. Aren't these politicians applying for a job? And aren't we hiring them?" Another agreed, wanting the candidates to produce "a check list of sorts." Prospective presidents would check off their positions on various issues. One interviewee wanted the list to be organized in columns: "These are the topics and these are the men. And this is how we feel about every topic. Neatly organized."[38]

For more than five decades voters have reviewed the "check lists" of accomplishments submitted by their chief executives with some satisfaction. Even in the midst of Watergate, 57 percent disagreed with the statement "As the government is now organized and operated, I think it is hopelessly incapable of dealing with all the crucial problems facing the country today."[39]

By the onset of the Reagan presidency, the "consensus politics" of Lyndon Johnson was no more. Ironically, it was a thirty-eight-year-old assistant secretary of labor in the Johnson administration who had forecast its demise. Daniel Patrick Moynihan told Theodore H. White during the 1964 campaign:

Maybe we're entering a new phase of government. Maybe the old legislative politics is coming to an end, the time when you passed a new law which set up a new bureau with a new appropriation to run new machinery. What lies ahead may be problems not answerable by law or by government at all. But that's nothing you can discuss now in 1964—that's years ahead.[40]

By 1980 the "new phase of government" that Moynihan foresaw had come to pass. Voters no longer believed that the federal establishment consisted of governors acting on behalf of the governed, but that it was dominated by a privileged few who were carelessly throwing away precious federal dollars. Surveys taken by the University of Michigan Center for Social Research tracked the growing disillusionment. In 1958, 18 percent agreed with the statement "The government is run by a few big interests looking out for themselves"; by 1980, 77 percent agreed. Moreover, the percentage who believed that "the government cannot be trusted to do what is right most of the time" stood at 25 percent in 1958, and at 66 percent in 1982. And the proportion of respondents who thought "quite a few [of the people running the government] don't seem to know what they are doing" stood at 28 percent in 1964, 45 percent in 1970, and 63 percent in 1980.[41]

The desire of "we, the people" to regain control of the government from the ineptitude of political elites became so powerful that it created its own peculiar historical revisionism. When asked in 1986 what John Kennedy meant when he proclaimed in his 1961

TABLE 4

Public Preference in Regard to the Vesting of Government Power,
1936, 1981, 1987

Preference	1936[a]	1981[b]	1987[c]
Federal government	56%	36%	34%
State government	44	64	63
No opinion	—	—	3

Note: Text of question: "Which theory of government do you favor: concentration of power in the federal government or concentration of power in the state government?"

[a] George Gallup, survey, 1936.   [b] George Gallup, survey, September 18–21, 1981.
[c] Decision/Making/Information, survey for the Republican National Committee, April 21–23, 1987.

Inaugural Address, "Ask not what your country can do for you, ask what you can do for your country," some of the responses were truly startling. One person said, "He's trying to remind the American people that they should try to be more responsible for themselves, and not be dependent on somebody taking over their responsibilities, such as providing you with benefits whenever you need it . . . Once you get on that track, why should you go back, because government is taking care of all your responsibilities."[42] A Democrat added, "I believe we are doing what we can for our country. We are not accepting any government programs and so-called handouts by being middle class."[43]

As the bill of particulars grew longer, the Roosevelt version of American federalism was itself reversed. A 1936 Gallup poll had found a majority favored a "concentration of power in the federal government"; in 1981 a majority favored a concentration of power in state government. Six years later the public remained solidly committed to the decentralization of political power (table 4). Older voters, whose political experiences began during the heyday of the New Deal, were somewhat less supportive of the states, preferring them to the federal government by a margin of only 13 percentage points. Younger voters, whose formative years occurred during the Reagan era, favored the states by 32 percentage points.[44]

A new brand of "consensus politics" was emerging. Eighty-three percent of a national sample told polltaker Louis Harris that they agreed with Reagan's inaugural proclamation that the size and influence of the federal government should be curbed.[45] Sixty-seven percent of the respondents in a 1981 Gallup survey believed state governments were more understanding of community needs; just 15 percent viewed the federal government this way.[46] Seventy-five percent in a 1982 Decision/Making/Information poll thought it was important for Reagan to transfer taxing and spending powers from the federal government to state governments, and 59 percent judged him a success in accomplishing that objective.[47]

Armed with these impressive figures, Reagan went before Congress in 1982 and proposed a program he dubbed "New Federalism." It was, he said, the most dramatic reversal in the relationship between the federal government and the states in fifty years: forty-seven billion dollars in federal programs would be returned to the states. To ease the transition, twenty-eight billion dollars would be available to local officials over a ten-year period to finance theretofore federally sponsored programs. After a decade, the states could abolish the programs or assume their full costs.[48]

The public strongly supported Reagan's New Federalism. A *Los Angeles Times* survey found 79 percent approving the plan and a mere 14 percent disapproving. The same poll also revealed that among Reagan's goals of cutting spending on social services, increasing defense expenditures, reducing government regulations, and delegating more power to state and local governments, 44 percent—a plurality—chose the last goal as the most important.[49]

Despite considerable public support, Reagan's New Federalism never received a congressional hearing, much less become part of the nation's legal code. No matter. It became law by default. The enormous budget deficits that Reagan produced not only prevented Democrats from enacting new programs but forced those who favored Franklin Roosevelt's mode of governance to search for alternatives while they defended the status quo. In a memo to the Democratic Policy Commission, pollster Brad Bannon wrote, "To many voters the Democratic style of government is to meet the nation's problems by fighting for programs that voters consider irrelevant or even worse, that they consider responsible for a national crisis of confidence that gripped the nation in the late 1960s and 1970s."[50]

The Right Meets the Left

As time passed Franklin Roosevelt and Ronald Reagan appeared to be "bookend presidents": one expanded and the other confined the limits of the federal government.[51] Each tried to make the system work, and in his own way each succeeded. Eventually, a new political agenda took hold, one that consisted of restraining federal responsibilities and returning power to state and local governments, and to the individual. It stemmed from the resentment voters had toward a federal establishment that had come to be seen as dominated by uncaring, dim-witted bureaucrats. A former school teacher captured the mood: "People are being screwed by the establishment."[52] Another agreed: "There's just thousands and thousands of white collar workers [in Washington] who do nothing but shuffle paper and don't do anything that's of any value to anyone. And they get a pay increment, they get incredible benefits, for what? It's just flab, it's just waste."[53]

The revolt against big government, which fueled Reaganism, extended to big business. An Iowa nurse said, "Big business, they should be able to cut back, too, and I don't see their profits cutting back any . . . that doesn't seem fair to me."[54] Another Iowan concurred: "That's the way I feel about Caterpillar [the tractor firm that had closed down]. Let them go. We've given them tax breaks, we've given them everything. Let them go."[55]

The revolt against bigness of every sort resulted in a corresponding longing for community. Pollster Yankelovich reported that his surveys showed the public's "search for community"—namely, the desire to compensate for the impersonal and threatening aspects of modern life by seeking identification with others—grew from 32 percent in 1973 to 47 percent at the start of the 1980s.[56] Since then the revolt against bigness has become entrenched. According to a 1986 CBS News/New York Times poll, 51 percent believe the federal government "creates more problems than it solves." The same poll showed 63 percent believing that state and local governments do the best job of coping with most of the problems they face.[57] Reagan pollster Wirthlin found majorities in 1986 were willing to turn some important federal responsibilities over to the private sector: 70 percent thought private industry, not the federal government, should continue producing electricity; 61 percent said private firms should provide insurance for U.S. companies doing business overseas; 50 percent thought industry should guarantee home loans. Wirthlin also found 67 percent agreed with the statement "In the '60s and '70s, it was the federal government growing beyond our control that strongly contributed to the collapse of our economy, of confidence in our institutions, and a shaking of the very roots of our freedom."[58]

A year later Wirthlin showed 50 percent believing local governments were most sensitive to their needs; just 26 percent selected state governments; and only 16 percent thought the federal government could be best described that way.[59]

Nowhere is the evidence of a substantial change in the political agenda more evident than in the rhetoric of Democratic party leaders. In a surprising role reversal, they are currently saying "me-too." Democrat Paul Tsongas, at that time a senator from Massachusetts, told a National Press Club audience in 1982 that the Democratic party must allow "a kind of cleansing realism to work its way in." He bluntly declared that his party "should take the best of what [Reagan] did and embrace that without embarrassment," adding that if the Democrats were to be returned to the White House, "not all the spending cuts [Reagan initiated] are going to be restored."[60]

Even the stalwarts joined the chorus. House Speaker Tip O'Neill said: "You just can't go the old New Deal road. The 1980s are a time of change, and the Democratic party has to respond to the people."[61] Still others found pleasure in denouncing the New Deal, believing that voters associated it with big government. New York Mayor Edward Koch branded his former House colleagues as "kneejerk liberals," saying, "I don't believe in half their crap. That government has to become bigger. That government is better if it does more. It's the New Deal out of the thirties, that government solves all problems. I once believed that. I have *contempt* for government."[62] This was a 180-degree "hard about" for Koch, who, as a Democratic congressman, received a 100 percent approval rating from the liberal Americans for Democratic Action.

Koch's reversal was subsequently echoed by another prominent New Yorker, Mario Cuomo. The day after the 1984 election, Cuomo told an interviewer:

One of the Senators . . . is supposed to have said, "We have read all of Governor Cuomo's speeches and they are New Deal." I laughed. What are you when you reduce public employees by 9,000? What are you when you say [that] need should be the criterion [for welfare benefits]? What are you when you can come out for a tax cut? What are you when you refuse to raise the basic taxes? What are you when you spend more on your defense budget, which we call corrections, than any governor in history?[63]

The answer to Cuomo's litany of questions is *reelected*. His 64.6 percent of the vote in 1986 was the greatest in New York history—a victory so enormous that the New Deal refusenik captured nearly half of the votes of those who said they had supported Reagan in 1984.[64]

Other Democrats trimmed their sails. Kathleen Kennedy Townsend, the daughter of the late Robert Kennedy, said in her losing 1986 campaign for Congress, "[It's] not just what government programs can do, but what each of us can do in our own lives." Her brother Joseph P. Kennedy II, who won his race for a House seat that year, declared, "The days of taxing and spending, taxing and spending are over."[65] Southern Democrats led by former Virginia Governor Chuck Robb, former Arizona Governor Bruce Babbitt, Missouri Congressman Richard Gephardt, and Georgia Senator Sam Nunn formed the Democratic Leadership Council. The purpose of the organization was not so much to mount a counterattack against the Reagan Revolution as to acknowledge its staying power by urging their fellow partisans to adapt to it or face defeat at the polls.

The party heeded the advice of its leaders. A 1986 report issued by the Democratic National Committee proclaimed a "Democratic Creed," a set of commandments that could have been written by Reagan himself: "the freedom to make personal choices is at the heart of the American dream"; "individuals must be responsible for their own lives"; "opportunity is the key to a free society"; "a growing economy is the foundation of a society that is both dynamic and just"; "achievement and progress are central to the expectations of Americans"; "strong state and local governments are essential"; "America must be strong to deter aggression and keep the peace."[66]

Congressional Democrats are following their party's creed. William Proxmire, chairman of the Senate Banking Committee, has suggested revoking the Glass-Steagall Banking Act, a landmark New Deal law that separated investment from commercial banking and created the Federal Deposit Insurance Corporation. Proxmire said he had not decided whether or not to overturn the law, but "there is a strong case for its outright repeal."[67] Paul Simon has introduced a "Guaranteed Job Opportunity Program," an idea similar to Roosevelt's Works Progress Administration. Simon's variant provides thirty-two weeks of minimum-wage employment while recipients receive counseling and training in locating permanent jobs in the private sector. A contender for the Democratic presidential nomination in 1988, Simon said he is the true heir to his party's traditional values: "I stand . . . as a Democrat, not as a neo-anything, as one who is not running away from the Democratic tradition of caring and daring and dreaming."[68] But the Illinois Democrat provided the following rationale for his jobs program: private sector jobs for the poor would strengthen families, deter crime and drug abuse, and stimulate business.[69] Such a program would not have been inconceivable in Roosevelt's day, but surely this is not the rationale that would have been used then. A senior congressional aide describes the Democratic party's 1987 legislative agenda as a "pursuit of liberal ends by conservative means."[70]

The Clean Water Act of 1987 provides another illustration of Reaganism's staying power. It passed the Democratically controlled Congress overwhelmingly, despite a veto by Reagan, who denounced its excessive cost. Lost in the headlines of Congress's rebuff to the executive was the bill's elimination of federal construction grants for sewage treatment plants and the transfer of these funds to the states.[71]

Democratic mayors no longer look to Washington for help, but practice their own versions of community politics. New York's Koch has proposed the largest tax abatement program in the country. Boston's Raymond Flynn relies upon private building contractors to construct low-cost housing projects. And San Antonio's Henry Cisneros has turned to industrialists for additional dollars.[72]

Governors are also getting into the act. Just three states in 1970 had overseas offices to drum up business; by 1980 the number had grown to thirty.[73] A Massachusetts industrial science agency has lent over $3 billion to businesses. Michael Dukakis proudly touts his state's services to the private sector: "There isn't much we won't do for a company that's willing either to expand or relocate in one of our target areas—heavy investments in older downtowns, direct stuff in addition to financing ... At any one time we'll have a hundred and fifty or two hundred of these projects going."[74] David Broder calls this "New Deal-Making politics."[75]

The involvement of state and local governments in areas heretofore reserved for private enterprise reflects a trend toward the removal of political disputes from the public domain. Political scientist E. E. Schattschneider wrote in 1971:

A long list of ideas concerning individualism, free private enterprise, localism, privacy, and economy in government seems to be designed to privatize conflict or to restrict its scope or to limit the use of public authority to enlarge the scope of conflict. A tremendous amount of conflict is controlled by keeping it so private that it is almost completely invisible.[76]

Schattschneider's observation has come to pass. The housing aspirations of the poor are now in the hands of volunteers from local businesses and churches; the stomachs of the hungry are filled by local citizens working in soup kitchens; the dying do so with dignity in neighborhood hospice programs. Aleen Zimberoff Bayard is one of a growing number of activists seeking private solutions to national problems. In 1985 she and several friends started the Entertainment Action Team (EAT) whose mission is to "end hunger in Chicago through self-sufficiency."[77] The group auctioned a part-ownership in an Arabian horse in order to buy a cafe that will serve as a restaurant-training program for homeless teenagers. Says Bayard: "Our group believes people want to help themselves. We're saying, 'Money doesn't solve the problem.' We are really apolitical. Fat government is the problem."[78]

In another part of Chicago a seventy-three-year-old woman joined a tenants association. She explained her new commitment this way: "I was craving more real, human contact with my neighbors. For years and years, I let myself get accustomed to the no-eye-contact, live-in-your-own world ways we'd come to regard each other. I decided that even at my own age, it was worth struggling out of that to something better, something more like community."[79]

In many neighborhoods across the United States the Left and the Right have met each other. As Reaganism continues its ascendancy, its reach extends far into the nation's political future.

The Implications of Reaganism

Television talk show host David Frost plans a series of prime-time interviews in 1988 with the would-be presidents, the first such in-depth conversations he has held in two decades. In 1968 Frost asked Richard Nixon, Hubert Humphrey and George Wallace, "Do you believe in your country right or wrong?" At the time the Vietnam War was raging, campus protests were mounting, and Lyndon Johnson was hiding out in the White House. It was a relevant inquiry.

Frost does not plan to repeat the question in 1988. It is irrelevant. Other topics, some literally matters of life and death, form the top tier of issues for the 1988 presidential campaign: the plague of AIDS, the scourge of international terrorism, the madness of nuclear weaponry, a shortage of energy, the enormous federal budget deficits, and despoiling of the environment. The Democratic and Republican candidates will, of course, dispute some of the specific decisions made by Reagan during his years in office. Democrats will charge that he was inept in his handling of the Iran-Contra affair, and that many of his domestic and foreign policies were woefully inadequate. Republicans will attack the Democrats' "tax and spend, tax and spend" policies.

But the two parties will not argue over the basic aspects of Reaganism itself. Each of the issues cited above will be debated and solved in the web of the traditional values structure woven during the Reagan era. Reaganism is now a political fact of life that transcends party. As time passes, the Reagan legacy will be increasingly evident in two principal areas: the types of persons who will seek the presidency and the manner in which future endeavors by American leaders will be undertaken.

The Democrats' Dilemma

In a dire March 1987 memo Democratic pollster Patrick Caddell warned that "only a minor political earthquake" will enable the Democrats to win back the White House in 1988:

The unpleasant truth is this: The party has never been weaker in our lifetime, and the array of obstacles and trends has never been more alarming . . . As Democrats, we have been victims of self-delusion—the delusion that ours is still the nation's majority party, that a generation of national defeats can be explained by unique defects of candidate, circumstance, tactics, or calculation and that victory is only a quick fix away.[80]

By every conceivable measure the Roosevelt-Truman-Kennedy-Johnson era of reasonably assured Democratic occupancy of the White House is over. Since 1968 Republicans have won 77 percent of the electoral votes cast, compared with the Democrats' 21 percent. Twenty-three states, with a total of 202 electors, have been won by the GOP every time.[81] The Democrats have managed to snag the three paltry electoral votes of the national capital, but only once in five elections have they won the right to preside there. Caddell notes that a successful 1988 Democratic ticket will have to outperform Mondale and Ferraro by nine percentage points. Only Eisenhower, who offered himself to disillusioned voters in the midst of an unresolved Korean War, and Carter, who offered himself to disillusioned voters in the wake of Watergate, were able to outscore their party's previous nominees by nine points.[82] Stuart Eizenstat commented, "It will take an extraordinary candidate and set of circumstances for the Democrats to win the Presidency in the foreseeable future."[83]

To collect the necessary 270 electoral votes to win the White House, the Democrats must crack the Republican base in the South and West. To do so, their nominee must adhere to a significantly different value structure from that of Mondale and his predecessors. The Democrats' choice in 1988 will inevitably be someone with "new ideas" that represent to some extent the values and the governing principles of Reagan. Former Colorado Senator Gary Hart says, "Mr. Reagan isn't in the White House just because of his charm. He's there, in large part, because of his ideas. We may disagree with those ideas, but we won't beat something with nothing."[84] Daniel Patrick Moynihan echoes Hart: "The Republicans simply left us behind. They became the party of ideas and we were left, in Lord Macaulay's phrase, 'The Stupid Party.'"[85]

To avoid being a leader of "The Stupid Party," the next Democratic standard-bearer will have to present new approaches to old problems. That requires a concoction of two parts Reaganism mixed together with one part of the party's old-time religion. In 1988 the result may be more than a "dime's worth of difference" between the Democratic and Republican presidential candidates. But it is not likely to be the dollar's worth of difference that Reagan and Mondale offered voters in 1984.

New Paths to the White House

At the 1787 Philadelphia convention that formulated the Constitution, Massachusetts delegate Elbridge Gerry suggested that state governors appoint the president because they could best determine the qualities the chief magistrate should possess. Gerry's idea was not approved, but a variant of it was practiced initially.[86] Throughout much of the nineteenth century and into the early twentieth, several governors, including Franklin Pierce, Rutherford B. Hayes, Grover Cleveland, William McKinley, Theodore Roosevelt, Warren G. Harding, and Calvin Coolidge, went from the governor's house to the White House.

The political powers of state chief executives became badly corroded during and after Franklin Roosevelt's time. Governors were no longer sought after for the White House job. One lamented,

"We don't have sovereign states anymore. All we have are a bunch of provinces . . . We are becoming conveyor belts for policies signed, sealed, and delivered in Washington."[87] Members of Congress, especially senators, had an "inside track" to the Oval Office. Harry Truman, Estes Kefauver, John Kennedy, Hubert Humphrey, Richard Nixon, Lyndon Johnson, Robert Kennedy, Eugene McCarthy, and George McGovern form part of the very lengthy list. Many of these seekers of the presidency, no doubt because of their Washington experience, sought to extend the federal government's reach into the lives of ordinary Americans.

In the 1970s the governors regained some of their lost prestige. Georgia's former governor Carter won the 1976 Democratic presidential nomination competing against California's Governor Edmund G. Brown. On the Republican side, California's former Governor Reagan nearly took the top slot away from Gerald Ford. Four years later two former governors squared off in the general election. Carter and Reagan were not aberrations; instead, they simply were reblazing an old trail to the White House.

The rewriting of the federal compact during the Reagan presidency has enhanced the powers and prestige of state governors. After a dozen years as governor of Washington State, Daniel Evans was leaving with some regret: "In the last four years I've seen the beginnings of change, and I guess I'm a little reluctant to leave office now since I see that things are beginning to come back our way."[88] Nevada Governor Paul Laxalt vacated the position only to claim a Senate seat three years later. But he quickly became bored. The drone of debate in the Senate chamber reminded him of the difference between being an executive and a legislator. Herman Talmadge, also a former governor and senator, put it this way: "The governor makes decisions and executes them. A senator makes decisions and talks about them. There's a big difference."[89]

The path from state capital to national capital is being trod upon once again in 1988. The fifty-first presidential election has more candidates than usual who are, or have been, governors: Bruce Babbitt and Michael Dukakis on the Democratic side, Pierre duPont on the Republican.[90] The fact that there are three former or incumbent governors actively seeking the presidency stands in sharp contrast to the last time the country saw an open seat in the Oval Office, 1968. Then all of the Democratic players came from the Senate: Hubert Humphrey, Robert Kennedy, Eugene McCarthy, and George McGovern. On the Republican side two governors, Nelson Rockefeller and George Romney, unsuccessfully pursued that party's nomination.

As the list of presidents grows to include more men and women whose political origins are in town halls, community organizations, local businesses, and state capitals—not the national capital—the importance attached to these formative neighborhood experiences is likely to increase.[91]

Reverberations in the "Echo Chamber"

Anyone who occupies the Oval Office is in an echo chamber of sorts, listening and responding to the vox populi. As the public has demanded, and been given, a rewriting of the federal compact, the exhortations from the White House differ markedly from those in the recent past. Instead of proposing new federal programs, presidents echo the voters' cry for a less obtrusive but involved federal government by inspiring local communities to tackle tough problems. These changed reverberations are heard, for example, in Ronald and Nancy Reagan's "Just say no" admonitions against drug usage. In the first-ever joint address by a president and a first lady, Ronald Reagan told his television audience, "If your friend or neighbor or a family member has a drug or alcohol problem, don't turn the other way. Go to his help or to hers. Get others involved with you—clubs, service groups, and community organizations—and provide support and strength."[92]

A similar initiation came in 1983 when the Department of Education released a study by the National Commission on Excellence in Education entitled *A Nation at Risk*. The commission's report card on the nation's public schools consisted of mostly failing grades. But instead of a massive federal effort to revamp curricula, commission members urged parents, teachers, students, and local communities to do more:

Our goal must be to develop the talents of all to their fullest. Attaining that goal requires that we expect and assist all students to work to the limits of their capabilities. We should expect schools to have genuinely high standards rather than minimum ones, and parents to support and encourage their children to make the most of their talents and abilities.[93]

The commissioners declared that "state and local officials, including school board members, governors, and legislators, have *the primary responsibility* for financing and governing the schools."[94] The federal government's role, they said, was "to identify the national interest in education," that is, to shine a spotlight on the problems facing the nation's public schools.[95] Parents were told to be "a *living* example of what you expect your children to honor and to emulate," and students were told to have "high expectations for yourself and convert every challenge into an opportunity."[96]

One year after the report was made, each state had formed a task force to study the problems in its schools with the following nationwide results: forty-seven changed teacher certification procedures; thirty-five raised high school graduation requirements; twenty-one reevaluated classroom textbooks; eight lengthened the school day; and seven expanded the school year. The private sector also got involved. Local businesses "adopted" neighborhood schools, and executives worked with teachers and students to improve the quality of classroom instruction. From the White House Reagan applauded these activities by creating the President's Academic Fitness Award that he gave to 220,000 high school graduates in 1984 who had consistently attained high grades.[97]

Future presidents are likely to emulate Reagan's approach. During his brief run for the White House, Democrat Joseph Biden lauded the Ford Motor Company for having "achieved amazing increases in productivity and quality." Biden argued that the principal duty of the next president must be "to convince all our citizens that they can and must shape their own future and the nation's future":

No new law or government program can make other firms follow Ford's example, nor could they make other unions show the same openness to change and innovation. But the president always has his "bully pulpit" and he should not hesitate to use it vigorously to promote such productive ideas.[98]

The new politics of localism, as practiced by Reagan and his successors, means that the "bully pulpit" of the presidency will continue to be used to persuade a Congress and a people. But it will not be a forum to address the needs of a national "family," as in the past. Instead, the next president will cajole individuals and neighborhoods into acting on important national problems.

The Regent and the Vox Populi

The use of traditional American values by candidates for high political office did not begin with Ronald Reagan. Others have employed them over the years with mixed success. Joseph Persico, who wrote speeches for Nelson Rockefeller, once described how his boss would extol "the brotherhood of man under the fatherhood of God." Persico coined the acronym BOMFOG to describe Rockefeller's preference for platitudes.[99] But Rockefeller's pitch did not resonate with much of the electorate. In part, this was due to his penchant for facts over symbols. Persico says that if Rockefeller, not Roosevelt, had delivered the Inaugural Address of 1933 instead of "one-third of a nation ill-housed, ill-clad, ill-nourished" we might have had "32.2 percent in substandard housing, 29.9 percent inadequately clothed."[100]

Reagan would not have so miscalculated. He, more than most presidents, understood that voters respond to symbols and phrases that evoke commonly held values. Reagan has followed this rule of politics so assiduously that, in effect, he has become a regent entrusted by the voters with making the values of family, work, neighborhood, peace, and freedom a greater reality in their lives.

Reagan's regency has created confusion about his historical legacy. ABC News correspondent Ted Koppel says, "[We] will have to wait until the footlights dim and the houselights go up again, before determining whether the play was any good at all."[101] The observation points to a significant difference between Reagan and his predecessors. Heretofore it has been presidential actions that have usually shaped history's final judgments. Descriptors are often simply a line or two in the history books. For George Washington, "He was the Father of the Country." For Abraham Lincoln, "He saved the Union and freed the slaves." For Franklin Roosevelt, "He launched the New Deal and fought World War II." Only John Kennedy's brief tenure is summarized by a word, "Camelot," which describes not actual accomplishments but a mood.[102]

Like Kennedy, Reagan's exiting line will probably be different from the rest. His former communications director, Patrick Buchanan, suggests it will be "Restored America's spirit and economy, built the great space shield and drove the Communists out of North America."[103] But Buchanan's lengthy and optimistic sentence focuses on deeds, not atmospherics. Ronald Reagan's legacy lies not so much in his actions as president, but in the "sense of return" he has given the American people in their values. Today, the traumas of Vietnam, Watergate, and the disappointing presidencies of Johnson, Nixon, Ford, and Carter are being placed, rightly or wrongly, in a values perspective.

American voters are often of two minds. They are idealists who can respond positively to a return to values. They are also resolute pragmatists who wait, often not patiently, to see if a president's policies will work. In 1980 voters wanted their ideals reaffirmed—so much so that they were willing to suspend disbelief to make these perceptions a reality. This longing reflected the intense desire in each human being to resolve questions of values. In Tom Robbins' novel *Even Cowgirls Get the Blues*, one of the characters rhetorically asks, "You really don't believe in political solutions do you?" The startling response: "I believe in political solutions to political problems. But man's primary problems aren't political; they're philosophical. Until humans can solve their philosophical problems, they're condemned to solve their political problems over and over and over again. It's a cruel, repetitious bore."[104]

Ronald Reagan helped many Americans solve their philosophical—that is, values—problems by giving them the answers they had always wanted to find. In doing so, he did not charm a gullible electorate. In political scientist V. O. Key's famous words, "Voters are not fools."[105] Reagan has been largely successful in communicating his values to a majority of the populace because these perceptions already were in alignment with their own.

That was not always the case. During the depths of the 1982–83 recession, Reagan's popularity fell significantly below that of Carter's at a comparable period in his presidency, and was substantially below that of presidents since Dwight Eisenhower.[106] Gallup polls taken in early 1983 found Walter Mondale defeating Reagan in the trial heats.[107] But when the economy improved, so did Reagan's personal standing with the voters. Thus, values he so often espoused began to resonate with a majority that held sway in an unprecedented forty-nine of fifty states in 1984.

Nearly 150 years ago Alexis de Tocqueville wrote, "The most outstanding Americans are seldom summoned to public office, and it must be recognized that this tendency has increased as democracy has gone beyond its previous limits. It is clear that during the last fifty years the race of American statesmen has strangely shrunk."[108] In the late twentieth century voters continue to choose among shrunken statesmen. They did so in 1980 and 1984, and they will undoubtedly select again from among imperfect candidates in 1988. But many Americans remain devoted to the values of family, work, neighborhood, peace, and freedom. If a president can persuade the voters that his policies adhere to those cherished values and that, if adopted, these values will become an even greater reality for most Americans, then that president can move the country.

NOTES

INTRODUCTION

1. Stephen E. Ambrose, *Nixon: The Education of a Politician, 1913–1962* (New York: Simon & Schuster, 1987), 541–42.
2. *The Tower Commission Report* (New York: Bantam Books and Times Books, 1987).
3. Quoted in Roland Evans and Robert Novak, *Lyndon B. Johnson: Exercise of Power* (New York: New American Library, 1968), 514–15.
4. Tip O'Neill with William Novak, *Man of the House: The Life and Political Memoirs of Speaker Tip O'Neill* (New York: Random House, 1987), 348.
5. Decision/Making/Information, postelection survey for the Republican National Committee, 7–10 November 1984.
6. Harold D. Lasswell, *Politics: Who Gets What, When, How* (New York: Meridian Books, 1958).
7. Lou Cannon, "Why the Band Has Stopped Playing for Ronald Reagan," *Washington Post*, 21 December 1986, D-1.
8. O'Neill, with Novak, *Man of the House*, 331.
9. George F. Will, "The Presidency in the American Political System," *Presidential Studies Quarterly* (Summer 1984): 324–30.
10. Mario M. Cuomo, *Newsday* Education Symposium, State University of New York, Old Westbury, 4 March 1987.
11. Ronald Reagan with Richard G. Huebler, *Where's the Rest of Me?* (New York: Duell, Sloan and Pearce, 1965), 13.
12. Reagan, with Huebler, *Where's the Rest of Me?*, 18.
13. The Jennings-Koppel Report, "Ronald Reagan: Memo to the Future," ABC News broadcast, 23 April 1987.
14. Ibid.
15. Quoted in Paul D. Erickson, *Reagan Speaks: The Making of an American Myth* (New York: New York University Press, 1985), 115.

1. THE (UN)MAKING OF RONALD REAGAN

1. Knute Rockne, "Gipp the Great," *Colliers*, 22 November 1930, 14–15.
2. Michael R. Steele, *Knute Rockne: A Bio-Bibliography* (Westport, Conn.: Greenwood Press, 1983), 20.
3. Rockne, "Gipp the Great," 15.
4. Steele, *Knute Rockne: A Bio-Bibliography*, 18–20, 169.
5. Rockne, "Gipp the Great," 15.
6. Steele, *Knute Rockne: A Bio-Biography*, 23.
7. Ibid., Wells Trombley, quoted.
8. Garry Wills, *Reagan's America: Innocents At Home* (Garden City, New York: Doubleday, 1981), 120.

9. Steele, *Knute Rockne: A Bio-Bibliography*, 230.

10. Rockne, "Gipp the Great," 15.

11. *Knute Rockne—All American*, Warner Brothers picture, 1940.

12. Wills, *Reagan's America*, 121.

13. Art Kleiner, "Master of the Sentimental Sell," *New York Times Magazine*, 14 December 1986, 72.

14. Ibid.

15. Rockne, "Gipp the Great," 15.

16. Ronald Reagan, Address to the Graduates at Notre Dame University, South Bend, Ind., 17 May 1981.

17. Ibid.

18. Anne Edwards, *Early Reagan: The Rise to Power* (New York: William Morrow, 1987), 219.

19. Ibid., 220.

20. Reagan was well aware of the meaning of the phrase "art imitates life." On March 30, 1981, John Hinckley attempted to assassinate him. Hinckley fell in love with actress Jody Foster after watching her performance (several times over) in the film *Taxi Driver*. To impress the actress, Hinckley fired on Reagan and several others the very day that the Academy Awards were announced.

21. Paul D. Erickson, *Reagan Speaks: The Making of an American Myth* (New York: New York University Press, 1985), 106.

22. Ibid., 108.

23. Ibid.

24. Michael Rogin, *Ronald Reagan, the Movie and Other Episodes in Political Demonology* (Berkeley: University of California Press, 1987), 42.

25. Ronald Reagan, radio address to the nation on the observance of Mother's Day, 7 May 1983.

26. Ibid., 5–6.

27. Wills, *Reagan's America*, 124.

28. Ibid., 412.

29. "Reagan Sheds a Tear," *New York Times*, 27 September 1984.

30. Ibid.

31. Ronald Reagan, "Remarks at a White House Luncheon for Members of the Baseball Hall of Fame," 27 March 1981.

32. Edwards, *Early Reagan*, 137.

33. William A. Henry III, *Visions of America: How We Saw the 1984 Election* (Boston: Atlantic Monthly Press, 1985), 9.

34. Erickson, *Reagan Speaks*, 64–65.

35. Ibid., 2.

36. William A. Galston, *One Year to Go: Citizen Attitudes in Iowa and New Hampshire* (Washington, D.C.: The Roosevelt Center for American Policy Studies, 1987), 20. This is a report based on sixty-five focus interviews conducted in Iowa and New Hampshire on January 12 and January 20–21, 1987.

37. Ronald Reagan, remarks on arrival at West Lafayette, Indiana, 9 April 1987.

38. Quoted in Rogin, *Ronald Reagan, the Movie*, 7.

39. Rockne, "Gipp the Great," 15.

40. Quoted in Emmet John Hughes, *The Living Presidency* (New York: Coward McCann and Geoghegan, 1973), 89.

41. *Connecticut Mutual Life Report on American Values in the '80s: The Impact of Belief* (Lanham, Md.: University Press of America, 1981), 27.

42. Quoted in Henry, *Visions of America*, 9.

43. Bernard Weinraub, "The Reagan Legacy," *New York Times Magazine*, 22 June 1986, 13.

44. "In Their Own Words: How the Iran-Contra Affair Took Shape," *New York Times*, 28 February 1987, 8.

45. Lance Morrow, "Charging Up Capitol Hill," *Time*, 20 July 1987.

46. "Transcript of Hart Statement Withdrawing His Candidacy," *New York Times*, 9 May 1987, 9.

47. "Morality Among the Supply-Siders," *Time*, 25 May 1987, 18–19.

48. Wills, *Reagan's America*, 121.

49. Ibid.

50. CBS News/*New York Times* surveys cited in *The Polling Report*, Volume 3, Number 11, 1 June 1987. Latest survey is that of 18–21 May 1987. Those who believe Reagan's accounting equalled 59 percent; those who disbelieved him equalled 24 percent. The remainder did not know or had no opinion.

51. Wyman had just won an Oscar for her role in the movie *Johnny Belinda*.

52. Quoted in Wills, *Reagan's America*, 161.

53. Laurence Leamer, *Make-Believe: The Story of Nancy and Ronald Reagan* (New York: Dell Books, 1984).

54. Aljean Harmetz, "Crossing the Line to Stardom: Talent Isn't Enough," *New York Times*, 7 June 1987, 42.

55. Kirk Douglas, "Let's Leave Make-Believe at the Movies," *Parade*, 23 August 1987, 4.

56. Stephen Ambrose, *Nixon: The Education of a Politician, 1913–1962* (New York: Simon and Schuster, 1987), 613–14.

57. T. S. Eliot, *The Complete Poems and Plays, 1909–1950* (New York: Harcourt, Brace and Company, 1958), 58.

58. Sam Donaldson, *Hold On, Mr. President!* (New York: Random House, 1987), 91.

59. "Representative Ferraro Reconsiders Remark About Religion," *New York Times*, 16 July 1984, A-1.

60. Interview with Walter Mondale on the NBC News broadcast "Meet the Press," 7 April 1985.

61. O'Neill with Novak, *Man of the House*, 357.

62. Garry Wills, "What Happened?" *Time*, 9 March 1987, 40.

63. Daniel J. Boorstin, *The Image: Or What Happened to the American Dream* (New York: Atheneum, 1962), 6.

64. Richard B. Wirthlin, "Meet the Press," NBC News broadcast, 19 July 1987.

gpt-4

2. VISIONS AND VALUES

1. Yelena Bonner, "A Quirky Farewell to America," *Newsweek*, 2 June 1986, 45.

2. New Hampshire automobile license plates include the motto "Live Free or Die."

3. Quoted in Lee Iacocca, "What Liberty Means to Me," *Newsweek*, 7 July 1986, 18.

4. Robert Lane, *Political Ideology: Why the Common Man Believes What He Does* (New York: Free Press, 1962), 24.

5. "Foreign Roots on Native Soil," *U.S. News and World Report*, 7 July 1986, 31.

6. Quoted in ABC News, "Liberty Weekend Preview," 2 July 1986.

7. Gilbert K. Chesterton, *What I Saw in America* (New York: Dodd, Mead, 1922), 8.

8. The phrase "the American dream" was coined by James Trunslow Adams during the Great Depression in James Trunslow Adams, *The Epic of America*, (Boston: Little, Brown, 1935), 174.

9. Ibid., 174.

10. Ronald Reagan, news conference, Washington, D.C., 28 June 1983.

11. Richard Nixon, Acceptance Speech, Republican National Convention, Chicago, 28 July 1960. *New York Times*, 29 July 1960, 9.

12. Mario M. Cuomo, *Diaries of Mario M. Cuomo* (New York: Random House, 1984), 219.

13. Quoted in Terry W. Hartle, "Dream Jobs?" *Public Opinion* (September/October 1986): 11.

14. Roper Organization for the *Wall Street Journal*, mid-October 1986, reported in *The Polling Report*, 23 February 1987, 1. Text of question: "I'm going to read you some possible descriptions or definitions of The American Dream, and for each one I'd like you to tell me if that's very much what you understand The American Dream to mean, or sort of what it means, or not what it means." The percentages cited in the text are those who answered "very much." Multiple responses were allowed.

15. Max Berger, *The British Traveller in America, 1836–1860*, (New York: Columbia University Press, 1943), 54–55.

16. *Knute Rockne—All American*, Warner Brothers motion picture, 1940.

17. Richard Nixon, Acceptance Speech, Republican National Convention, Miami, 8 August 1968. *New York Times*, 9 August 1968, 20.

18. Michel-Guillaume-Jean de Crevecoeur, *Letters from an American Farmer, 1782* in Henry Steele Commager, ed., *Living Ideas in America*, (New York: Harper & Brothers, 1951), 21.

19. *Knute Rockne—All American*, Warner Brothers motion picture, 1940.

20. National Opinion Research Center, University of Chicago, General Social Surveys, 1972–1984. Text of the 1984 question: "America has an open society. What one achieves in life no longer depends on one's family background, but on the abilities one has and the education one requires." Forty percent responded "strongly agree"; 44 percent, "somewhat agree"; 13 percent, "somewhat disagree"; 2 percent "strongly disagree."

21. National Opinion Research Center, University of Chicago, General Social Surveys, 1972–1987. Text of the 1987 question: "Some people say that people get ahead by their own hard work; others say that lucky breaks or help from other people are more important. Which do you think is most important?" Sixty-six percent responded "hard work"; 18 percent, "hard work, luck equally important"; 15 percent "luck most important."

22. Martin Luther King, "I Have a Dream," address at the Lincoln Memorial, 28 August 1963, reprinted in the *New York Times*, 28 August 1983, 28.

23. Decision/Making/Information, survey for the Free Congress Foundation, 4–5 November 1981.

24. "American Values: Change and Stability: A Conversation with Daniel Yankelovich," *Public Opinion* (December/January 1984): 6.

25. Sixty-five percent believe that "someone who is against churches and religion should be allowed to speak in the community"; "an admitted Communist," 56 percent; "someone who believes blacks are inferior," 58 percent; "an admitted homosexual," 64 percent; "someone who advocates doing away with elections and letting the military run the country," 54 percent. Likewise, those who do not favor removing a book from the public library with the views of "someone who is against churches and religion" is 60 percent; "an admitted Communist," 57 percent; "someone who believes blacks are genetically inferior," 61 percent; "an admitted homosexual," 56 percent; "someone who advocates doing away with elections and letting the military run the country," 56 percent. Source: National Opinion Research Center, combined General Social Surveys, 1972–1987.

26. James Q. Wilson, "A Guide to Reagan Country: The Political Culture of Southern California," *Commentary* (May 1967): 40.

27. Cited in Lance Morrow, "Freedom First," *Time*, 16 June 1986, 29.

28. U.S. Bureau of the Census, *Statistical Abstract of the United States: 1986*, 106th edition (Washington, D.C.: U.S. Government Printing Office, 1985), 458.

29. Quoted in Lane, *Political Ideology*, 69.

30. Andrew H. Malcolm, "What Five Families Did After Losing the Farm," *New York Times*, 4 February 1987, A-1.

31. Cited in Everett Carll Ladd, *The American Polity* (New York: Norton, 1987), 67.

32. Survey by Civic Service, 5–18 March 1981.

33. National Opinion Research Center, University of Chicago, General Social Surveys, 1972–1984. Text of the 1984 question: "Differences in social standing between people are acceptable because they basically reflect what people made out of the opportunities they had." Sixteen percent responded, "strongly agree"; 55 percent, "somewhat agree"; 20 percent, "somewhat disagree"; 5 percent "strongly disagree."

34. Garry Wills, *Inventing America* (New York: Vintage Books, 1978), xxii.

35. Daniel J. Boorstin, *The Genius of American Politics* (Chicago: University of Chicago Press, 1953), 14.

36. Louis Hartz, *The Liberal Tradition in America*, (New York: Harcourt Brace Jovanovich, 1955), 58.

37. Quoted in Thomas E. Cronin, *The State of the Presidency* (Boston: Little, Brown, 1980), 161.

38. Remarks by the president and first lady in a national television address on drug abuse and prevention, Washington, D.C., 14 September 1986.

39. National Opinion Research Center, University of Chicago, combined General Social Surveys, 1972–1987.

40. "Proceedings of the State Conference on Immigration in Massachusetts Industries," *Bulletin of the Department of Education* (5 November 1920).

41. Cited in Edward B. Fiske, "With Old Values and New Titles, Civics Courses Make a Comeback," *New York Times*, 7 June 1987, 1.

42. Alexis de Tocqueville, *Democracy in America*, Richard D. Heffner, ed. (New York: New American Library, 1956), 90.

43. James Madison, "Federalist Number Ten," in Alexander Hamilton, John Jay, and James Madison, *The Federalist*, Edward Mead Earle, ed. (New York: Modern Library, 1937), 55.

44. Ibid., 53–54.

45. National Opinion Research Center, University of Chicago, General Social Surveys, 1972–1987. Text of question: "Which of these statements comes closest to your feelings about pornography laws?" Forty-one percent responded, "There should be laws against the distribution of pornography whatever the age"; 52 percent said, "There should be laws against the distribution of pornography to persons under 18"; 6 percent, "There should be no laws forbidding the distribution of pornography."

46. Thomas Hobbes, *Leviathan* (New York: Collier Books, 1962), 100.

47. Quoted in Arthur M. Schlesinger, *A Thousand Days* (New York: Greenwich House, 1983), 105–6.

48. James Reston, "Liberty and Authority," *New York Times*, 29 June 1986, E-23.

49. Morton J. Frisch, ed., *Selected Writings and Speeches of Alexander Hamilton* (Washington, D.C.: American Enterprise Institute, 1985), 316.

50. Quoted in Edward Meade Earle's introduction to Alexander Hamilton, John Jay, and James Madison, *The Federalist*, xiii. Historian Claude Bowers agreed that Hamilton's goal was to "cripple" the states. See Claude G. Bowers, *Jefferson and Hamilton: The Struggle for Democracy in America* (Boston: Houghton Mifflin, 1925), 31.

51. Quoted in Ted Morgan, *FDR: A Biography* (New York: Simon & Schuster, 1985), 38.

52. Quoted in Richard Reeves, *The Reagan Detour* (New York: Simon & Schuster, 1985), 19.

53. Quoted in Robert F. Kennedy, *To Seek a Newer World* (New York: Doubleday, 1967), 56.

54. Morgan, *FDR*, 365.

55. Tocqueville, *Democracy in America*, 194.

56. "The Themes of 1984 with Governors Mario Cuomo and George Deukmejian," *Public Opinion* (December/January 1984): 20.

57. Ronald Reagan, State of the Union Address, Washington, D.C., 27 January 1987.

58. *Olmstead v. U.S.*, 279 U.S. 849 (1925): 476. Justice Brandeis wrote a dissenting opinion in this case.

59. Henry Steele Commager, ed., *Living Ideas in America* (New York: Harper & Brothers, 1951), xviii.

60. Quoted in Reeves, *The Reagan Detour*, 43.

61. Reagan-Carter debate, Cleveland, 29 October 1980.

62. Quoted in Reston, "Liberty and Authority."

63. Herbert Croly, *The Promise of American Life* (New York: Archon Books reprint, 1963), 29.

64. Quoted in Hughes, *The Living Presidency*, 32.

65. Ibid., 23.

66. Adams, *The Epic of America*, 198.

67. Richard Nixon, Acceptance Speech, 1968.

68. Walter Mondale, Acceptance Speech, Democratic National Convention, San Francisco, 19 July 1984.

69. Clinton Rossiter, *The American Presidency* (New York: New American Library, 1960), 103.

70. Cited in Carl Sandburg, *Abraham Lincoln, Volume Three: The War Years* (New York: Dell, 1954), 661.

71. Richard B. Wirthlin, "Final Report of the Initial Actions Project," 29 January 1981. Wirthlin was quoting Thomas E. Cronin. See Cronin, *State of the Presidency* (Boston: Little, Brown, 1980), 84.

72. Quoted in Hughes, *The Living Presidency*, 40.

73. Decision/Making/Information, postelection study for the Republican National Committee, November 1980.

74. Woodrow Wilson, *Constitutional Government in the United States* (New York: Columbia University Press, 1908), 54–61.

75. Hughes, *The Living Presidency*, 273.

3. A TRANSFORMING ELECTION

1. Quoted in Theodore H. White, *America in Search of Itself: The Making of the President, 1956–1980* (New York: Harper & Row, 1982), 276.

2. The gentleman's name was Breen, not Green.

3. Samuel Lubell, *The Future of American Politics* (New York: Harper & Row, 1965), 13.

4. Richard B. Wirthlin, *Reagan for President: Campaign Action Plan*, unpublished campaign document, 29 June 1980, 31.

5. Decision/Making/Information, panel study for the Reagan for President Committee, December 1979.

6. Patrick H. Caddell, "Crisis of Confidence—Trapped in a Downward Spiral," *Public Opinion* (October/November, 1979): 5. In 1959 the "step ladder of opinion" looked as follows: respondents on a scale of 1 to 10 placed themselves at 6.5 five years earlier (1955), 6.7 today (1959), and 7.4 five years thence (1964). In 1979, for the first time, the ladder turned

downward: respondents saw themselves at 5.7 on the ladder five years earlier (1974); 4.7 today (1979); and 4.6 for five years thence (1984).

7. Emil Reich, *Success among the Nations* (New York: Harper and Brothers, 1904), 265–66.

8. Quoted in Patrick H. Caddell, "Crisis of Confidence—Trapped in a Downward Spiral," 55.

9. Decision/Making/Information, survey for the Free Congress Foundation, 4–5 November 1981. Forty-five percent blamed the family's decline on a lowering of parental standards and permissiveness; 31 percent cited parents' having to work.

10. Wirthlin, *Reagan for President*, 35–36.

11. *Connecticut Mutual Life Report on American Values in the '80's: The Impact of Belief*, 86–97.

12. S. Robert Lichter and Stanley Rothman, "Media and Business Elites," *Public Opinion* (October/November 1981): 44.

13. Ibid., 43. Ninety-four percent of the media elites voted for Johnson in 1964; 87 percent for Humphrey in 1968; 81 percent for McGovern and Carter in 1972 and 1976, respectively.

14. Quoted by Jimmy Carter in the so-called "Malaise Speech," Washington, D.C., 15 July 1979.

15. *Connecticut Mutual Life Report on American Values in the '80's*, 202.

16. Richard Nixon, address to the nation, Washington, D.C., 15 August 1971.

17. Decision/Making/Information, surveys for the Reagan for President Campaign, 1975.

18. Wirthlin, *Reagan for President*, 31.

19. Jimmy Carter, Acceptance Speech, Democratic National Convention, New York, 15 July 1976, author's personal tape recording.

20. Quoted in Charles McDowell, "Television Politics: The Medium Is the Revolution," Paul Duke, ed., in *Beyond Reagan: The Politics of Upheaval*, (New York: Warner Books, 1986), 266.

21. Jimmy Carter, *Why Not the Best?* (New York: Bantam Books, 1976), 4.

22. Edwin Newman, NBC News, 3 November 1976, author's personal tape recording.

23. Surveys taken by the Gallup Organization, 18–21 March 1977 and 4–7 August 1978.

24. Quoted in Arthur M. Schlesinger, Jr., *A Thousand Days: John F. Kennedy in the White House* (New York: Fawcett Books, 1965), 67.

25. Speech by Francis X. Bellotti to the Massachusetts Democratic State Convention, 16 May 1986.

26. James Fallows, "The Passionless Presidency," *Atlantic Monthly* (May 1979): 42.

27. Ibid., 38.

28. Arthur M. Schlesinger, *Kennedy or Nixon: Does It Make Any Difference?* (New York: Macmillan, 1960).

29. Barry M. Goldwater, Acceptance Speech, Republican National Convention, San Francisco, 16 July 1964.

30. Social Security benefits were indexed to rise with the inflation rate in 1972.

31. For a further discussion of this, see Vincent J. Burke and Vee Burke, *Nixon's Good Deed: Welfare Reform* (New York: Columbia University Press, 1974).

32. Samuel H. Beer, "Ronald Reagan: New Deal Conservative?" *Society* (January/February 1983): 44.

33. Quoted in William A. Schambra, "Progressive Liberalism and American 'Community'," *Public Interest* (Summer 1985): 41.

34. Robert F. Kennedy, *To Seek a Newer World*, 8 and 56.

35. Ibid., 57.

36. Ibid., 61.

37. Theodore H. White, *The Making of the President, 1964* (New York: New American Library, 1965), 366.

38. White, *America in Search of Itself*, 154.

39. Alexander Hamilton, "Federalist Number 70," in Hamilton, Jay, and Madison, *The Federalist*, 454.

40. Wirthlin, *Reagan for President*, 34.

41. Quoted in "FDR," ABC News Transcript (New York: Journal Graphics) 29 January 1982, 14.

42. Survey taken by the Gallup Organization, 21–24 July 1978.

43. Fallows, "The Passionless Presidency," 42.

44. Jimmy Carter, *Keeping Faith* (New York: Bantam Books, 1982), 117.

45. Jimmy Carter, address to the nation, Washington, D.C., 15 July 1979. Carter never actually used the term malaise. It was a moniker placed on the speech first by Edward Kennedy, later by Reagan.

46. 1980 Democratic National Platform.

47. Reagan-Carter debate, Cleveland, 29 October 1980.

48. William Schneider, "The Democrats in '88," *Atlantic Monthly* (April 1987): 54.

49. Schlesinger, *A Thousand Days*, 70.

50. See Fred I. Greenstein, *The Hidden-Hand Presidency: Eisenhower as Leader* (New York: Basic Books, 1982).

51. See Michael Beschloss, *Mayday: Eisenhower and the U-2 Affair* (New York: Harper & Row, 1986).

52. Decision/Making/Information, survey for the Reagan for President campaign, December 1979.

53. Ronald Reagan, Acceptance Speech, Republican National Convention, Detroit, 17 July 1980.

54. "Face Off: A Conversation with the Presidents' Pollsters, Patrick Caddell and Richard Wirthlin," *Public Opinion* (December/January 1981): 2.

55. Quoted in Lars-Erik Nelson, "As for Confidence: A Lot of Americans See an Uncertain Future," *Providence Journal*, 5 August 1986, A-15.

56. Ronald Reagan, Acceptance Speech, Republican National Convention, Detroit, 17 July 1980.

57. 1980 Republican National Platform.

58. Helene von Damm, *Sincerely, Ronald Reagan* (Ottawa, Ill.: Green Hill Publishers, 1976), 84.

59. Ronald Reagan, "A Vision for America," television broadcast, 3 November 1980.

60. Wirthlin, *Reagan for President*, 152.

61. Ibid., 164.

62. Decision/Making/Information, survey for the Reagan for President Campaign, June 1980.

63. Wirthlin, *Reagan for President*, 12.

64. Quoted in Emmet John Hughes, *The Living Presidency*, 20.

65. Reagan, with Huebler, *Where's The Rest of Me?*, 303. This is an excerpt from a speech Reagan made hundreds of times on the lecture circuit during the 1960s.

66. Quoted in Schambra, "Progressive Liberalism," 46.

67. Ronald Reagan, "A Vision for America," television broadcast, 3 November 1980.

68. "Five Republican Leaders Speak Out," *U.S. News and World Report*, 29 August 1977, 24.

69. 1980 Republican National Platform.

70. Hugh Sidey, "A Conversation with Reagan," *Time*, 3 September 1984.

71. Quoted in Everett Carll Ladd, *Where Have All the Voters Gone?* (New York: Norton, 1982), 111.

72. Decision/Making/Information, postelection survey, November 1980.

73. Decision/Making/Information, survey, June 1980.

74. Wirthlin, *Reagan for President*, 21.

75. Daniel Patrick Moynihan quoting John F. Kennedy on "Larry King Live," CNN broadcast, 24 February 1986.

76. White, *America in Search of Itself*, 300.

77. Peter D. Hart Associates and Lynch Research, Inc., "Report to the Democratic Congressional Campaign Committee," August 1983.

78. Decision/Making/Information, late October survey for the Reagan for President Campaign, cited in Richard B. Wirthlin, "The Final Report of the Initial Actions Project," 29 January 1981, 11.

79. Wirthlin, "Final Report of the Initial Actions Project," 31.

80. Louis Harris and Associates, postelection survey, November 1980.

81. Decision/Making/Information, postelection survey, November 1980.

82. Louis Harris and Associates, postelection survey, November 1980.

83. Decision/Making/Information, postelection survey, November 1980.

84. Alfred Marshall, *Principles of Economics: An Introductory Volume*, 8th ed. (London: Macmillan, 1936), iii.

85. *Connecticut Mutual Life Report on American Values in the '80's*, 30.

4. THE ENCORE

1. Mondale Campaign Manager Jim Johnson quoted in Peter Goldman and Tony Fuller, *The Quest for the Presidency, 1984* (New York: Bantam Books, 1985), 347.

2. Francis X. Clines, "Mondale Seen Ahead in Only Four States," *New York Times*, 26 October 1984, A-17.

3. Mondale quoted in Bernard Weinraub, "Thousands Crowd Garment District to Cheer Mondale," *New York Times*, 2 November 1984, A-1, and Goldman and Fuller, *The Quest for the Presidency*, 347.

4. White, *The Making of the President, 1964*, 400.

5. "Mondale, in Summation, Evokes Dr. King's Goal," *New York Times*, 5 November 1984, B-17.

6. Bernard Weinraub, "Grinning, Fist Clenched Mondale Ends Campaign," *New York Times*, 6 November 1984, A-23.

7. 1984 Democratic National Platform.

8. 1984 Republican National Platform.

9. Richard B. Wirthlin, "Final Report of the Initial Actions Project," 29 January 1981, 1.

10. See Jonathan Moore, ed., *The Campaign for President 1980 in Retrospect* (Cambridge, Mass.: Ballinger, 1982), 252–53.

11. David Stockman, "Avoiding a GOP Economic Dunkirk," in William Greider, *The Education of David Stockman and other Americans* (New York: E. P. Dutton, 1982), 149.

12. Ronald Reagan, address to Congress, Washington, D.C., 18 February 1981.

13. Ronald Reagan, Remarks at Building and Construction Trades (AFL-CIO) National Conference, Washington, D.C., 30 March 1981.

14. Ronald Reagan, "Economic Report of the President's Annual Message to Congress," Washington, D.C., 10 February 1982.

15. Leslie H. Gelb, "Reagan Foreign Policy: Shifting Aim," *New York Times*, 26 October 1984, A-18.

16. Thomas Ferguson and Joel Rogers, *Right Turn: The Decline of the Democrats and the Future of American Politics* (New York: Hill and Wang, 1986), 124.

17. For an excellent article on this subject, see Samuel H. Beer, "Ronald Reagan: New Deal Conservative?" *Society* (January/February 1983): 40–44.

18. David A. Stockman, *The Triumph of Politics: Why the Reagan Revolution Failed* (New York: Harper & Row, 1986), 111–12.

19. Ferguson and Rogers, *Right Turn*, 129.

20. Ibid., 131.

21. Jack Germond and Jules Witcover, *Blue Smoke and Mirrors* (New York: Viking Press, 1981).

22. John Kenneth White, interview with Thomas P. O'Neill, Washington, D.C., 22 September 1982.

23. Quoted in the 1984 Republican National Platform.

24. Reagan, "Economic Report of the President's Annual Message to Congress."

25. William J. Baroody, Jr., American Enterprise Institute Memorandum, Summer 1985.

26. Ibid.

27. Ronald Reagan, 1985 State of the Union Address, Washington, D.C., 6 February 1985.

28. Ronald Reagan, 1982 State of the Union Address, Washington, D.C., 26 January 1982.
29. Ronald Reagan, "'We Will Lift America Up,'" *New York Times*, 26 September 1984, D-22.
30. Wills, *Reagan's America*, 356–57.
31. Ronald Reagan, 1984 State of the Union Address, Washington, D.C., 25 January 1984.
32. "The Themes of 1984 with Governors Mario Cuomo and George Deukmejian," *Public Opinion*, December/January 1984, 20.
33. William A. Schambra, "Progressive Liberalism and American 'Community,'" *The Public Interest* (Summer 1985): 46.
34. Geraldine Ferraro, "'Our Better Instincts' Versus Appeals to Self-Interest," *New York Times*, 28 September 1984.
35. John Kenneth White, interview with John Rendon, Potsdam, New York, 30 April 1984.
36. Quoted in Fay S. Joyce, "Mondale Campaign Adopts Some Tactics from Reagan," *New York Times*, 26 October 1984, A-17.
37. Schambra, "Progressive Liberalism, 31.
38. Ferraro, "'Our Better Instincts' Versus Appeals to Self Interest."
39. Ibid.
40. 1984 Democratic National Platform.
41. Walter Mondale, Acceptance Speech, Democratic National Convention, San Francisco, 19 July 1984, author's tape recording.
42. Goldman and Fuller, *The Quest for the Presidency, 1984*, 347.
43. Mondale, Acceptance Speech.
44. Gary Hart, *A New Democracy: A Democratic Vision for the 1980s and Beyond* (New York: Quill, 1983), 8.
45. Ibid.
46. Ibid.
47. 1984 Republican National Platform.
48. Walter Mondale, "'The Issues Are With Us,'" *New York Times*, 11 October 1984, B-13.
49. Mondale, Acceptance Speech.
50. Geraldine Ferraro, Acceptance Speech, Democratic National Convention, San Francisco, 19 July 1984.
51. Mario Cuomo, "A Case for the Democrats, 1984: A Tale of Two Cities," Keynote Speech to the Democratic National Convention, San Francisco, 16 July 1984.
52. Schambra, "Progressive Liberalism," 46.
53. Ibid.
54. 1984 Democratic National Platform.
55. Ibid.
56. Lyndon Johnson, "To Fulfill These Rights," commencement address, Howard University, Washington, D.C., 4 June 1965.
57. Jesse Jackson, speech to Democratic National Convention, San Francisco, 17 July 1984, author's tape recording.
58. Paul M. Barrett, "The Caucus-Happy Democrats," *Washington Monthly* (April 1985): 24–29.

59. William A. Galston, *One Year to Go: Citizen Attitudes in Iowa and New Hampshire* (Washington, D.C.: The Roosevelt Center for American Policy Studies, 1987), 32.

60. Ronald Reagan, 1982 State of the Union Address, Washington, D.C., 26 January 1982.

61. Ronald Reagan, radio address to the nation on the observance of Mother's Day, 7 May 1983.

62. Ronald Reagan, address to the nation announcing the Reagan-Bush candidacies for reelection, 29 January 1984.

63. Schambra, "Progressive Liberalism," 46.

64. Roger Ailes, "Is There a Republican Realignment?" transcript of remarks at a conference sponsored by the Americans for Responsible Government, Washington, D.C., 1 October 1985, 61.

65. Quoted in Arthur M. Schlesinger, *A Thousand Days*, 64.

66. Reagan-Mondale debate on domestic policy, Louisville, 7 October 1984, author's tape recording.

67. Mondale, Acceptance Speech.

68. Ronald Reagan, Acceptance Speech, Republican National Convention, Dallas, 23 August 1984.

69. Ronald Reagan, address to the nation announcing the Reagan-Bush candidacies for reelection, 29 January 1984.

70. Jeane Kirkpatrick, speech, Republican National Convention, reprinted in *New York Times*, 21 August 1984, A-22.

71. Reagan, "'We Will Lift America Up.'"

72. Merle Miller, *Lyndon: An Oral Biography* (New York: Ballantine Books, 1980), 673.

73. League of Women Voters, "Official Transcript, 1980 Presidential Debates," Cleveland, 28 October 1980.

74. "Final Report of the Initial Actions Project," Decision/Making/Information, unpublished transition document, 29 January 1981, 9.

75. Decision/Making/Information, postelection study for the Republican National Committee, 7–10 November 1984.

76. CBS News/*New York Times* poll, 8–14 November 1984.

77. Richard B. Wirthlin, *Campaign Action Plan*, unpublished confidential campaign document, August 1983, 56.

78. Franklin Roosevelt collected 523 electoral votes in 1936 to Alfred Landon's 8. Reagan won 525 electoral votes in 1984 to Mondale's 13.

79. J. C. Archer, G. T. Murauskas, F. M. Shelley, E. R. White, and P. J. Taylor, "Counties, States, Sections, and Parties in the 1984 Presidential Election," *Professional Geographer* (August 1985): 279.

80. ABC News, exit poll, 6 November 1984.

81. CBS News/*New York Times*, exit poll, 6 November 1984.

82. Ibid.

83. Ibid.

84. Ibid.

85. Goldman and Fuller, *The Quest for the Presidency*, 451.

86. Decision/Making/Information, postelection survey for the Republican National Committee, 7–10 November 1984. Text of question: "Now

I'd like to get your feelings toward some people and organizations in politics. I'm going to read you some names and I'd like you to rate each one on a scale from 0 to 100, where the worst possible one, in your judgment, would get a rating of 0, while the best possible person or organization would get a rating of 100. Most items, of course, would be rather somewhat in between those extremes. Remember, we just want to know *your* opinion, with 0 being the *worst* possible rating and 100 being the *best*. If I name someone or something you don't know too much about, just tell me and we'll go on to the next one. The first/next name is Ronald Reagan [Walter Mondale]."

87. Decision/Making/Information, postelection survey for the Republican National Committee, 7-10 November 1984. Text of the question: "Now let's talk about Walter Mondale and Ronald Reagan. I'm going to read you several statements describing the Presidential candidates. Some of these statements will be favorable; others will be unfavorable. For each one, please tell me whether the statement best describes Ronald Reagan or Walter Mondale."

88. Decision/Making/Information, postelection studies, 1972, 1976 and 1984.

89. Pro-Reagan voters cited as reasons for their vote Reagan's job performance, 42 percent; the issues, 29 percent; Reagan's leadership, 12 percent; his personality, 8 percent; partisan vote (e.g., "he's a Republican"), 5 percent; other miscellaneous reasons, 4 percent. Pro-Mondale voters gave the following reasons for supporting him: his position on the issues, 44 percent; his leadership, 23 percent; partisan vote (e.g., "he's a Democrat"), 15 percent; his personality, 8 percent; other miscellaneous reasons, 10 percent. Source: Decision/Making/Information, postelection survey for the Republican National Committee, 7-10 November 1984. Text of question: "Why did you vote for Ronald Reagan [or Walter Mondale]?"

90. Richard B. Wirthlin, Decision/Making/Information, unpublished report to the Republican National Committee, November 1984, 59.

91. Reagan, 1984 Acceptance Speech.

92. "Mondale Praises Representative Ferraro after Meeting," *New York Times*, 17 June 1984, A-18.

93. "Younger Voters Tending to Give Reagan Support," *New York Times*, 16 October 1984, A-1.

5. THE PARTIES: US AGAINST THEM

1. Paul Kirk, address on C-SPAN, 1 April 1985.

2. Jimmy Carter, Acceptance Speech, Democratic National Convention, New York, 15 July 1976.

3. "A Dream Deferred," *Newsweek*, 30 December 1985, 20.

4. Arthur M. Schlesinger, *The Cycles of American History* (Boston: Houghton, Mifflin, 1986), 23-48.

5. Peter Jennings, "The Presidential Election: Smoke and Mirrors," in ABC News, *The '84 Vote* (New York: American Broadcasting Company, 1985), xxxix.

6. Thomas B. Edsall, "Even the Democrats Say the Republicans Have Caught Up," *Washington Post National Weekly Edition*, 12 August 1985, 11.

7. John Kenneth White, interview with Peter D. Hart, Washington, D.C., 5 August 1985.

8. Roosevelt lost only Maine and Vermont. Thus, the adage: "As goes Maine so goes Vermont."

9. David S. Broder and George Lardner, "Did Anybody See a Mandate Go By?" *Washington Post National Weekly Edition*, 19 November 1984, 10.

10. Dennis Hale and Mark Landy, "Are Critical Elections Extinct?" *Boston College Bi-Weekly*, 15 November 1984.

11. Quoted in Walter Dean Burnham, *The Current Crisis in American Politics* (New York: Oxford University Press, 1982), 14.

12. Thomas B. Edsall, Speech to the Committee for Party Renewal, Eagleton Institute, Rutgers University, New Brunswick, New Jersey, 14 January 1987.

13. Interview with Paul E. Maslin, Washington, D.C., 5 December 1984.

14. Peter Tauber, "Notes on a Brief Campaign," *New York Times Magazine*, 31 May 1987, 55.

15. William Schneider provides a superb analysis of the political distinctions between "us" and "them" in "The New Shape of American Politics," *Atlantic Monthly* (January 1987): 39–54.

16. Quoted in James MacGregor Burns, *Roosevelt: The Lion and the Fox* (New York: Harcourt, Brace, & World, 1956), 271.

17. Ted Morgan, *FDR: A Biography* (New York: Simon and Schuster, 1985), 362.

18. Quoted in Burns, *Roosevelt*, 274.

19. Morgan, *FDR*, 440.

20. Quoted in Burns, *Roosevelt*, 283.

21. Ibid.

22. Quoted in Stefan Lorant, *The Presidency: A Pictorial History of Presidential Elections from Washington to Truman* (New York: Macmillan, 1951), 591.

23. Quoted in Julie Nixon Eisenhower, *Pat Nixon: The Untold Story* (New York: Simon and Schuster, 1986), 86.

24. The phrase "mental pictures" is Richard Trilling's. See Richard J. Trilling, "Party Image and Electoral Behavior," *American Politics Quarterly*, Vol. 3, No. 3 (July 1975): 285.

25. Gallup poll, 3–8 August 1951. Text of question: "Suppose a young person, just turned 21, asked you what the Republican party (Democratic party) stands for today—what would you tell them?" The number-one Republican response, 16 percent, was "for the privileged few, moneyed interests." The number-one Democratic response, 19 percent, was "for the working man, for the public benefit, for the common man."

26. Gallup poll, 1–6 June 1946. Text of question: "As you feel today, which political party—the Democratic or Republican—can better handle the problems of keeping wages high?" Democrats, 53 percent; Republicans, 26 percent; makes no difference, 21 percent.

27. Gallup poll, 18–23 June 1948. Text of question: "Do you think the

Republican party is run by a few big businessmen of the country?" Yes, 47 percent; no, 37 percent; no opinion, 16 percent.

28. Gallup poll, 20–25 January 1955. Text of question: "Which political party—the Democratic or the Republican—do you think serves the interests of the following groups best?" Professional and business: Republicans, 57 percent; Democrats, 21 percent. Skilled workers: Republicans, 21 percent; Democrats, 53 percent. Unskilled workers: Republicans, 15 percent; Democrats, 61 percent.

29. "Reagan Stumps for Two Gubernatorial Candidates in the Middle West," *New York Times*, 25 September 1986, D-24.

30. The Kennedy-Rossiter anecdote is found in Everett Carll Ladd, *The American Polity* (New York: Norton, 1987), 167.

31. Theodore H. White, *The Making of the President, 1960* (New York: Signet Books, 1961), 371.

32. Quoted in Theodore H. White, *The Making of the President, 1968* (New York: Atheneum Publishers, 1969), 359.

33. Ibid.

34. Ibid.

35. Richard M. Nixon, *RN: The Memoirs of Richard Nixon* (New York: Grosset & Dunlap, 1978), 456.

36. Quoted in Fred Barnes, "Meet Mario the Moderate," *New Republic*, 8 April 1985, 19.

37. "Democratic Official Switches," *New York Times*, 25 June 1985, A-16.

38. "Reagan Stumps for Two Gubernatorial Candidates in the Middle West," D-24.

39. John Kenneth White, interview with V. Lance Tarrance, Houston, 22 March 1985.

40. The story is told in E. J. Dionne, "Catholics and the Democrats: Estrangement but not Desertion" in Seymour Martin Lipset, ed., *Party Coalitions in the 1980s* (San Francisco: Institute for Contemporary Studies, 1981), 308.

41. CBS News/*New York Times*, poll, 8–14 November 1984.

42. Data cited in Thomas E. Cavanaugh and James L. Sundquist, "The New Two-Party System," in John E. Chubb and Paul E. Peterson, eds., *The New Direction in American Politics* (Washington, D.C.: Brookings Institution, 1985), 50.

43. Decision/Making/Information, postelection survey for the Republican National Committee, November 1986.

44. Ibid.

45. Louis Harris and Associates, survey, 5–8 April 1986.

46. *Time*/Yankelovich, Clancy and Shulman, survey, 8–10 September 1986.

47. Decision/Making/Information, postelection survey for the Republican National Committee, November 1986.

48. Paul Maslin, "A Democratic Year . . . But Will It Stick?", *Polling Report*, 1 September 1985.

49. White, interview with Tarrance.

50. ABC News/*Washington Post*, exit poll, 6 November 1984.
51. Yankelovich, Skelly and White, poll for *Time* taken in September 1985.
52. CBS News/*New York Times*, poll, 28 September–1 October 1986.
53. *Time*/Yankelovich, Clancy and Shulman, poll, 8–10 September 1986.
54. Louis Harris and Associates, poll, 5–8 April 1986.
55. Ibid.
56. Decision/Making/Information, postelection survey for the Republican National Committee, November 1986.
57. White, interview with Hart.
58. Decision/Making/Information, selected surveys for the Reagan for President Campaign and the Republican National Committee, 1980–1986.
59. The August 1987 figures are as follows: Democrats, 47 percent; Republicans, 40 percent; independents, 12 percent. These figures include those independents who said they "leaned toward" one party or the other. These data were supplied to the author by the Wirthlin Group, formerly known as Decision/Making/Information.
60. Quoted in Jack W. Germond and Jules Witcover, "GOP Gain of Five Governors Possible in 1986," *National Journal*, 14 December 1985, 2873.
61. Interview with Donald Roch, Providence, 22 October 1979. Cited in John Kenneth White, *The Fractured Electorate: Political Parties and Social Change in Southern New England* (Hanover, N.H.: University Press of New England, 1983), 79.
62. Decision/Making/Information, 1974 postelection study. Text of question: "Looking ahead to elections *for President* over the next twenty years or so, there will be five presidential elections. How many elections for president do you think the Republican party candidate will win: none, one, two, three, four or all five?" Responses: none, 10 percent; one, 18 percent; two, 40 percent; three, 15 percent; four, 2 percent; five, 2 percent.
63. Market Opinion Research, postelection survey, November 1974.
64. Decision/Making/Information, merge of surveys taken for the Republican National Committee, 5 November 1986 to 29 January 1987. Those surveyed total 17,700.
65. Decision/Making/Information, surveys taken for the Reagan for President Campaign and the Republican National Committee, latest 20–23 October 1986.
66. Ibid.
67. "Conversion Rites," *New York Times*, 21 October 1985, A-16.
68. White, interview with Hart.
69. Zachary Taylor, who hailed from Louisiana, was the Whig party nominee for president in 1848.
70. White, interview with Maslin.
71. Cited in "Moving Right Along? Campaign '84's Lessons for 1988: An Interview with Peter Hart and Richard Wirthlin," *Public Opinion* (December/January 1985): 62.
72. Ibid.

73. Cited in James A. Dyer, David B. Hill, Arnold Vedlitz, and Stephen N. White, "The Partisan Transformation of Texas" (Paper presented at the annual meeting of the American Political Science Association, New Orleans, 29 August–1 September 1985.)

74. ABC News, exit poll, November 6, 1984.

75. Wayne King, "Republican Inroads Put Texas On Edge," *New York Times*, 25 February 1985, A-10.

76. White, interview with Hart.

77. Quoted in "State Political Parties Are Playing A New Role," *New York Times*, 16 June 1985, E-20.

78. ABC News, exit poll, 4 November 1986.

79. Ibid.

80. Ibid.

81. "Is There A Republican Realignment?," conference sponsored by Americans for Responsible Government, Washington, D.C., 1 October 1985.

82. Decision/Making/Information, postelection surveys for the Republican National Committee, 1980 and 1984.

83. CBS News, exit poll, 6 November 1984.

84. Decision/Making/Information, survey for the Reagan for President Campaign, June 1980.

85. Among those aged fifty-five to sixty-four, Democrats totalled 53 percent; Republicans, 32 percent. For those aged sixty-five or older, Democrats numbered 51 percent while Republicans held at 35 percent. Source: Decision/Making/Information, merged data from studies done for the Republican National Committee, 5 November 1986 to 29 January 1987. Those surveyed total 17,700.

86. John Kenneth White, interview with Richard B. Wirthlin, Washington, D.C., 6 December 1984.

87. Patrick Caddell, "What Is Needed Is an Indirect Approach," memo reproduced in Peter Goldman and Tony Fuller, *The Quest for the Presidency, 1984* (New York: Bantam Books, 1985), 426.

88. William A. Galston and Mark J. Rovner, *Southern Voices/Southern Views: A Report on Focus Groups Conducted by the Roosevelt Center for American Policy Studies* (Washington, D.C.: The Roosevelt Center for American Policy Studies, 1987), 11.

89. Survey conducted by William R. Hamilton and Staff for Larry Sabato and AMPAC, cited in *The Polling Report*, 20 October 1986, 3.

90. "Jersey Democrats Urged to Replace Old Heroes," *New York Times*, 5 March 1985, B-2.

91. Morgan, *FDR*, 440.

92. Juan Williams, "Social Security and the Politics of Perception: 'Ripoff' by the Elderly?" *Washington Post National Weekly Edition*, 4 March 1985, 11.

93. Ibid., 10.

94. The estimate is by Kimball Brace, president of Election Data Services, Inc. See Richard Cohen, "The Big Shift," *National Journal*, 7 February 1987, 320.

95. Ibid.

96. Under the 1992 Electoral College projections, the Kennedy vote count would read 279 votes; Nixon, 244. This excludes the District of Columbia, which did not vote for president in 1960. The Twenty-Third Amendment, which gave Washington, D.C., three electoral votes, was ratified in 1961. Presumably, the District of Columbia would vote Democratic, raising Kennedy's margin to 282 electoral votes.

97. Ibid.

98. Cited in Richard Wirthlin and John White, "From Political Poverty to Parity: The Restoration of the Republican Party?" *Public Opinion* (January/February 1987): 60.

99. A. James Reichley, "The Rise of National Parties," in Chubb and Peterson, *The New Directions in American Politics*, 199.

100. These figures exclude Minnesota and Nebraska, which have nonpartisan state legislatures. Of the divided states: 24 percent have Democratic governors and Republican legislatures, 35 percent have Republican governors and Democratic legislatures. In fact, of the eight newly elected Republican governors in 1986, five face state legislatures in which the Democrats control both houses. Source: Walter Dean Burnham, "Elections Dash GOP Dreams of Realignment," *Wall Street Journal*, 26 November 1986.

101. Richard Nixon, memorandum, "The Only Question Is the Magnitude," quoted in Goldman and Fuller, *The Quest for the Presidency, 1984*, 451.

102. Richard L. Berke, "Study Says PACs Play Growing Election Role," *New York Times*, 6 April 1987, D-31.

103. Randall B. Ripley and Grace A. Franklin, *Congress, the Bureaucracy, and Public Policy* (Homewood, Ill.: Dorsey Press, 1984), 45.

104. Randall B. Ripley, *Congress: Process and Policy* (New York: Norton, 1983), 263.

105. Thomas Ferguson and Joel Rogers, "The Myth of America's Turn to the Right," *Atlantic Monthly* (May 1986), 50.

106. *Los Angeles Times*, survey, 12–15 October 1984.

107. Tom Wicker, "A Party of Access?" *New York Times*, 25 November 1984, E-17.

108. Thomas B. Edsall, speech to the Committee for Party Renewal, Eagleton Institute, Rutgers University, New Brunswick, N.J., 14 January 1987.

109. ABC News/*Washington Post*, survey, 15–19 January 1987.

110. Kenneth E. John, "More People View Democrats as the Party of Prosperity," *Washington Post National Weekly Edition*, 9 March 1987, 37.

111. The precise number of interviews was 4,244, conducted between 25 April and 10 May 1987. Each interview was conducted in the respondent's home and lasted 70 minutes. Of these respondents, 1,903 were reinterviewed by telephone between 1 and 13 September 1987.

112. Enterprisers were married, of northern European ancestry, suburban. They make up 10 percent of the adult population and 16 percent of likely voters in 1988. They were 99 percent white, 60 percent male, 40 percent

female. Ninety-nine percent said they were Republicans or leaned toward the Republican party. Moralists were regular churchgoers, and a large number were born-again Christians. They were mostly nonurban, constituting 11 percent of the adult population and 14 percent of likely voters in 1988. They were 94 percent white, 45 percent male, 55 percent female. Ninety-nine percent said they were Republicans or leaned toward the Republican party.

113. Upbeats were middle-income, with little or no college education, and under forty years of age. They constituted 9 percent of the adult population and 9 percent of likely voters in 1988. Ninety-four percent were white, 44 percent male, 56 percent female. Sixty-six percent were Republicans or leaned toward the Republican party. Disaffecteds were middle-aged and middle-income respondents often facing personal financial pressures. They make up 9 percent of the adult population and 7 percent of those likely to vote in 1988. Ninety-five percent were white, 57 percent male, 43 percent female. Forty-four percent were Republicans or leaned toward the Republican party.

114. New Dealers were blue-collar, union members, older, and religious. They make up 11 percent of the adult population and 15 percent of those likely to vote in 1988. Eighty-eight percent were white, 45 percent male, 55 percent female. Ninety-nine percent were Democrats or leaned toward the Democratic party. The '60s Democrats were well educated and married. They constituted 8 percent of the adult population and 11 percent of those likely to vote in 1988. Eighty-three percent were white, 38 percent male, 62 percent female. Ninety percent were Democrats or leaned toward the Democratic party. Seculars were well-educated, middle-aged, professional workers. They make up 8 percent of the adult population and 9 percent of likely voters in 1988. Ninety-five percent were white, 51 percent male, 49 percent female. Sixteen percent favored the Republicans or leaned toward the Republican party; 77 percent were Democrats or leaned toward the Democratic party. The passive poor were less well educated, older, poor, and most lived in the South. They make up 7 percent of the adult population and 6 percent of those likely to vote in 1988. Sixty-three percent were white, 48 percent male, 52 percent female. Eighty-seven percent were Democrats or leaned toward the Democratic party. The partisan poor were urban, poorly educated, low-income respondents who lived in the South. They make up 9 percent of the adult population and 9 percent of likely voters in 1988. Fifty-eight percent where white, 44 percent male, 66 percent female. Ninety-eight percent were Democrats or leaned toward the Democratic party.

115. Bystanders were under thirty years of age, poorly educated, and with an almost total lack of interest in current affairs. They make up 11 percent of the adult population and none were likely to vote in 1988. Eighty-two percent were white, 46 percent male, 54 percent female. Twenty-nine percent were Republicans or leaned toward the Republican party; 33 percent were Democrats or leaned toward the Democratic party. Followers were young, poorly educated, blue-collar workers, with little religious commitment. They make up 7 percent of the adult population and 4 percent

of those likely to vote in 1988. Sixty-nine percent were white, 47 percent male, 53 percent female. Twenty-three percent were Republicans or leaned toward the Republican party; 55 percent were Democrats or leaned toward the Democratic party.

116. Norman Ornstein, "How to Win in '88: Meld the Unmeldable," *U.S. News and World Report*, 12 October 1987, 33.

6. ECHOES IN THE MARKETPLACE

1. "Born in the U.S.A." was not the first of the "patriotic" tunes to become popular in the Reagan era. In 1980, Neil Diamond released a song called "America."

2. Dave Marsh, *Glory Days: Bruce Springsteen in the 1980s* (New York: Pantheon Books, 1987), 255.

3. George F. Will, "Bruce Springsteen's U.S.A.," *Washington Post*, 13 September 1984, 19.

4. Ibid.

5. Ibid.

6. Ronald Reagan, "Remarks at a Reagan-Bush Rally," Hammonton, N.J., 19 September 1984.

7. Marsh, *Glory Days*, 259.

8. Ibid.

9. Ibid.

10. Ibid., 264.

11. Ibid., 265.

12. Ibid., 208.

13. Ibid.

14. Ibid., 424.

15. George McGovern also used it—perhaps more appropriately—in his ill-fated 1972 presidential campaign as a theme song.

16. Joe Klein, *Woody Guthrie: A Life* (New York: Alfred A. Knopf, 1980), 434.

17. Marsh, *Glory Days*, 260.

18. Ibid., 29.

19. The reviewer was Grecil Marcus, whose article was presciently titled "Born in the U.S.A." Cited in Marsh, *Glory Days*, 145.

20. Ibid., 263–64.

21. Ibid., 264.

22. Ibid., 338.

23. Jeffrey Simpson, "Living beside a Cultural and Economic Colossus," *New York Times*, 24 August 1986, E-3.

24. Ibid.

25. Jack Valenti, "And the Winner Is . . . American Movies, Television, and Videos," *Public Opinion* (February/March 1986): 14.

26. "Pop Goes the Culture," *Time*, 16 June 1986, 71.

27. Ibid., 73.

28. Ibid.

29. Ibid.

30. Aljean Harmetz, "Crossing the Line to Stardom," *New York Times*, 7 June 1987, 42. Clearly, Nicholson was a major box-office attraction, as the movie *One Flew Over the Cuckoos Nest* demonstrated.

31. Ibid.

32. "Experts Study the Habits of the Genus Baby Boomer," *New York Times*, 21 April 1986, B-6. Recently, Caddell has been interested in the return of the 1960s rock group, "The Monkees." Caddell has advised Democratic presidential candidate Joseph Biden that a 1960s sensibility was appearing in the 1980s—a sensibility that, according to Caddell, was reflected in the reemergence of "The Monkees." See "Joe Biden's 'Petulant Genius,'" *U.S. News and World Report*, 21 September 1987, 25.

33. Quoted by Richard Wirthlin in a luncheon address to the American Marketing Association, Washington, D.C., 31 March 1987.

34. See Randall Rothenberg, "The Boom in Political Consulting," *New York Times*, 24 May 1987, F-6. Decision/Making/Information was the former name of Wirthlin's firm; in 1987 it was changed to the Wirthlin Group.

35. "Experts Study the Habits of Genus Baby Boomer," B-6.

36. Joe McGinniss, *The Selling of the President, 1968* (New York: Pocket Books, 1970).

37. DeGaulle was ousted from power on 27 April 1969.

38. "'Revolution' in Advertising," *Syracuse Post-Standard*, 4 June 1987, D-1.

39. "The Bunny Is Hopping," *U.S. News and World Report*, 18 May 1987.

40. Ibid.

41. "Fundamentalists Wound Men's Magazines," *Providence Journal*, 7 September 1986, F-1.

42. Quoted in "American Values: Change and Stability, A Conversation with Daniel Yankelovich," *Public Opinion* (December/January 1984): 8.

43. "The Bunny Is Hopping."

44. "Pop Goes the Culture," 74.

45. American culture in 1942 is depicted in James MacGregor Burns, *Roosevelt: The Soldier of Freedom* (New York: Harcourt Brace Jovanovich, 1970), 271.

46. Franklin D. Roosevelt, Inaugural Address, Washington, D.C., 20 January 1945.

47. Jimmy Carter, address to the nation, Washington, D.C., 15 July 1979.

48. The "bad-years" theme may be making a comeback as the Reagan presidency ends. Economist Ravi Batra has written *The Great Depression of 1990* (New York: Simon and Schuster, 1987). The book has registered on the *New York Times* "best-sellers" chart.

49. The Jennings-Koppel Report, "Ronald Reagan: Memo to the Future," ABC News broadcast, 23 April 1987.

50. *Knute Rockne—All American*, Warner Brothers motion picture, 1940.

51. The themes of Reagan's movie career are well-documented in William A. Henry III, *Visions of America: How We Saw the 1984 Presidential Election* (Boston: Atlantic Monthly Press, 1985), especially 9–12.

52. Ibid., 10–11.

53. Ibid., 11.
54. Ibid., 164.
55. Ronald Reagan, 1986 State of the Union Address, Washington, D.C., 4 February 1986.
56. Lee Iacocca with William Novak, *Iacocca: An Autobiography* (New York: Bantam Books, 1984), xv.
57. Ibid., xvi.
58. Robert Lacey, *Ford: The Men and the Machine* (New York: Ballantine Books, 1986), 689–90.
59. Ibid., 690.
60. Ibid., 668–69. Actually, the office had been previously used by the retired chairman of the board of the Ford Motor Company, Ernest R. Breech.
61. "Madonna Rocks the Land," *Time*, 27 May 1985.
62. Ben Stein, " 'Miami Vice': It's So Hip You'll Want to Kill Yourself," *Public Opinion* (October/November 1985): 43.
63. "Cosby, Inc.," *Time* magazine, 28 September 1987, 56. Overall ratings for "The Cosby Show" in the 1986–1987 season equalled 34.9 in the A. C. Nielson ratings. That figure was the best for any television series since "Bonanza" in 1964–65.
64. Ibid., 60.
65. Ibid.
66. Ibid., 58.
67. Leigh Brown, "Where America Feels at Home: The Sitcom Living Room," *New York Times*, 29 January 1987, C-1.
68. "Cosby, Inc.," 60.
69. Ibid., 56.
70. "Overextending the Family," *Newsweek*, 24 November 1986, 76.
71. Ibid.
72. "The Consequence of Ideas: The Reagan Revolution and Beyond, An Interview with Jeane Kirkpatrick, Michael Novak, and Herbert Stein," *Public Opinion* (Summer 1986): 20.
73. Tamar Lewin, "New Sex Mores Are Chilling TV Ardor," *New York Times*, 8 March 1987, H-29.
74. Ibid.
75. Ibid.
76. The new respect even extends to popular music. Springsteen biographer Dave Marsh chronicles the band's admiration for its leader—a feeling so deep that they and the fans often referred to him as "The Boss." See Marsh, *Glory Days*, 22.
77. John Kenneth White, interview with Richard Wirthlin, Washington, D.C., 6 December 1984. Young voters deeply resented those whom they perceived as authoritarian—persons like Christian fundamentalist Jerry Falwell.
78. Vincent Canby, "Peggy Sue Visits a Changeless Past," *New York Times*, 19 October 1986, H-1.
79. "Remembering Hamburger Hill," *Newsweek*, 14 September 1987, 83.
80. Canby, "Peggy Sue Visits a Changeless Past." Some who monitor cultural trends believe that the values Reagan has espoused may be losing

their grip. *Platoon* has grossed $100 million at the box office. Seemingly typecast from the 1970s, *Platoon* richly details the American experience in Vietnam—replete with blood and guts but no victory.

7. A SENSE OF RETURN

1. Richard Grenier, "Around the World in American Ways," *Public Opinion* (February/March 1986): 58.

2. Conservative Canadian Prime Minister John G. Difenbaker held office from 1957 to 1963. In 1979, conservative Joe Clark won the office but managed to hold it for only nine months.

3. Bernard Weinraub, "The Reagan Legacy," *New York Times Magazine*, 22 June 1986, 19.

4. William A. Galston, *One Year to Go: Citizen Attitudes in Iowa and New Hampshire* (Washington, D.C.: Roosevelt Center for American Policy Studies, 1987), 30. This report is based on a series of sixty-five focus interviews conducted in Iowa and New Hampshire on 12 and 20–21 January 1987.

5. Louis Harris, *Inside America* (New York: Vintage Books, 1987), 305.

6. Weinraub, "The Reagan Legacy," 13.

7. Ibid., 21.

8. Helen Dewar, "Democrats Are Charging Full Speed Ahead More Slowly, *Washington Post National Weekly Edition*, 23 March 1987, 11.

9. "Future Uncertain for State's Democrats," *California Journal* (March 1987): 121.

10. *Programme of the German Green Party* (London: Heretic Books, 1983), 36–37.

11. "Meetings in City Back Atomic Freeze," *New York Times*, 27 May 1982, B-1.

12. Proceedings of the Green Organizing Planning Meeting, Macalester College, St. Paul, Minn., 10–12 August 1984.

13. See Eric F. Goldman, *The Tragedy of Lyndon Johnson* (New York: Alfred A. Knopf, 1969), 51.

14. Summary of speech to General Electric employees in Reagan with Huebler, *Where's the Rest of Me?*, 303.

15. Goldman, *The Tragedy of Lyndon Johnson*, 51.

16. In his Inaugural Address of March 3, 1801, Thomas Jefferson said, "We are all Republicans, we are all Federalists." The Johnson quotation is taken from his State of the Union Address, Washington, D.C., 4 January 1965.

17. Lyndon B. Johnson, Inaugural Address, Washington, D.C., 20 January 1965.

18. Ladd, *The American Polity*, 322.

19. Quoted in Larry Sabato, *Goodbye to Good-time Charlie: The American Governorship Transformed* (Washington, D.C.: Congressional Quarterly, 1983), 161.

20. 1936 Democratic National Platform, as reprinted in the *New York Times*, 26 June 1936, 1.

21. Ibid.

22. Ibid.

23. Ibid. For every Supreme Court justice over the age of seventy, Roosevelt wanted to appoint, with the consent of the Senate, another justice.

24. 1936 Republican National Platform, as reprinted in the *New York Times*, 12 June 1936, 1.

25. Ibid.

26. Ibid.

27. Ibid.

28. Robert A. Nisbet, *The Sociological Tradition* (New York: Basic Books, 1966); Nisbet, *Tradition and Revolt* (New York: Random House, 1968); Nisbet, *The Quest for Community* (New York: Oxford University Press, 1953); Nisbet, *Social Change and History* (New York: Oxford University Press, 1969).

29. Quoted in Daniel Yankelovich, *New Rules: Searching for Self-Fulfillment in a World Turned Upside Down* (New York: Random House, 1981), 226.

30. James MacGregor Burns, "The President Behind the Candidate," *Life*, 9 October 1964, 96.

31. Goldman, *The Tragedy of Lyndon Johnson*, 276.

32. The Comprehensive Employment and Training Act.

33. *Wyatt* v. *Stickney* (1972).

34. *Hamilton* v. *Schiro* (1970).

35. Raoul Berger, *Government by Judiciary: The Transformation of the Fourteenth Amendment* (Cambridge, Mass.: Harvard University Press, 1977).

36. Abraham Lincoln, address, Gettysburg, Penna., 19 November 1863.

37. Galston, *One Year to Go*, 35.

38. Ibid.

39. Decision/Making/Information, 1974 postelection study.

40. White, *The Making of the President, 1964*, vii.

41. University of Michigan, Center for Social Research, selected surveys, 1958, 1964, 1970, 1980, and 1982.

42. Stanley B. Greenberg, "Plain Speaking: Democrats State Their Minds," *Public Opinion* (Summer 1986): 48.

43. Ibid.

44. Decision/Making/Information, survey for the Republican National Committee, 21–23 April 1987. The age cohorts cited are those between seventeen and twenty-four years, and those over sixty-five years.

45. Louis Harris and Associates, survey, 22–25 January 1981.

46. Gallup, survey, 18–21 September 1981. Text of question: "Which do you think is more understanding of the real needs of the people of this community—the Federal government in Washington or the government of this state?" Federal government, 15 percent; state government, 67 percent; same, 9 percent, no opinion, 9 percent.

47. Decision/Making/Information, survey for the Republican National Committee, 4–11 November 1982. Text of questions: "During the last two years, Ronald Reagan has talked about several things he hopes to accomplish as President. For each goal that I read tell me whether you generally think it is extremely important, somewhat important . . . or not important

at all." Goal: "Transferring taxing and spending powers from the federal government to the state governments." Extremely important, 33 percent; somewhat important, 42 percent; not important, 18 percent; no opinion, 7 percent. "Now I'm going to read that same list again. This time would you please tell me how successful you think Ronald Reagan has been in accomplishing that goal; that is, has he been very successful, somewhat successful, or not successful at all?" Very successful, 9 percent; somewhat successful, 50 percent; not at all successful, 28 percent; no opinion, 13 percent.

48. Ronald Reagan, 1982 State of the Union Address, Washington, D.C., 26 January 1982.

49. *Los Angeles Times*, poll, 3–7 January 1982. Text of questions: "Do you approve or disapprove of President Reagan's proposal to give more power to state and local governments?" Responses: approve, 79 percent; disapprove, 14 percent; not sure, 7 percent. "Which one of these proposals do you think is the most important: reducing spending on social services . . . increasing military spending . . . removing many government regulations . . . or giving more power to state and local governments? Is there one of these proposals that you think is very important?" Responses: services, 32 percent; military, 37 percent; government regulation, 19 percent; state power, 44 percent; not sure, 10 percent.

50. Brad Bannon, memo to members of the Democratic Policy Commission, 8 November 1985.

51. The term "bookend presidents" is Charles O. Jones'. See Weinraub, "The Reagan Legacy," 14.

52. Galston, *One Year to Go*, 15.

53. Ibid., 25.

54. Ibid., 15.

55. Ibid., 16.

56. Yankelovich, *New Rules*, 251.

57. CBS News/*New York Times*, survey, 19–23 January 1986.

58. Decision/Making/Information, survey for the Republican National Committee, 11–12 January 1986.

59. Decision/Making/Information, survey for the Republican National Committee, 23 April 1987. Text of question: "Recently, there has been much discussion about the functions performed at the three levels of government—federal, state and local. I am going to read you some phrases, both positive and negative, that are sometimes used to describe government. For each one that I read, please tell me whether you feel that phrase best describes the federal, state or local government . . . Is most sensitive to my needs."

60. Paul E. Tsongas, speech, National Press Club, Washington, D.C., 5 October 1982.

61. John Kenneth White, interview with Thomas P. O'Neill, Jr., Washington, D.C., 22 September 1982.

62. Quoted in Ken Auletta, "Profile: Mayor Edward I. Koch," *New Yorker*, 10 September 1979, 79.

63. Barnes, "Meet Mario the Moderate," 18.

64. CBS News/*New York Times*, exit poll, 4 November 1986. Of those

who voted for Reagan in 1984, 46 percent sided with Cuomo in 1986, and 49 percent voted for Cuomo's Republican opponent.

65. "The Kennedys: A New Generation Moves Up," *Newsweek*, 8 September 1986, 20.

66. *New Choices in a Changing America: The Report of the Democratic Policy Commission to the Democratic National Committee* (Washington, D.C.: Democratic National Committee, 1986), 2.

67. Nathaniel C. Nash, "For Proxmire, the Fleece Goes On," *New York Times*, 28 September 1987, B-6.

68. Phil Gailey, "Simon Declares, Embracing Democrats' Activist History," *New York Times*, 19 May 1987, A-20.

69. Ibid.

70. Dewar, "Democrats Are Charging," 11.

71. Ibid.

72. Sabato, *Goodbye to Good-time Charlie*, 194.

73. Ibid.

74. Quoted in William Schneider, "The Democrats in '88," *Atlantic Monthly* (April 1987): 49.

75. Ibid.

76. E. E. Schattschneider, *The Semi Sovereign People: A Realist's View of Democracy in America* (Hinsdale, Ill.: The Dryden Press, 1975 reprint), 7. This book was first published in 1960.

77. "A Change in the Weather," *Time*, 30 March 1987, 31.

78. Ibid.

79. Yankelovich, *New Rules*, 253.

80. Kevin Sack, "Democrats Need a 'Quake' to Win, Pollster Says," *Atlanta Constitution*, 20 March 1987, 1.

81. See Everett Carll Ladd, "On Mandates, Realignments, and the 1984 Presidential Election," *Political Science Quarterly*, vol. 11 (Spring 1985): 18. The states the Republicans have won consistently since 1968 are Alaska, Arizona, California, Colorado, Idaho, Illinois, Indiana, Iowa, Kansas, Montana, Nebraska, Nevada, New Hampshire, New Jersey, New Mexico, North Dakota, Oregon, South Dakota, Utah, Vermont, Virginia, and Wyoming.

82. Sack, "Democrats Need a 'Quake," 1. Historically, the only presidential nominees who increased their party's vote by 9 percentage points and went on to win the presidency were Andrew Jackson in 1828, William Henry Harrison in 1840, Warren G. Harding in 1920, and Franklin D. Roosevelt in 1932.

83. Weinraub, "The Reagan Legacy," 21.

84. Edward Walsh, "Once More with Hart," *Washington Post National Weekly Edition*, 9 February 1987, 15.

85. Quoted in Richard Reeves, *The Reagan Detour* (New York: Simon and Schuster, 1985), 32.

86. Sabato, *Goodbye to Good-time Charlie*, 196.

87. Ibid., 161.

88. Ibid.

89. Ibid., 190.

90. Former Republican governor Paul Laxalt made an abortive run at the 1988 Republican presidential nomination in 1987. On the Democratic side, there was considerable speculation in late 1987 that New York Governor Mario Cuomo would be a late entrant into the 1988 Democratic presidential contest. There remain a number of members of Congress (and former members) who are seeking the presidency in 1988, including Robert Dole, Jack Kemp, Richard Gephardt, Paul Simon, and Albert Gore.

91. New York Governor Mario Cuomo is a good example of a successful 1980s politician who got his start in political life by mediating a neighborhood dispute. See Mario M. Cuomo, *Forest Hills Diary: The Crisis of Low Income Housing* (New York: Random House, 1974).

92. Remarks by the president and the first lady in a national television address on drug abuse prevention, Washington, D.C., 14 September 1986.

93. *A Nation at Risk* (Washington, D.C.: Superintendent of Documents, U.S. Government Printing Office, 1983), 13.

94. Ibid., 32.

95. Ibid., 33.

96. Ibid., 35-36.

97. Ronald Reagan, radio address to the nation on education, Camp David, Maryland, 12 May 1984.

98. E. J. Dionne, "Biden, Offering 1988 Vision, Says American Dream Is Evaporating," *New York Times*, 15 May 1987, A-18.

99. Joseph Persico, *The Imperial Rockefeller: A Biography of Nelson A. Rockefeller* (New York: Simon and Schuster, 1982), 227.

100. Ibid., 226.

101. "The Jennings-Koppel Report: Memo to the Future," ABC News broadcast, 23 April 1987.

102. For an analysis of this point see Lewis J. Paper, *The Promise and the Performance: The Leadership of John F. Kennedy* (New York: Crown Publishers, 1975).

103. Patrick J. Buchanan, "A Conservative Makes a Final Plea," *Newsweek*, 30 March 1987, 26.

104. Tom Robbins, *Even Cowgirls Get the Blues* (Boston: Houghton Mifflin, 1976), quoted in Yankelovich, *New Rules*, preface.

105. V. O. Key, *The Responsible Electorate: Rationality in Presidential Voting, 1936-1962* (New York: Vintage Books, 1966), 7.

106. A Gallup poll conducted from 10-13 December 1982 found Reagan's approval rating stood at 41 percent. This is in sharp contrast to Reagan's recent predecessors. After two years in office, Carter's approval rating stood at 51 percent; Nixon's, 52 percent; Kennedy's, 76 percent; Eisenhower's, 69 percent. Text of the Gallup question: "Do you approve or disapprove of the way [name of president] is handling his job as President?"

107. A Gallup survey conducted 29 April to 2 May 1983 found Mondale defeating Reagan in a trial presidential heat, 49 percent to 43 percent. Reagan lost even more decisively to Democrat John Glenn, 54 percent to 37 percent.

108. Tocqueville, *Democracy in America*, 182.

FURTHER READINGS

SELECTED BOOKS

A Nation at Risk. Washington, D.C.: Superintendent of Documents, U.S. Government Printing Office, 1983.

Adams, James Truslow. *The Epic of America.* Boston: Little, Brown, 1935.

Ambrose, Stephen E. *Nixon: The Education of a Politician, 1913–1962.* New York: Simon and Schuster, 1987.

Barrett, Laurence I. *Gambling with History: Reagan in the White House.* Garden City, NY: Doubleday, 1983.

Bell, Daniel. *The End of Ideology.* Glencoe, Ill.: Free Press, 1960.

Berger, Max. *The British Traveller in America, 1836–1860.* New York: Columbia University Press, 1943.

Berger, Raoul. *Government by Judiciary: The Transformation of the Fourteenth Amendment.* Cambridge, Mass.: Harvard University Press, 1977.

Boorstin, Daniel J. *The Genius of American Politics.* Chicago: University of Chicago Press, 1953.

Boorstin, Daniel J. *The Image: Or What Happened to the American Dream.* New York: Atheneum, 1962.

Bowers, Claude G. *Jefferson and Hamilton: The Struggle for Democracy in America.* Boston: Houghton Mifflin, 1925.

Broder, David, Lou Cannon, Haynes Johnson, Martin Schram, Richard Harwood, and the staff of the *Washington Post. The Pursuit of the Presidency 1980.* New York: Berkley Books, 1980.

Burke, Vincent J. and Vee Burke. *Nixon's Good Deed: Welfare Reform.* New York: Columbia University Press, 1974.

Burns, James MacGregor. *Roosevelt: The Lion and the Fox.* New York: Harcourt, Brace, and World, 1956.

Burns, James MacGregor. *Roosevelt: The Soldier of Freedom.* New York: Harcourt Brace Jovanovich, 1970.

Califano, Joseph A., Jr. *Governing America: An Insider's Report from the White House and the Cabinet.* New York: Simon and Schuster, 1981.

Cannon, Lou. *Reagan.* New York: G. P. Putnam's Sons, 1982.

Carter, Jimmy. *Keeping Faith.* New York: Bantam Books, 1982.

Carter, Jimmy. *Why Not the Best?* New York: Bantam Books, 1976.

Chubb, John E., and Paul E. Peterson, eds. *The New Direction in American Politics.* Washington, D.C.: Brookings Institution, 1985.

Chesterton, Gilbert K. *What I Saw in America.* New York: Dodd, Mead, 1922.

Commager, Henry Steele. *Living Ideas in America.* New York: Harper and Brothers, 1951.

Connecticut Mutual Life Report on American Values in the '80s: The Impact of Belief. Lanham, Md.: University Press of America, 1981.

Croly, Herbert. *The Promise of American Life.* New York: Archon Books reprint, 1963.

Cronin, Thomas E. *The State of the Presidency.* Boston: Little, Brown, 1980.

Cuomo, Mario M. *Diaries of Mario Cuomo.* New York: Random House, 1984.

Donaldson, Sam. *Hold On, Mr President!* New York: Random House, 1987.

De Tocqueville, Alexis. *Democracy in America.* Reprint. New York: New American Library, 1956.

Dugger, Ronnie. *On Reagan: The Man and His Presidency.* New York: McGraw-Hill, 1983.

Duke, Paul, ed. *Beyond Reagan: The Politics of Upheaval.* New York: Warner Books, 1986.

Earle, Edward Mead, ed. *The Federalist.* New York: Modern Library, 1937.

Edwards, Anne. *Early Reagan: The Rise to Power.* New York: William Morrow, 1987.

Eisenhower, Julie Nixon. *Pat Nixon: The Untold Story.* New York: Simon and Schuster, 1986.

Erickson, Paul D. *Reagan Speaks: The Making of an American Myth.* New York: New York University Press, 1985.

Evans, Roland, and Robert Novak. *Lyndon B. Johnson: Exercise of Power.* New York: New American Library, 1968.

Ferguson, Thomas, and Joel Rogers. *Right Turn: The Decline of the Democrats and the Future of American Politics.* New York: Hill and Wang, 1986.

Frish, Morton J., ed. *Selected Writings of Alexander Hamilton.* Washington, D.C.: American Enterprise Institute, 1985.

Galston, William A. *One Year to Go: Citizen Attitudes in Iowa and New Hampshire.* Washington, D.C.: The Roosevelt Center for American Policy Studies, 1987.

Galston, William A., and Mark J. Rovner, *Southern Voices/Southern Views: A Report on Focus Groups Conducted by the Roosevelt Center for American Studies.* Washington, D.C.: The Roosevelt Center for American Policy Studies, 1987.

Germond, Jack, and Jules Witcover. *Blue Smoke and Mirrors.* New York: Viking Press, 1981.

Goldman, Eric F. *The Tragedy of Lyndon Johnson.* New York: Alfred A. Knopf, 1969.

Goldman, Peter, and Tony Fuller. *The Quest for the Presidency, 1984.* New York: Bantam Books, 1985.

Greenstein, Fred I. *The Hidden-Hand Presidency: Eisenhower as Leader.* New York: Basic Books, 1982.

Greider, William. *The Education of David Stockman and Other Americans.* New York: E. P. Dutton, 1981.

Harris, Louis. *Inside America.* New York: Vintage Books, 1987.

Hart, Gary. *A New Democracy: A Democratic Vision for the 1980s and Beyond.* New York: Quill, 1983.

Hartz, Louis. *The Liberal Tradition in America.* New York: Harcourt Brace Jovanovich, 1955.

Henry, William A., III. *Visions of America: How We Saw the 1984 Election.* Boston: Atlantic Monthly Press, 1985.

Honomichl, Jack. *Honomichl of Marketing Research.* Lincolnwood, Illinois: NTC Business Books, 1986.

Hughes, Emmet John. *The Living Presidency.* New York: Coward, McCann and Geoghegan, 1973.

Iacocca, Lee, with William Novak. *Iacocca: An Autobiography.* New York: Bantam Books, 1984.

Jennings, Peter, and David Brinkley. *The '84 Vote.* New York: American Broadcasting Company, 1985.

Kennedy, Robert F. *To Seek a Newer World.* New York: Doubleday, 1967.

Key, V.O. *The Responsible Electorate: Rationality in Presidential Voting, 1936–1962.* New York: Vintage Books, 1966.

Klein, Joe. *Woody Guthrie: A Life.* New York: Alfred A. Knopf, 1980.

Lacey, Robert. *Ford: The Men and the Machine.* New York: Ballantine Books, 1986.

Ladd, Everett Carll. *The American Polity.* New York: Norton, 1987.

Ladd, Everett Carll. *Where Have All the Voters Gone?* New York: Norton, 1982.

Lane, Robert. *Political Ideology: Why the Common Man Believes What he Does.* New York: Free Press, 1962.

Lasswell, Harold D. *Politics: Who Gets What, When, How.* New York: Meridian Books, 1958.

Leamer, Laurence. *Make-Believe: The Story of Nancy and Ronald Reagan.* New York: Dell Books, 1984.

Lipset, Seymour Martin, ed. *Party Coalitions in the 1980s.* San Francisco: Institute for Contemporary Studies, 1981.

Lowi, Theodore J. *The End of Liberalism.* New York: Norton, 1969.

Lubell, Samuel. *The Future of American Politics.* New York: Harper & Row, 1965.

Marsh, Dave. *Glory Days: Bruce Springsteen in the 1980s.* New York: Pantheon Books, 1987.

McGinniss, Joe. *The Selling of the President, 1968.* New York: Pocket Books, 1970.

Miller, Merle. *Lyndon: An Oral Biography.* New York: Ballantine Books, 1980.

Moore, Jonathan, ed. *The Campaign for President: 1980 in Retrospect.* Cambridge, Mass.: Ballinger Publishing Company, 1982.

Morgan, Ted. *FDR: A Biography.* New York: Simon and Schuster, 1985.

Neustadt, Richard. *Presidential Power: The Politics of Leadership from FDR to Carter.* New York: John Wiley and Sons, 1980.

New Choices in a Changing America: The Report of the Democratic Party Policy Commission to the Democratic National Committee. Washington, D.C.: Democratic National Committee, 1986.

Nixon, Richard M. *RN: The Memoirs of Richard Nixon*. New York: Grosset and Dunlap, 1978.

O'Neill, Thomas P., with William Novak. *Man of the House: The Life and Political Memoirs of Speaker Tip O'Neill*. New York: Random House, 1987.

Paper, Lewis J. *The Promise and the Performance: The Leadership of John F. Kennedy*. New York: Crown Publisher, 1975.

Persico, Joseph E. *The Imperial Rockefeller: A Biography of Nelson A. Rockefeller*. New York: Simon and Schuster, 1982.

Programme of the German Green Party. London: Heretic Books, 1983.

Public Papers of the Presidents of the United States, Ronald Reagan, 1981. Washington, D.C.: U.S. Government Printing Office, 1982.

Public Papers of the Presidents of the United States, Ronald Reagan, 1982, Volumes I and II. Washington, D.C.: U.S. Government Printing Office, 1983.

Public Papers of the Presidents of the United States, Ronald Reagan, 1983, Volume I. Washington, D.C.: U.S. Government Printing Office, 1984.

Public Papers of the Presidents of the United States, Ronald Reagan, 1983, Volume II. Washington, D.C.: U.S. Government Printing Office, 1985.

Public Papers of the Presidents of the United States, Ronald Reagan, 1984, Volume I. Washington, D.C.: U.S. Government Printing Office, 1986.

Reagan, Ronald, with Richard G. Huebler. *Where's the Rest of Me?* New York: Duell, Sloan and Pearce, 1965.

Reeves, Richard. *The Reagan Detour*. New York: Simon and Schuster, 1985.

Reich, Emil. *Success among the Nations*. New York: Harper and Brothers, 1904.

Rogin, Michael. *Ronald Reagan, the Movie and Other Episodes in Political Demonology*. Berkeley, Cal.: University of California Press, 1987.

Rossiter, Clinton. *The American Presidency*. New York: New American Library, 1960.

Sabato, Larry. *Goodbye to Good-time Charlie: The American Governorship Transformed*. Washington, D.C.: Congressional Quarterly, Inc., 1983.

Schattschneider, E.E. *The Semi-Sovereign People: A Realist's View of Democracy in America*. Hinsdale, Ill.: The Dryden Press, 1975 reprint.

Schlesinger, Arthur M. *A Thousand Days: John F. Kennedy in the White House*. New York: Fawcett Books, 1965.

Schlesinger, Arthur M. *Kennedy or Nixon: Does It Make Any Difference?* New York: MacMillan, 1960.

Schlesinger, Arthur M. *The Cycles of American History*. Boston: Houghton Mifflin, 1986.

Steele, Michael R. *Knute Rockne: A Bio-Bibliography*. Westport, Conn.: Greenwood Press, 1983.

Stockman, David A. *The Triumph of Politics: Why the Reagan Revolution Failed*. New York: Harper & Row, 1986.

Tower Commission Report. New York: Times Books and Bantam Books, 1987.

Von Damm, Helene. *Sincerely, Ronald Reagan.* Ottawa, Ill.: Green Hill Publishers, 1976.

White, John Kenneth. *The Fractured Electorate: Political Parties and Social Change in Southern New England.* Hanover, N.H.: University Press of New England, 1983.

White, Theodore H. *America in Search of Itself: The Making of the President 1956–1980.* New York: Harper & Row, 1982.

White, Theodore H. *The Making of the President, 1960.* New York: Signet Books, 1961.

White, Theodore H. *The Making of the President, 1964.* New York: New American Library, 1965.

White, Theodore H. *The Making of the President, 1968.* New York: Atheneum Publishers, 1969.

Wills, Garry. *Inventing America.* New York: Vintage Books, 1978.

Wills, Garry. *Reagan's America: Innocents At Home.* Garden City, N.Y.: Doubleday, 1981.

Wilson, Woodrow. *Constitutional Government in the United States.* New York: Columbia University Press, 1908.

Yankelovich, Daniel. *New Rules: Searching for Self-Fulfillment in a World Turned Upside Down.* New York: Random House, 1981.

SELECTED ARTICLES

"A Change in the Weather." *Time,* 30 March 1987.

"American Values: Change and Stability: A Conversation with Daniel Yankelovich." *Public Opinion,* December/January 1984.

Archer, J.C., G.T. Murauskas, F.M. Shelley, E.R. White, and P.J. Taylor. "Counties, States, Sections, and Parties in the 1984 Presidential Election." *Professional Geographer,* Volume 37, Number 3 August 1985.

Auletta, Ken. "Profile: Mayor Edward I. Koch." *New Yorker,* 10 September 1979.

Barnes, Fred. "Meet Mario the Moderate." *New Republic,* 8 April 1985.

Barrett, Paul M. "The Caucus-Happy Democrats." *Washington Monthly,* April 1985.

Beer, Samuel H. "Ronald Reagan: New Deal Conservative?" *Society,* Volume 20, Number 2 (January/February 1983).

Bonner, Yelena. "A Quirky Farewell to America." *Newsweek,* 2 June 1986.

Burns, James MacGregor. "The President Behind the Candidate." *Life,* 9 October 1964.

Caddell, Patrick H. "Crisis of Confidence—Trapped in a Downward Spiral." *Public Opinion,* October/November 1979.

"Cosby, Inc." *Time,* 28 September 1987.

Easterbrook, Gregg. "Ideas Move Nations." *Atlantic Monthly,* May 1979.

Fallows, James. "The Passionless Presidency." *Atlantic Monthly,* May 1979.

"Face Off: A Conversation with the Presidents' Pollsters Patrick Caddell and Richard Wirthlin." *Public Opinion,* December/January 1981.

"Five Republican Leaders Speak Out." *U.S. News and World Report,* 29 August 1977.

"Future Uncertain for State's Democrats." *California Journal*, March 1987.

Greenberg, Stanley B. "Plain Speaking: Democrats State Their Minds." *Public Opinion*, Summer 1986.

Grenier, Richard. "Around the World in American Ways." *Public Opinion*, February/March 1986.

Harmetz, Aljean. "Crossing the Line to Stardom: Talent Isn't Enough." *New York Times*, 7 June 1987.

Hartle, Terry W. "Dream Jobs?" *Public Opinion*, September/October 1986.

Kleiner, Art. "Master of the Sentimental Sell." *New York Times Magazine*, 14 December 1986.

Ladd, Everett Carll. "On Mandates, Realignments, and the 1984 Presidential Election." *Political Science Quarterly*, Spring 1985.

Lichter, S. Robert, and Stanley Rothman. "Media and Business Elites." *Public Opinion*, October/November 1981.

"Morality Among the Supply-Siders." *Time*, 25 May 1987.

"Moving Right Along? Campaign '84's Lessons for 1988: An Interview with Peter Hart and Richard Wirthlin." *Public Opinion*, December/January 1985.

"Pop Goes the Culture." *Time*, 16 June 1986.

Rockne, Knute. "Gipp the Great." *Colliers*, 22 November 1930.

Schambra, William A. "Progressive Liberalism and American 'Community'." *Public Interest*, Number 80 (Summer 1985).

Schneider, William. "The Democrats in '88." *Atlantic Monthly*, April 1987.

Schneider, William. "The New Shape of American Politics." *Atlantic Monthly*, January 1987.

Sidey, Hugh. "A Conversation with Reagan." *Time*, 3 September 1984.

Simpson, Jeffrey. "Living Beside a Cultural and Economic Colossus." *New York Times*, 24 August 1986.

Stein, Ben. "'Miami Vice': It's So Hip You'll Want to Kill Yourself." *Public Opinion*, October/November 1985.

Tauber, Peter. "Notes on a Brief Campaign." *New York Times Magazine*, 31 May 1987.

"The Consequence of Ideas: The Reagan Revolution and Beyond: An Interview with Jeane Kirkpatrick, Michael Novak, and Herbert Stein." *Public Opinion*, Summer 1986.

"The Themes of 1984 with Governors Mario Cuomo and George Deukmejian." *Public Opinion*, December/January 1984.

Trilling, Richard J. "Party Image and Electoral Behavior." *American Politics Quarterly*, Volume 3, Number 3, (July 1975).

Valenti, Jack. "And the Winner Is . . . American Movies, Television, and Videos." *Public Opinion*, February/March 1986.

Vogel, David. "The Inadequacy of Contemporary Opposition to Business." *Daedalus*, Volume 109, Number 3 (Summer 1980).

Weinraub, Bernard. "The Reagan Legacy." *New York Times Magazine*, 22 June 1986.

White, John Kenneth. "Our Three-Party System." *Election Politics*, Fall 1986.

White, John Kenneth. "Shattered Images: Political Parties in the 1980s." *Public Opinion*, December/January 1984.

White, John Kenneth. *Shifting Coalitions in American Politics* (monograph). Washington, D.C.: American Academy of Higher Education, 1986.

Will, George F. "Bruce Springsteen's U.S.A." *Washington Post*, 13 September 1984.

Will, George F. "The Presidency in the American Political System." *Presidential Studies Quarterly*, Summer 1984.

Wills, Garry. "What Happened?" *Time*, 9 March 1987.

Wilson, James Q. "A Guide to Reagan Country: The Political Culture of Southern California." *Commentary*, May 1967.

Wirthlin, Richard, and John White. "From Political Poverty to Parity: The Restoration of the Republican Party?" *Public Opinion*, January/February 1987.

SELECTED POLLS

Decision/Making/Information, panel study for the Reagan for President Committee, December 1979.

Decision/Making/Information, postelection studies 1972, 1974, 1976, 1980, and 1984.

Decision/Making/Information, survey for the Free Congress Foundation, 4–5 November 1981.

Decision/Making/Information, surveys for the Reagan for President Campaign, 1975.

Decision/Making/Information, survey for the Reagan for President Campaign, June 1980.

National Opinion Research Center, University of Chicago, combined General Social Surveys, 1972–1987.

The Wirthlin Group, selected surveys for the Republican National Committee, 1987.

University of Michigan, Center for Social Research, selected surveys, 1958, 1964, 1970, 1980, and 1982.

SELECTED SPEECHES

Bellotti, Francis X. Address to the Massachusetts Democratic State Convention. Springfield, Massachusetts, 16 May 1986.

Carter, Jimmy. Acceptance Speech. Democratic National Convention, New York, 15 July 1976.

Carter, Jimmy. Acceptance Speech. Democratic National Convention, New York, 14 August 1980.

Carter, Jimmy. Address to the Nation. Washington, D.C., 15 July 1979.

Cuomo, Mario M. "A Case for the Democrats, 1984: A Tale of Two Cities." Keynote Speech to the Democratic National Convention, San Francisco, 16 July 1984.

Cuomo, Mario M. Address at *Newsday* Education Symposium. State University of New York, Old Westbury, New York, 4 March 1987.

Edsall, Thomas B. Speech to the Committee for Party Renewal. Eagleton Institute, Rutgers University, New Brunswick, New Jersey, 14 January 1987.

Ferraro, Geraldine. Acceptance Speech. Democratic National Convention, San Francisco, 19 July 1984.

Ferraro, Geraldine. "'Our Better Instincts' Versus Appeals to Self-Interest." Reprinted in the *New York Times*, 28 September 1984.

Goldwater, Barry M. Acceptance Speech. Republican National Convention, San Francisco, 16 July 1964.

King, Martin Luther, Jr. "I Have A Dream." Address at the Lincoln Memorial, 28 August 1963. Reprinted in the *New York Times*, 28 August 1983.

Kirkpatrick, Jeane J. Speech to the Republican National Convention, Dallas. Reprinted in the *New York Times*, 21 August 1984.

Jackson, Jesse L. Speech to the Democratic National Convention. San Francisco, 17 July 1984.

Johnson, Lyndon B. Inaugural Address. Washington, D.C., 20 January 1965.

Johnson, Lyndon B. "To Fulfill These Rights." Commencement Address, Howard University, Washington, D.C., 4 June 1965.

Mondale, Walter F. Acceptance Speech. Democratic National Convention, San Francisco, 19 July 1984.

Mondale, Walter F. "'The Issues Are With Us'." Reprinted in the *New York Times*, 11 October 1984.

Nixon, Richard M. Acceptance Speech. Republican National Convention, Chicago, 28 July 1960.

Nixon, Richard M. Acceptance Speech. Republican National Convention, Miami, 8 August 1968.

Nixon, Richard M. Address to the Nation. Washington, D.C., 15 August 1971.

Reagan, Ronald. "A Vision for America." Television broadcast, 3 November 1980.

Reagan, Ronald. Acceptance Speech. Republican National Convention, Detroit, 17 July 1980.

Reagan, Ronald. Acceptance Speech. Republican National Convention, Dallas, 23 August 1984.

Reagan, Ronald. Address to Congress. Washington, D.C., 18 February 1981.

Reagan, Ronald. Address to the Graduates. Notre Dame University, South Bend, Indiana, 17 May 1981.

Reagan, Ronald. Address to the Nation Announcing the Reagan-Bush Candidacies for Reelection. 29 January 1984.

Reagan, Ronald. Economic Report of the President's Annual Message to Congress, Washington, D.C., 10 February 1982.

Reagan, Ronald. Inaugural Address. Washington, D.C., 20 January 1981.

Reagan, Ronald. Inaugural Address. Washington, D.C., 21 January 1985.

Reagan, Ronald. Radio Address to the Nation on Education. 12 May 1984.

Reagan, Ronald. Radio Address to the Nation on the Observance of Mother's Day. 7 May 1983.

Reagan, Ronald. Remarks at Building and Construction Trades (AFL-CIO) National Conference. Washington, D.C., 30 March 1981.

Reagan, Ronald, and Nancy Reagan. Remarks by the President and the First Lady on Drug Abuse Prevention. Washington, D.C., 14 September 1986.

Reagan, Ronald. 1982 State of the Union Address. Washington, D.C., 26 January 1982.

Reagan, Ronald. 1984 State of the Union Address. Washington, D.C., 25 January 1984.

Reagan, Ronald. 1985 State of the Union Address. Washington, D.C., 6 February 1985.

Reagan, Ronald. 1986 State of the Union Address. Washington, D.C., 4 February 1986.

Reagan, Ronald. 1987 State of the Union Address. Washington, D.C., 27 January 1987.

Reagan, Ronald. "'We Will Lift America Up'." Reprinted in the *New York Times*, 26 September 1984.

Roosevelt, Franklin D. Inaugural Address. Washington, D.C., 20 January 1945.

Tsongas, Paul E. Speech to the National Press Club. Washington, D.C., 5 October 1982.

SELECTED INTERVIEWS

Hart, Peter D. Washington, D.C., 5 August 1985.

Maslin, Paul E. Washington, D.C., 5 December 1984.

Mondale, Walter F. Interview broadcast on "Meet the Press," 7 April 1985.

O'Neill, Thomas P. Washington, D.C., 22 September 1982.

Rendon, John. Potsdam, New York, 30 April 1984.

Tarrance, Lance. Houston, 22 March 1985.

Wirthlin, Richard B. Washington, D.C., 6 December 1984.

OTHER PRINTED MATTER

"Is There a Republican Realignment?" Conference sponsored by the Americans for Responsible Government, Madison Hotel, Washington, D.C., 1 October 1985.

Bannon, Brad. Memo to Members of the Democratic Policy Commission, 8 November 1985.

Baroody, William J., Jr. American Enterprise Institute Memorandum, Summer 1985.

Democratic National Platform, 1936. Reprinted in the *New York Times*, 26 June 1936.

Democratic National Platform, 1980. Washington, D.C.: Democratic National Committee, 1980.

Democratic National Platform, 1984. Washington, D.C.: Democratic National Committee, 1984.

Dyer, James A., David B. Hill, Arnold Vedlitz, and Stephen N. White. "The Partisan Transformation of Texas." Paper presented at the annual meeting of the American Political Science Association, New Orleans, 29 August-1 September 1985.

"FDR," ABC News transcript. New York: Journal Graphics, Inc., 29 January 1982.

Hart, Peter D. Report to the Democratic Congressional Campaign Committee, August 1983.

Republican National Platform, 1936. Reprinted in the *New York Times*, 12 June 1936.

Republican National Platform, 1980. Washington, D.C.: Republican National Committee, 1980.

Republican National Platform, 1984. Washington, D.C.: Republican National Committee, 1984.

"Ronald Reagan: Memo to the Future." Jennings-Koppel Report. ABC News broadcast, 23 April 1987.

Wirthlin, Richard B. Final Report of the Initial Actions Project, 29 January 1981. Unpublished transition document.

Wirthlin, Richard B. Reagan for President: Campaign Action Plan, 29 June 1980. Unpublished confidential campaign document.

Wirthlin, Richard B. Campaign Action Plan, August 1983. Unpublished confidential campaign document.

INDEX

ABC News/*Washington Post* (poll), 85, 99
Abortion, 41, 42, 83. *See also* Lifestyles
Acquired Immune Deficiency Syndrome (AIDS), 101, 111, 119, 137
Adams, James Truslow, 24, 34
Adams, John, 15
Adams, John Quincy, 24
Affirmative Action, 42. *See also* Equality
Agar, Herbert, 112
Ailes, Roger, 67
Alger, Horatio, 27
"All in the Family," 119–20
Ambrose, Stephen, 19
American Bar Association, 14
American dream, 23, 24–27, 28, 34, 35, 36, 40, 50, 51, 69, 73, 84, 107, 117. *See also* Presidency
American Federation of Labor-Congress of Industrial Organizations (AFL-CIO), 66
Anderson, John B., 37, 59
Andrews, Dana, 12
Atwater, Lee, 110
Avalon, Frankie, 112

Babbitt, Bruce, 135, 140
Baker, Howard H., 70
Baker, James, 111
Bakker, Jim, 24
Bakker, Tammy, 24
Bannon, Brad, 132
Baroody, William J., Jr., 60
Bartles and Jaymes, 9–10, 18
Bayard, Aleen Zimberoff, 137
Bedtime for Bonzo, 113
Beggs, James, 17
Bellotti, Francis X., 44
Berger, Max, 25
Bierce, Ambrose, 52
Berlin, Irving, 106
Bernstein, Carl, 112
Biden, Joseph, 142

Blacks, 71, 77, 89, 93, 102
Blue-collar workers, 52
Bonner, Yelena, 23
Boorstin, Daniel, 21, 29
"Born-Again" Christians, 52, 71, 83, 100
Bosworth, Barry, 44
Brandeis, Louis, 33
Breaux, John, 92
Breech, Ernest R., 116
Broder, David, 136
Brown, Edmund G., 140
Brown, Kevin, 110
Brown, Pat, 52
Broyhill, James, 92
Brzezinski, Zbigniew, 44
Buchanan, Patrick, 19, 143
Burford, Anne, 17
Burns, James MacGregor, 79, 128
Burton, Philip, 98
Bush, George, 38, 59, 110
Butler, Shelby, 61

CBS News/*New York Times* (poll), 37, 84, 133
Caddell, Patrick H., 39, 50, 94, 109, 138
Canby, Vincent, 121
Carson, Charles, 61
Carson, Johnny, 103
Carter, Jimmy, 1, 6, 37, 38, 39, 42, 43, 44, 47, 57, 63, 68, 72, 74, 95, 115, 128, 143, 144; malaise and, 48, 112; 1976 election and, 42–43, 83, 90, 138, 140; 1980 election and, 37–39, 42–49, 50, 54–55, 90, 140
Catholics, 52, 89
Cavioli, Richard, 61
Central American Peace Project, 125
Chesterton, Gilbert K., 24
Christian, George, 91
Cisneros, Henry, 136
Clements, William, 92
Cleveland, Grover, 139
Commager, Henry Steele, 33

Connecticut Mutual Life Insurance Company (poll), 41, 55
Coolidge, Calvin, 79, 139
Cosby, Bill, 117–18. See also "Cosby Show, The"
"Cosby Show, The" 117–18, 119, 121. See also Cosby, Bill; Rashad, Phylicia
Croly, Herbert, 34, 36
Cruise, Tom, 109
Culture (U.S.), 6, 103–21
Cuomo, Mario M., 5, 16, 25, 33, 61–62, 64, 68, 83, 97, 134–35

D'Amato, Alfonse, 84, 97
Daniloff, Nicholas, 16
Davis, Betty, 116
Dean, "Dizzy," 13, 14
Deaver, Michael K., 17, 104
Decision/Making/Information, 27, 36, 39, 40, 87, 131, 132. See also Wirthlin, Richard B.
deCrevecoeur, Jean, 26
deGaulle, Charles, 110
Democratic Leadership Council, 135
Democratic party, 2, 3, 6, 12, 32–33, 44, 47–48, 51, 53, 54, 59, 63, 65–67, 68, 71, 74, 75, 79, 82, 83, 85, 86, 94, 98, 118, 126–27, 134, 135, 136, 138–39; identifiers, 51, 52, 76, 84, 85, 87, 89, 90, 94, 100; in Massachusetts, 124–25; 1980 platform of, 48; 1984 platform of, 57, 63–64, 65, 68; opposition to Reagan, 2, 61, 62. See also Elections; Political parties
Denton, Jeremiah, 92
Dessart, George, 119
deTocqueville, Alexis, 30, 31, 32, 46, 144
Deukmejian, George, 97
Dixon, Alan, 97
Doggett, Lloyd, 91
Donaldson, Sam, 20
Donovan, Hedley, 44
Douglas, Kirk, 19, 108
Drew, Elizabeth, 65
Dukakis, Michael S., 136, 140
duPont, Pierre, 140
Dylan, Bob, 43

East, John, 92
Eastwood, Clint, 111, 114
Economy, 46, 50, 57, 70, 80, 85, 86, 99. See also Inflation; "Misery Index"; Unemployment

Edsall, Thomas B., 76–77, 99
Education, 25, 66, 128, 141–42
Eisenhower, Dwight D., 49, 76, 128, 138, 144
Eizenstat, Stuart, 44, 123, 138–39
Elections, 51; in Canada, 122; in France, 122; in Great Britain, 122; in West Germany, 122; of 1960, 37, 45, 96; of 1964, 2, 125, 126; of 1968, 42, 45, 82, 90; of 1972, 39, 42, 82, 83; of 1976, 42, 43; of 1980, 11, 37–39, 49–55, 70, 122, 144; of 1984, 69–73, 90, 122, 144; of 1986, 92–93. See also Democratic party; Presidency; Republican party
Eliot, T. S., 20
Equality: of opportunity, 25–27, 28; of result, 65. See also Affirmative Action
Evans, Daniel, 140

Fairbanks, Douglas, 18
Fairness issues, 78, 79, 86, 89
Fallows, James, 44, 47
Family, 2, 4, 12, 21, 22, 31, 33, 50, 54, 57, 60, 61, 64, 65, 67, 69, 73, 103, 104, 117, 118, 121, 128, 144. See also Values
Farmer, James, 125
Federal Government, 3, 52, 53, 54, 57, 58, 59, 60, 78; public disillusionment with, 42, 47, 130, 131, 132, 134; relationship with states, 47, 59, 126–32
Ferraro, Geraldine A., 20, 62, 64, 67, 71, 105, 138
Ferrell, Trevor, 61
Fisher, Terry Louise, 119
Fonda, Jane, 124
Flynn, Raymond, 136
Ford, Gerald R., 1, 42, 47, 50, 90, 128, 140, 143
Ford, Harrison, 114
Ford, Henry II, 115, 125
Ford, Tyrone, 61
Fox, Michael J., 114, 118
Freedom, 2, 4, 21, 22, 24, 27, 29, 30–31, 32, 54, 57, 60, 61, 69, 73, 135, 144. See also Values
Frost, David, 137
Funicello, Annette, 112

Gallo, Ernest and Julio, 10
Gallup Poll, 37, 80, 84, 85, 99, 100, 110, 116, 131, 132, 144
Gardner, Ava, 18

Geldof, Bob, 125
Gephardt, Richard, 135
Gerry, Elbridge, 139
Gipp, George, 7–8, 9, 10, 11, 12, 15, 116
Glenn, John, 68
Goldman, Eric, 126
Goldsmith, Judy, 67
Goldwater, Barry M., 2, 45, 56, 58, 125, 126
Gore, Albert, 111
Gorbachev, Mikhail, 16, 20
Gramm, Phil, 91
Gramsci, Antonio, 76, 77
Green Party (U.S.), 124
Green Party (West Germany), 124, 125
Grenada, 61, 67
Griffin, Merv, 119
Gulick, Luther, 126
Guthrie, Woody, 106

Hale, Mother, 61
Haley, Alex, 112
Hamilton, Alexander, 31, 32, 34, 36, 47
Hamiltonian Nationalism, 31–36, 45, 46, 47, 48, 52, 60, 65, 68, 73
Hammer, Armand, 116
Handlin, Oscar, 40
Harding, Warren G., 139
Harmetz, Aljean, 109
Harris, Louis, 37, 54, 85, 123, 131
Hart, Gary, 16, 63, 74, 77, 139
Hart, Peter D., 54, 75, 86, 90, 91, 92
Hartz, Louis, 29
Hawkins, Paula, 92
Hayden, Tom, 124
Hayes, Rutherford B., 139
Hayworth, Rita, 18
Heclo, Hugh, 123
Hellcats of the Navy, 113
Helms, Jesse, 91
Henry, William A., III, 14
Heston, Charlton, 108
Hiss, Alger, 29
Homosexuality, 30, 41, 42, 101. *See also* Lifestyles
Hoover, Herbert, 78, 120
House Committee on Un-American Activities (HUAC), 29
Hunt, James, 91
Humphrey, Hubert H., 38, 42, 47, 51, 65, 82, 137, 140

Iacocca, Lee A., 27, 105, 109, 114–16

Inflation, 39, 46–47, 50, 54, 70. *See also* Economy; Unemployment
Iran-Contra Affair, 1–2, 14, 16, 17, 18, 19, 21, 22, 87, 99. *See also* Reagan, Ronald

Jackson, Andrew, 31
Jackson, Jesse, 65, 68, 77
Jefferson, Thomas, 24, 31, 32, 34, 43, 46, 59, 126
Jeffersonian Democracy, 31–36, 45, 59, 124
Jennings, Peter, 1, 5–6, 74–75, 113
Jews, 71
John Paul II (Pope), 116
Johnson, Lady Bird, 128
Johnson, Lyndon B., 1, 2, 3, 38, 45, 46, 47, 65, 68, 69, 71, 82, 91, 95, 137, 138, 140, 143; Great Society and, 1, 3, 46, 58, 95, 125–28, 130. *See also* Vietnam War
Jordan, Hamilton, 49
Jurges, Billy, 13, 14

Keene, Karlyn, 111
Kefauver, Estes, 140
Kelley, Kitty, 116
Kemp, Jack, 59
Kennedy, Edward M., 37, 38, 48, 54, 94, 121, 123
Kennedy, John F., 1, 3, 21, 37, 38, 44, 45, 49, 51, 52, 54, 56, 68, 69, 81, 82, 83, 88, 94, 95, 96, 130, 131, 138, 140, 143; New Frontier and, 3, 68, 128
Kennedy, Joseph P., II, 135
Kennedy, Robert F., 46, 94, 135, 140
Kerry, John, 76
Key, V.O., 144
Khomeini, Ayatollah, 3, 19
King, Martin Luther, Jr., 27, 77
Kings Row, 18, 113
Kirk, Paul, 74
Kirkpatrick, Jeane J., 69
Koch, Edward, 134, 136
Kohl, Helmut, 122
Koppel, Ted, 143
Knute Rockne—All American, 9, 11, 26, 113

Lacey, Robert, 115
Landon, Alfred, 69, 79, 127
Laski, Harold, 34
Lasswell, Harold, 3
Lavelle, Rita, 17

Laxalt, Paul, 140
Lee, Richard Henry, 32
Lennon, John, 110
Lewis, Huey, 111
Lewis, Jerry, 114
Lichter, S. Robert, 42
Lifestyles, 30, 31, 41–42, 82. *See also*
Abortion; Homosexuality; Religion
Lincoln, Abraham, 33, 35, 89, 129, 143
Lippmann, Walter, 33–34
Long, Russell, 92
Lubell, Samuel, 38

"M*A*S*H," 120
Madison, James, 31, 35
Madonna, 111, 116
Market Opinion Research, 88
Maslin, Paul, 77, 86, 90
Mattingly, Mack, 92
McCarthy, Eugene, 140
McGinniss, Joe, 110
McGovern, George, 28, 42, 56, 69, 71,
72, 82, 83, 140
McKinley, William, 139
Mannatt, Charles, 56
Marshall, Alfred, 55
Meese, Edwin, 17, 111
Melville, Herman, 29
"Miami Vice," 116–17
Michel, Bob, 75
"Misery Index," 50. *See also* Economy
Mitchell, John N., 45
Mondale, Walter F., 3, 6, 11, 20, 56, 57,
62, 67, 68, 71, 72, 105, 123, 138, 139,
144; 1984 election and, 56, 62, 66, 70,
75, 86, 90; values and, 63–69
Monroe, Marilyn, 18
Moore, Henson, 92
Morgan, John A., 97
Morrow, Lance, 16
Movies, 108, 109, 112, 113–14, 121
Moynihan, Daniel P., 53, 130, 139
Mudd, Roger, 38

National Education Association (NEA),
66, 128
National Opinion Research Center, 26–
27, 29, 31
National Organization for Women
(NOW), 66
Neighborhood, 2, 4, 21, 22, 46, 50, 54,
57, 60, 69, 73, 103, 104, 121, 128, 144.
See also Values

Newman, Edwin, 43
Nguyen, Jean, 61
Nicholson, Jack, 109
Nisbet, Robert, 127–28
Nixon, Richard M., 1, 16, 19, 23, 25, 26,
29, 35, 37, 39, 42, 44, 45, 47, 51, 56, 62,
69, 71, 72, 76, 80, 81, 82, 83, 88, 95, 96,
97–98, 118, 137, 140, 143;
administration of, 45, 128. *See also*
Watergate
Nofziger, Lyn, 17
Nolan, Martin, 106
North Carolina, state elections in, 91–
92, 93
North, Oliver, 7, 16, 67
Novak, Michael, 119
Novak, William, 115
"Nuclear Freeze" movement, 124
Nunn, Sam, 135

O'Neill, Thomas P. (Tip), Jr., 2, 4, 20–
21, 59, 134
Ornstein, Norman, 102

Parsons, Louella, 18
Patriotism, 50. *See also* Values
Patterson, Janet, 73
Peace, 2, 4, 21, 22, 54, 57, 60, 61, 72, 73,
144. *See also* Values
Persico, Joseph, 142, 143
Pickford, Mary, 18
Pierce, Franklin, 139
Pitt, William, 24
Playboy, 40, 110, 111, 118
Poindexter, John, 7, 16
Political Action Committees (PACs), 98
Political parties, 6, 32, 33, 51, 75, 77, 78,
84, 87, 123; parity party system, 76,
77, 96–102; realignment of, 75, 77;
values and, 77–84. *See also*
Democratic party; Republican party;
Values
Polls, 3, 17, 19, 24, 25, 26–27, 28, 29, 30,
31, 36, 37, 39, 40, 41, 42, 43, 47, 49, 51,
53, 54, 70, 71, 72, 76, 80, 85, 86, 93, 94,
95, 97, 99, 100, 116, 123, 130, 131, 132,
133, 134, 144
Pornography, 31, 111
Potter, Lora A., 72, 73
Presidency, 31, 81, 103, 129–30, 139–44;
American dream and, 34–36, 51;
elections and, 2, 11, 37–39, 49–55;
failures of, 1, 47; as symbol, 15–16, 61,

111–12; values and, 15. *See also* Elections; Reagan, Ronald
Protestants, 89
Proxmire, William, 135

Rashad, Phylicia, 117. *See also* "Cosby Show, The"
Reagan, Nancy, 11, 15, 18, 40, 113, 141
Reagan Revolution, 57, 58, 59, 122–25, 133, 135
Reagan, Ronald, 6, 25, 29, 33, 36, 37, 40, 49, 54, 57, 62, 68, 72, 75, 76, 77, 80, 83, 105, 106, 111, 115, 125, 126, 132, 136, 139, 140, 141; administration of, 58, 141–42; and Iran-Contra Affair, 1–2, 3, 17, 18, 19, 21, 22; and Jeffersonian Democracy, 33, 34, 52–54; and Republican party, 53, 62, 84, 85, 94, 95, 101; and U.S. culture, 103, 113–14, 117, 120–21; as "Great Communicator," 1, 4, 5, 61, 67, 68, 143–44; as Governor of California, 15–16, 50, 52; as "the Gipper," 7, 10–15, 17–21, 116; as storyteller, 12–15, 61; 1980 election of, 37–39, 49–55, 70, 140; 1984 election of, 68, 69–73; popular approval and, 2, 3, 4, 17, 19, 21, 22; values and, 2, 4, 12, 20; values strategy of, 49–54. *See also* Iran-Contra Affair; Presidency; Republican party; Values
Reich, Emil, 39–40
Reichley, A. James, 97
Religion, 30, 41, 50, 60. *See also* Lifestyles
Rendon, John, 62
Republican party, 6, 32, 33, 45, 53, 59, 62, 63, 69, 75, 79, 80, 82, 83, 84, 85, 86, 88, 92, 94, 96, 98, 118, 127, 138, 139; identifiers, 51, 76, 85, 87, 88, 89, 90, 93, 100; 1980 platform of, 50, 53, 64; 1984 platform of, 57. *See also* Elections; Political parties; Reagan, Ronald
Reston, James, 31
Reuther, Walter, 125
Rice, Donna, 16
Rice, Grantland, 9
Riney, Hal, 10, 18
Ritter, Bruce, 61
Robb, Chuck, 135
Robbins, Tom, 122, 144
Roch, Don, 88

Rockefeller, Nelson A., 140–41, 142, 143
Rockne, Knute, 7, 8, 9, 10, 15, 17, 26
Rockwell, Norman, 5, 16, 21
Roiphe, Anne, 118
Romney, George, 141
Rooney, Mickey, 18
Roosevelt, Franklin D., 3, 32, 33, 36, 45, 48, 51, 52, 69, 71, 73, 74, 75, 77, 78, 79, 80, 81, 82, 83, 84, 86, 94, 95, 96, 102, 112, 113, 120, 128, 132, 138, 139, 143; New Deal and, 3, 34, 60, 74, 78, 127, 135; 1936 election of, 75, 79
Roosevelt, Theodore, 139
Roper Organization, 25
Rossiter, Clinton, 35, 81
Roth, William, 59
Rothman, Stanley, 42
Royko, Mike, 12
Ruff, Howard, 112
Russell, Richard, 125

Sajak, Pat, 118, 119
Sanford, Terry, 92
Sarbanes, Paul, 74
Schattschneider, E. E., 136, 137
Schlesinger, Arthur M., 45, 74
Schroeder, Pat, 21, 74
Scott, John, 112
Sevareid, Eric, 44
Shamie, Ray, 76
Sheehy, Gail, 112
Siegel, Mark, 95
Simon, Paul, 135, 136
Simpson, Jeffrey, 107, 108
Sinatra, Frank, 116
Skutnik, Lenny, 61
South, politics in, 89–93, 94. *See also* Southern whites
Southern whites, 52, 83, 89–90, 93. *See also* South, politics in
Springsteen, Bruce, 28, 103–7, 109
Squier, Bob, 110
Stein, Ben, 116–17
Stevenson, Adlai, 82
Stewart, James, 16
"Sting," 109
Stockman, David, 57, 58

Talmadge, Herman, 140
Tarrance, Lance, 84, 86
Tauber, Peter, 74, 77
Teeter, Robert, 87
Television, 67, 68, 112, 116–20

Terkel, Studs, 25
Texas, state elections in, 90–91, 92, 93
Thatcher, Margaret, 122
Thompson, James, 97
Tower Commission, 1
Townsend, Kathleen Kennedy, 135
Tracy, Spencer, 38
Travolta, John, 18
Trudeau, Garry, 61, 121
Trujillo, Stephen, 61
Truman, Harry S, 3, 34, 51, 52, 68, 69,
    71, 82, 83, 128, 138, 140
Tsongas, Paul, 134
Turner, Lana, 18
Turner, Tina, 116

Unemployment, 50, 65, 70, 71, 78. See
    also Economy; Inflation

Valenti, Jack, 108
Values, 6, 10, 23, 24, 27, 29, 33, 41, 43,
    52, 60, 61, 63, 73, 113, 121; Carter and,
    43; Mondale and, 63–69; political
    parties and, 77–84, 100–2; Reagan
    and, 2, 4, 5, 6, 12, 14, 16, 18, 20, 21, 22,
    49–54, 57, 60, 143–44. See also
    Culture (U.S.); Family; Freedom;
    Neighborhood; Patriotism; Peace;
    Political parties; Reagan, Ronald;
    Work
Vance, Ethel, 112
Vanocur, Sander, 93
Vietnam War, 2, 5, 38, 42, 43, 46, 47, 82,
    105, 110, 121, 137, 143. See also Johnson,
    Lyndon B.
Volpe, John, 88
Voorhis, Jerry, 80

Wallace, George C., 45, 46, 137
Washington, George, 15, 75, 76, 143
Watergate, 1, 5, 16, 39, 42, 43, 46, 47, 62,
    95, 130, 138, 143. See also Nixon,
    Richard M.
Wayne, John, 16, 19
Wexler, Anne, 44
White, Leonard D., 126
White, Mark, 92
White, Theodore H., 81, 130
White, Vanna, 118
Wick, Charles Z., 108
Wicker, Tom, 99
Will, George F., 4, 103, 104, 105
Wills, Garry, 17, 21, 29
Wilson, James Q., 28
Wilson, Woodrow, 36, 76
Winthrop, John, 62
Wirthlin, Richard B., 19, 22, 36, 37, 42–
    43, 51, 54, 70, 72, 76, 85, 86, 87, 88, 90,
    94, 109, 110, 120, 133, 134. See also
    Decision/Making/Information
Wirthlin Group, 110
Woodward, Bob, 112
Work, 2, 4, 12, 21, 22, 26, 49, 50, 54, 57,
    60, 61, 69, 73, 103, 121, 144. See also
    Values
Wyman, Jane, 17, 18, 40

X, Malcolm, 77

Yankelovich, Daniel, 27, 85, 86, 133
Yeager, Chuck, 116
Young voters, 71, 82, 88, 93–96, 131

Zoglin, Richard, 117
Zschau, Ed, 97
Zucker, Merrie, 95